ADDITIONAL PRAISE FOR *THE SYMPTOM IS NOT THE WHOLE STORY*

"I consider Daniel Araoz's book a creative achievement of great significance. This is a 'must' for all mental health professionals who would like to grasp the essence of psychoanalysis and its application to understanding human behavior and its dysfunction. Dr. Araoz's in-depth knowledge of the field and extensive experience in psychodynamic therapy enriches the importance of his work. He provides all practitioners with astute and succinct explanations of the principles of psychoanalysis that will transform the client's understanding of his condition and view of life to a healthy state of being."

—THE REV. DR. NISHAN J. NAGARIAN, LMHC, Clergy and Associate Professor of Education, C.W. Post Campus, Long Island University

"In *The Symptom Is Not the Whole Story*, Dr. Araoz brings together the many facets of training and practicing in psychotherapy that have dominated his own experience over a lifetime's dedication to his work as a counselor educator, hypnotherapist, and marriage and family therapist. That he should now show us how psychoanalysis has a crucial role in our own training and practice as professional counselors/psychotherapists will be a lasting contribution in our field.

"Psychoanalysis came to be viewed in many negative ways, causing many to discard it as narrow, biased, useless. In the old adage, there was a tendency to throw out the baby with the bathwater, to fail to see the positive possibilities and wisdom in psychoanalytic theory. As is true with much of the work in our field, psychotherapy is and always will be a dynamic, ever-changing, ever-growing process. Dr. Araoz makes this abundantly clear and, in doing so, brings psychoanalysis into the twenty-first century. Most importantly, his ideas and recommendations make psychoanalysis, especially in its understanding of the unconscious, accessible to all who grow in their own training and assist others to do so in their work with clients. Psychoanalytic techniques and understandings have significant applications in the repertoire of counselors/psychotherapists in whatever may be their areas of practice and specialization. Dr. Araoz brings all of us closer to putting them into practice and, ultimately, becoming better practitioners as a result."

—CAROLYN S. HEWSON, Ph.D., Counseling and Development Department, Professor Emeritus, C.W. Post Campus, Long Island University

"This book makes a major contribution to the field of mental health counseling, in particular to the training needs of mental health professionals. Araoz's thoughtful and readable text serves as a basic primer for the introduction and application of psychoanalytic understanding, principles, and techniques in therapeutic practice. Beginning counselors, for example, will learn how to expand their awareness of the dynamics inherent in the counseling relationship so that they can integrate theoretical concepts and interview skills with an attunement to their own and their clients' feelings as they work to understand presenting problems as often representative of more profound character structure. I highly recommend this book as a classic companion to any beginning mental health professional's library."

—**ROBERT DURFEY**, Ph.D., Fiorello H. LaGuardia Community College, City University of New York

THE SYMPTOM IS NOT THE WHOLE STORY

{ *Psychoanalysis for*
Non-Psychoanalysts }

DANIEL ARAOZ

Other Press • New York

Copyright © 2006 Daniel Araoz

Production Editor: Mira S. Park
Text design: Natalya Balnova

This book was set in 10.7 pt. Janson Text by Alpha Graphics of Pittsfield, NH.

10 9 8 7 6 5 4 3 2 1

Library of Congress Cataloging-in-Publication Data

Araoz, Daniel L., 1930–
   The symptom is not the whole story : psychoanalysis for non-psychoanalysts / Daniel Araoz.
      p. ; cm.
   Includes bibliographical references.
   ISBN-13: 978-1-59051-217-3 (alk. paper)
   ISBN-10: 1-59051-217-0 (alk. paper)
   1. Psychoanalysis—Popular works.   I. Title.
   [DNLM: 1. Psychoanalytic Theory—Case Reports.
2. Psychoanalytic Therapy—Case Reports.   3. Unconscious
(Psychology)—Case Reports.
WM 460 A662s 2006]
RC508.A73 2006
616.89'17—dc22
                                              2006007098

To my grandchildren Kaylee, Malcolm,
Luke, Ava, Emma, and Juliet
May their unconscious help them
always to live a full life.

and

To the memory of Ross Thalheimer, Ph.D.
Inspiration, role-model, mentor, and founder of
the American Institute for Psychotherapy and
Psychoanalysis, Inc.

NOTE

To avoid sexist language I alternatively use feminine and masculine genders in pronouns throughout the book. I also use the terms "client" and "patient" as well as "counseling" and "therapy" interchangeably.

Contents

Chapter 2

TOOLS FOR KNOWING AND DOING

Chapter 3

BRANCHES FROM THE MAIN TRUNK

Chapter 4

STRESS AND PSYCHOANALYSIS

Chapter 5

DEFENSES AGAINST ANXIETY

Chapter 14

WORKING THROUGH AND ACTING OUT

Chapter 15

PSYCHOANALYSIS AND THE GOOD LIFE

Chapter 16

REALITY, PSYCHODYNAMICS, AND SEX

FOREWORD

What Dostoyevsky once famously said about the Russian character—
that it is broad—might also be said of Daniel Araoz. In the thirty-
plus years since I first met him, I've experienced him at one time or
another, sometimes simultaneously, as a teacher, educator, psychoanalytic theorist, and—most of all—as a colleague. In all of his professional personae, he has never been less than an enthusiastically
collaborative and nurturing presence.

Since contemporary psychoanalysis often tends to be either
theoretically factious or half-heartedly interdisciplinary, it is refreshing to encounter someone like Daniel Araoz, who combines
solid scholarship with the kind of eclectic and dynamic open-
mindedness that is the signature of a creative thinker. Not surprisingly, his new book, *The Symptom Is Not the Whole Story*, is the
embodiment of what might be termed clinical wisdom. His views
do not seem concocted or intellectually labored but appear to be
the mature, organic residue of someone who has immersed himself in a world of psychoanalytic insights, has acquired vast clinical
experience along the way, and is bolstered by a strong commitment
to the work at hand. The theoretical positions he arrives at, accordingly, not only avoid the distance of detachment, but also are

animated by and reflective of who he is as a person. His presence truly inhabits the book.

In these pages he has set himself the admirable and challenging task of demystifying the unconscious. To do that, he needs to bring it out of the closet. Quickly, the reader sees that the storied psychoanalytic dynamic unconscious is not simply a seething cauldron of dark impulses. It is not something to be feared. It is something, instead, to be respected, reflected upon, listened to, guided by, and, above all, engaged with.

It is hard to appreciate how different this orientation is from the prevailing attitude of our contemporary culture. I can still remember the day, twenty-five years ago, when I was just starting my formal training to be a psychotherapist. Our teacher had asked us, "How many of you have ever seen the movie *Spellbound*? If you have, you can get a pretty good idea of what Americans used to think of therapy." In this 1945 Hitchcock classic, Ingrid Bergman, as the beautiful psychiatrist, falls hopelessly in love with her handsome patient, played by the irresistible leading man, Gregory Peck, cures him of his amnesia, and saves him from a date with the electric chair for a murder he did not commit. To prove his innocence, she must first help him flee from the police to buy time and figure out who the real killer is. When she does, in the movie's harrowing final scene, she takes her life in her hands in order to confront and expose the man she suspects. To those of us who had seen this movie, as I had, our teacher's point could not have been more obvious. Back then, the typical American moviegoer did not even have the crudest idea of what actually takes place in the therapist's office.

Yet over sixty years later, judging from some of our popular culture's biggest recent hits, the observation seems just as valid. For we have the beautiful Dr. Melfi becoming so emotionally and dangerously involved with her patient, Mob boss Tony Soprano, that at one point she is forced to leave her practice and go into hiding. We have an enraged Robin Williams as the psychologist Sean, in *Good Will Hunting* (1997), suddenly seizing by the throat his startled patient (Matt Damon) who had been mercilessly baiting him, and pinning him to the wall. "If you ever disrespect my wife again . . . I will end you," growls Williams, in effect threatening to kill his own patient. We have the ever-adorable, wisecracking Billy Crystal as the bemused, benighted shrink who is ruthlessly bullied by his Mob-boss patient (Robert DeNiro) in *Analyze This* (1999), while simultaneously being tricked by the Feds into secretly wearing a wire. We have the terrifying Hannibal Lecter who either cures or eats his patients. One could go on and on with a list that only expands as we move backward in time. To an amazing extent, therapists have been portrayed in movies as killing the patient (*Dressed to Kill*), seducing patients (*Prince of Tides, Deconstructing Harry*), or being exposed as fools by their patients (in *What about Bob?* and a dozen others). What is striking is not the misperception that this reflects of what actually transpires between therapist and patient, but how well movies manage to flesh out the secret fantasies of their intended audience. For people are deeply suspicious of the ulterior motives of psychotherapists. Patients do wonder about what lurking, hidden sexual desires their shrinks may harbor for them. Therapists do feel the need to armor themselves against potential outbreaks of unconscious rage and hostility from the more disturbed members of their practice. Nor is this a case of art imitating life, or life imitating art, although that does occur.

If it is true there is a widespread fear of the unconscious, then part of the art of psychotherapy will be to help patients listen without anxiety to the voices of their own unconscious. It is worth noting here, however, that the narrative voices of patients caught up in the process of psychotherapy are considerably less straightforward than narrative in its conventional sense. There is a notable lack of narrative unity, of an Aristotelian beginning, middle, and end. On the contrary, the narrative voices of patients—especially those who struggle to articulate, to give meaning to the more profound traumatic losses of their personal history—tend to be discontinuous, fragmented, muted, disguised, and often unconsciously derivative. And it is the task and challenge of the psychotherapist, in fact, to facilitate these muted voices—what Christopher Bollas (1987) in *The Shadow of the Object* has memorably called "a dead language" (the unknown known of their early childhood)—and bring them to life.

It is no small irony that the mental health profession itself has inadvertently colluded with the avoidance of the unconscious. Beguiled by the advances of biological psychiatry and the undeniable potency of psychotropic medications, it has often seemed to foster the contrary belief that the symptom is the whole story. In an age of the quick fix and instant gratification, it has in large measure turned away from the pursuit of a depth psychology as well as the classical sense of the prospective patient as an existential (if unconscious) participant in his or her own destiny. In place of these concepts one finds a growing fascination with what could justifiably be called the designated illness of our time—the trauma of survivors of an abused childhood: adult children of alcoholics, of sexual molesters, of batterers, of narcissists, and so on. And it is a further irony to observe how the very upper echelons of the mental health profession—the elite therapeutic training institutes—can also unwittingly collude in the negation of the complexity of unconscious dynamics. In my book, *The Dark Side of the Analytic Moon: A Memoir of Life in a Training Institute* (1996), I published the results of a personal ten-year study of the subculture of the analytic training institute, with my principal finding being that there is an unfortunate, pervasive neglect of the manifold creative dimensions that are indispensable to the development of the really outstanding therapist.

Partly to correct this, Araoz in this new book has moved outside the elitist training institutes and privileged halls of academe. The audience he aspires to speak with are those mental health practitioners who would be interested in exploring a more psychodynamic orientation to human behavior and its dysfunction. What is therefore offered here is an eminently practical tour of some of the conceptual mainstays of psychoanalysis. Beginning with Sigmund Freud, and moving on to the neo-Freudians, object-relations theorists, Kleinians, interpersonalists, and the revisionists, the author skillfully guides the reader through the principal psychoanalytic movements of the past century. Throughout, Daniel Araoz shows himself to be a wise teacher, and his obvious mastery of a complex and multidimensional field paves the way for the reader's eventual safe passage through what otherwise might be puzzling thickets of theory.

The book contains excellent summary chapters on ego psychology, anxiety, defense mechanisms, transference, and the superego. His discussion of the transition from hypnosis to hypnoanalysis is lucid and succinct. His chapters on psychoanalysis with couples and for sexual problems, as well as psychoanalysis with families and in groups, are masterful. I especially liked the many clinical vignettes, which could not be more user-friendly.

This, however, is an existential as well as a practical book. On a deeper level, the author invites the reader to join him in a meditation on an intellectual, emotional, psychological, intrapsychic, interpersonal, and polysemous passage—the story of our psyche—that is at one and the same time as up-to-date today and as old as the human race.

Although the central message that the dynamic unconscious is alive and well is not new, the messenger surely is.

To whom, then, is this book recommended? To all mental health professionals and every serious student of human nature.

Gerald Alper, Fellow, American Institute for Psychotherapy and Psychoanalysis, and author, among others, of *Self-Defense in a Narcissistic World* (2003); *Portrait of the Artist as a Young Patient* (1998); *The Puppeteers* (1994); and *Paranoia in Everyday Life: Fleeing the Terrorist Within* (2005).

INTRODUCTION

This book is for all mental health professionals who are not psycho-analysts. The readers for whom I have written this book include the vast number of counselors and therapists who are already effectively helping an incredibly large number of patients and clients, individu-ally, in groups and in families, through lectures and workshops, in hospitals, schools, agencies, and corporations, and in private prac-tice. Yet many of these therapists and counselors have not special-ized in psychoanalysis and psychodynamic therapy.

With this premise clearly in mind, I'd like to introduce to you my book on the unconscious as the core of psychoanalysis. Toward the end of my four years of psychoanalytic training, well over thirty years ago, I felt uncomfortable with the mystique that I sensed had grown up around psychoanalysis, although personally I found psy-choanalysis, both its concepts and the experience of it, liberating and enriching, mentally, emotionally, and spiritually. I still feel this—and perhaps with the maturity of age, even more so than I did then.

After having started my informal analytic training in Argen-tina in 1954, I finally finished it eighteen years later in the United States and was ready to spread the good news of psychoanalysis to the whole world. But unfortunately my attitude was not approved and welcomed. I felt that the general belief then was that psycho-analysis was not for the masses and that we, the club members, were special. Indeed, I agree that the experience of psychoanalysis (that is, to be in analysis) is not and should not be for everyone, and that to have gone through the experience of analysis is a special privi-lege of a small minority of humans. On the other hand, psychoana-lytic thinking, I thought then and still do now, is not the property of a few but should be the right of all humans. Those who talked in technical riddles did not make psychoanalysis available to the masses. Many still talk and write with obfuscations, keeping it eso-teric and mysteriously confusing. You still find practitioners and even patients who enjoy using exotic terms, thus separating them-selves from the rest of the world. This is reminiscent of religious fanaticism and as such does not make psychoanalysis user-friendly but less approachable.

This book is written for "the rest of the world," in the hope of making psychoanalysis accessible, first and foremost, to the many mental health workers without specialized training in this field (and who, consequently, are not psychoanalysts), and second, through them, to the rest of the world. In the past, with very few excep-tions, it was "either/or," as if they were telling you, "If you are not a psychoanalyst, stay away from it." However, there is a greater friendliness nowadays, a wider understanding that thinking psycho-analytically is beneficial to the individual, to families, to corpora-tions, and to the world at large: nations, cultures, religions. My intention is to interest every professional in the people-helping field in the fundamental concepts, principles, and applications of psycho-analysis so that they can enrich their lives and their clinical work by using the unconscious more effectively.

In sum, I affirm that to work fully psychoanalytically, at what I call second-level analysis, you need prolonged specialized training, including your own personal analysis. But I also assert that your work as a health provider will be enriched when you become aware of the unconscious (yours and the patient's) as well as when you begin thinking psychoanalytically and start to apply some of the techniques for working with the unconscious in your work. This is first-level analysis. There is an apparent contradiction when I tell you that to be a psychoanalyst you need very detailed training and then I invite you to try some of the psychoanalytic techniques. But notice carefully that first-level analysis stays in the area of recognizing the unconscious in everybody, questioning yourself about it in yourself and others, and becoming sensitive of unconscious possibilities and respectful of it and them. You know plenty of similar situations. For instance, it's not a problem for you to use mathematics without being a mathematician or to have political opinions without having a degree or being a recognized expert in political science. You can think of innumerable circumstances like these.

Also, you won't find in this book a systematic, logical presentation, mainly because there are excellent books on theory but also because I believe that to discuss the unconscious it is better to do it in a manner resembling free association. It is better because, even if it is not logically or sequentially organized, it respects the unconscious organization that initially is foreign territory to those less aware of the unconscious. My intention is for you to have a taste of what it is to work with the unconscious (first in yourself, as I keep emphasizing) so that you realize the need and advantage of learning more about it and psychoanalysis. This sensed need, I hope, will give birth to the beneficial outcome of your wanting to have the psychoanalytic experience, through self-analysis, reading, courses, and conferences, as well as through supervision of your clinical work. But—and this is especially important—you may want to have the unique experience of being in psychoanalysis yourself.

The basis of thinking psychoanalytically lies in the inclusion of the unconscious in one's thought. A knowledge of the unconscious reality in human life is essential to understand oneself and others, the individual as well as human events in general. If the ancient saying, *Historia magistra vitae* (History is the teacher of life), accurately represents Roman thinking, we can see that they believed that in order to understand human nature one has to find out what happened in the past and behind the scenes. What is hidden gives the true explanation of what is seen. And this attitude corrects the mistaken concept that psychoanalysis always finds others to blame, especially parents. The absurdity of that view is that genuine understanding supersedes judgment and condemnation. If a person is neurotic because of his maternal upbringing, psychoanalysis does not blame the mother because it knows that her neurosis can be understood by looking into her own history and so on.

There are numerous misunderstandings of this field. I find that many see it only as psychotherapy while others perceive a philosophy, a manner of understanding human behavior that lends itself to benefiting people when used as therapy. Both views are partially correct and, ideally, to know the totality of psychoanalysis will make a person a better practitioner. The philosophical aspect of it, mentioned at more length in Chapter 12, centers on self-knowledge, which is, paradoxically, considered essential in order to be a practitioner of this trade. The reader will be introduced to the philosophical aspect in order to make the practical side more meaningful and as a way to help practitioners assimilate this way of thinking into their own cognitive styles.

My hometown is Buenos Aires, a city where, in my time, reading and studying psychoanalytic books was more than a hobby, but was a serious avocation enjoyed by practically everybody, especially those in disciplines as diverse as law, medicine, education, engineering, architecture, accounting, astronomy, and anthropology, just to mention a few. Everybody was interested in psychoanalysis: cab drivers, retail salespeople, repair people, doormen. I remember several instances when a cabdriver or a doorman picked up a copy of Freud or Klein to defend his point or strengthen his argument. That was then, and I learned from it that one can usefully apply psychoanalysis to every occurrence in life. This book is an invitation to all the non-psychoanalysts in the helping professions to look into psychoanalysis, to allow it to enlarge their thinking so the unconscious can be included in their work, because understanding human problems from that perspective and employing it in helping suffering people can create changes for the better.

I also hope to contribute to the present change in perception regarding psychoanalysis among the general public, and even more so among other professionals. As Chapter 12 discusses, I want people to realize that psychoanalysis can mean not only a form of mental health treatment but also, and more importantly, a view of life, a philosophy; and that the form of treatment is not limited to the caricature of the patient on the couch and the bearded analyst with a heavy accent who sits out of the patient's range of vision saying very little and trying to remain a mystery to her. As a matter of fact, in the more than three decades since I became a psychoanalyst I have worked mostly in an office that had a "living room" arrangement, where I am facing the client, facilitating the client's interaction with me. I have not used the couch with more than about fifty patients in all these years.

Because of the numerous popular misconceptions about my work, I used to prefer to identify myself as a psychotherapist rather than a psychoanalyst. Just the word still elicits, even among professionals and educated people in general, all the erroneous images and misunderstandings learned in movies and novels. Now, the New York state licensing of psychoanalysts, I hope, will help correct the bias by presenting to the public regular people practicing the new licensed profession. This book is published also to celebrate the four new licenses offered in 2006 in New York (in Mental Health Counseling, Marriage and Family Therapy, Creative Arts Therapy, and Psychoanalysis), and to encourage professional counselors and psychotherapists of all persuasions to enrich their work with what they find in these pages. All that the three non-psychoanalytic mental health professionals need to benefit from this book is an inquisitive, open, curious mind. They can practice first-level analysis and in so doing, renew their professional enthusiasm and increase for their clients the beneficial outcome of their work.

Toward the end of his life, Freud commented hopefully on blending psychoanalysis with other forms of psychotherapy and counseling. I hope this book helps to make true the dream of the Master.

Daniel Araoz, EdD, ABPP, ABPH, NCC Fellow, American Institute for Psychotherapy and Psychoanalysis, NCPsyC.
April 2005

PART ONE | THE FUNDAMENTALS

Chapter 1
HOW CAN YOU USE PSYCHOANALYSIS?

The essence of the psychoanalytic perspective is to see beyond the seen, to understand more than what is evident, and to decode the meaning behind the metaphors of our existence. Its essence is to broaden both one's own and the client's inner experience and self-knowledge by recognizing the dynamics of thoughts and actions even in the trivia that make up most of our existence. All this and more is embodied in Freud's succinct formula, "to make the unconscious conscious." Psychoanalytic theory is based on the existence of the unconscious, and it touches the individual, psychotherapy, social conditions, criminal law, art, and practically every other aspect of being human. At the same time, psychoanalytical practice, the application of the theory, embraces great variations and methods, as Chapter 3 explains and as the entire book discusses.

The first level of psychoanalysis is self-knowledge
Anyone dealing with human problems can benefit from the psycho-analytic perspective. Like many ancient philosophies—Hinduism, Buddhism, Taoism, classical Greek and Roman schools of thought,

Kabala, Christian and Muslim mysticism—psychoanalysis is ulti-mately a program of self-enhancement and personal growth. All these self-transformation disciplines aim at increasing our awareness, ex-panding our consciousness, and refining our sensitivity to the sur-rounding reality. This is what this book is all about.

On the one hand, in any aspect of human behavior one can find the deeper dimension that depth psychology has examined for over a century. On the other, poets, artists, and philosophers in every culture and from time immemorial, centuries before Freud, have delved into this level of our experience in many different ways and by means of different languages or symbols. However, many in our society wrongly identify the unconscious with Freud as if he had discovered or invented it, and many "new" therapies deny its exis-tence—or at least its importance.

Symptom removal or psychotherapy?

Now that mental health counselors and marriage and family thera-pists are licensed professionals in practically every state of the Union, many practitioners would like to learn how to be more than symp-tom removers or emotional brushfire fighters. Many practitioners are curious about psychodynamics in themselves and in their clients. Unfortunately, most counseling and family-therapy programs offer them only a superficial and often negatively biased idea of psycho-analytic or psychodynamic therapy. A small survey I conducted sev-eral years ago showed that in the entire master's degree program in professional counseling, an average of one and a half classes were devoted exclusively to psychoanalytical theory, with a range of 0 to 3. It is not surprising then to hear ignorant comments from profes-sionals, such as "It does not make sense to delve into the client's past," or "When a client presents a problem it's unethical to look for 'more to it' than the presenting problem," or "Psychoanalysis has been proven to be unscientific and ineffective." Others talk about "wasting time" and "not getting anything done [that is, no concrete goals attained] in many sessions" of psychoanalysis. Still others, stating that they know about psychoanalysis, seem to believe that nothing has evolved in its theory and practice in the last century since Freud. As a matter of fact, many clinicians are completely unfamiliar with most of the great psychoanalytical theorists that came after Freud. They know the names, and surprisingly little more, of a few like Erik Erikson, Erich Fromm, Karen Horney, and perhaps Harry Stack Sullivan. That's about it. Don't even mention the great psychoanalytical authors from Europe and Latin America, like Bion, Winnicott, Lacan, Kernberg, or Etchegoyen. This negativism toward psychoanalytic thinking is unfair to the new mental health professionals who, because of lack of exposure, are barred from a powerful way of thinking about their clients and the issues that bother them. Because of this, all mental health practitioners will enrich their perspective by becoming aware and using psychodynamics in their thinking, although this does not mean that they will practice second-level psychoanalysis, as such.

The profession of psychoanalysis

The practice of second-level psychoanalysis requires serious, in-depth specialization. Without it, no one should use the title of psychoanalyst. As a matter of fact, from 2006 on, it is illegal to do so in New York State without a license in psychoanalysis. This is the very first time that this mental health specialization is legally recognized as an independent profession. To become a psychoanalyst, postgraduate training institutes offer a rigorous four-year program primarily centered on one's own psychoanalysis, not merely on classes and lectures. For example, the American Institute for Psychotherapy and Psychoanalysis, from which I graduated and became a Fellow in early 1972, and where I later taught for over a decade, required many more hours of personal analysis and supervision than of classes. Obviously then, to repeat for emphasis, this book is not for psychoanalysts but for those mental health practitioners who want to acquire a new way of considering neurotic behavior, human problems, and their remediation.

In touch with the human condition

My hope is that this book will give you, as one of these clinicians, a taste of current psychoanalytic thinking, or may perhaps even encourage some to experience and study psychoanalysis extensively, and open their eyes to the many new, applicable and useful developments in the field. These developments can be adapted to any form of counseling and psychotherapy because most of the symptoms we humans develop are consistent and meaningful, though it may not appear so at first sight. To focus only on the symptoms is to bypass the hidden inner conflict that most often explains and gives meaning to them. This existential suffering basically always reaches to the conflict between life and death, good and evil, "the flesh versus the spirit," wanting to know and fearing the truth. We are familiar with this fundamental conflict from the story of Adam and Eve, a masterpiece of symbolic presentation of the human condition. Though the conflict is expressed by the patient challengingly in neurotic behavior, its resolution is the seed of personal growth and marks the end of the symptom, which was the unconscious neurotic symbol. Precisely because the symptom is not the whole story, it is important and meaningful in itself, given that it takes us to the basic conflict of what our existence is all about. Human beings cannot avoid this inner struggle that all of us face sooner or later until we resolve it, and that differentiates us from all other animals on the planet. This existential conflict centers on our desire to be happy; "the pursuit of happiness" is not only our human right but also our human sentence and a burden we cannot get rid of, as Lacan (Dor 1999) teaches.

This unresolved inner conflict creates anxiety and often forces us to repeat in different scenarios, with different characters, the same script we learned early in life. This script may be made up of specific fears, insecurities, anger and frustration, impossible dreams, or many other such early feelings. Freud called this urge to reenact, as a way of handling the original, nonresolved anxiety, "the repetition compulsion" because, without realizing it, we reenact our early conflicts in new situations. And this is the reason for stating earlier that psychoanalysis is helpful in practically every aspect of human behavior.

Honest introspection

I cannot convince you of the unique value of psychoanalysis. You must experience it. In order to understand this in an experiential (as different from logical) manner, I suggest the following practical exercise. Focus your thinking on a recent encounter (last week, yesterday, or this morning) you had with a new person. Analyze it and find the explanation for the type of reaction you had toward that person. You'll discover that you felt comfortable or not; that you liked her or not; that the person reminded you of someone else, even if you didn't fully realize who that other person was. You felt afraid or threatened by the new person or you trusted her; you considered her someone you "can handle" or not. In reflecting on all this you'll recognize "unconscious" themes and connections that only you understand thoroughly because they come from your personal history; that is, these are not just the facts of historical reality but your unique perception and experience of those facts, your emotional reaction to them.

Because of the nature of psychoanalysis you cannot comprehend it unless and until you engage in this type of exercise, a point that unfortunately those who demand scientific evidence from psychoanalysis do not understand. They want objective, factual validation while psychoanalysis produces subjective, idiosyncratic evidence. The tools employed by the physical sciences do not work when studying subjectivity. For that, the best tool is still verbalized introspection (see Lothane 1994).

To explain further what I mean by this introspective and subjective mind exercise, here is a personal example of using psychoanalytic thinking to expand awareness. I went to my scheduled dental cleaning expecting the regular dental hygienist, Jennifer, to take care of my teeth. She is a bright, attractive, rather quiet, and very nice young woman who takes her job seriously and does it with gentleness and expertise. Instead of Jennifer, I was told that because she was on vacation, John, whom I had not met before, would take care of me. John is a big, youngish man with an easy smile and a firm handshake. I've always felt uncomfortable with big guys. Psychoanalytic thinking makes me suspect that the reason for my discomfort is related to the fact that I'm the oldest of five siblings in a Latin family and was taught not to let anyone overshadow me. I had to be "above the others." Big guys always put me on high alert. At a more primitive and consequently deeper level, I have a conflict with big men because of a simplistic sense of father loyalty (simplistic because it started very early in my life, when I saw my father as a giant—as all little boys see their father). This is what Freud explains symbolically with the myth of Oedipus. This time I did not feel the usual threat, in spite of John's size: his style of dental hygiene was direct, secure, and respectful. While I was rinsing my mouth, he made some comments that I agreed with regarding the news channel my dentist keeps on while patients are treated. I didn't see the big guy, John, as a threat to me but as a friend and protector, even with traits of a father substitute. I realized that age-wise he could be my son and I felt protective of him. I liked him, even though he is a big guy. I saw him first and foremost as someone who is doing a service for me, not as the big guy. Yet as I tried to point out, John's mere presence triggered in me early developmental issues; unconscious dynamics came to the fore and willy-nilly I regressed emotionally. Further, and essential to the understanding of this process, is that this regression happens all the time, that my experience is not unique, and that most people don't even realize what is going on in similar circumstances.

All this came to my mind. So what? Those who consider psychoanalysis irrelevant may ask, "What's the point of all this analyzing?" My response is that an insignificant encounter like this can raise one's consciousness and make one more aware of one's inner dynamics, as it did for me. In this insignificant event I recognized my compulsion to reenact and, thanks to my self-analysis, I was able to relate to John as he was, not as I perceived him to be because of my neurotic inner world. John, a former U.S. Army dental hygienist, became part of my life for a brief moment to help me, not to give me grief and cause any sort of trouble. His physical size became irrelevant; he was not going to "unseat" me; he was not my father's ghost. By analyzing this, I realized something that had earlier been too generalized in my awareness ("I feel uncomfortable with big guys"). Thanks to this analysis I became aware that the problem I have is not with big guys but with my misperceptions that come from different levels of my psyche. Before this experience I believed that "big guys" were the problem and I was not completely clear about the reasons why. Now I know more about myself. What did I gain? Self-knowledge, and with it the freedom to approach big guys without the "conviction" that I don't trust them or like them, the confidence to give big guys a chance, and the possibility for me of being enriched by the contact with a big guy, as I was by my one-hour contact with John.

Benefits of psychoanalytic thinking

Going back to the theme and purpose of this book, this type of intro-spective thinking makes the clinician more aware of what is going on inside of her own psyche: feelings, desires, associations, and memo-ries (the "psychodynamics") that, if ignored, can distract her from the client and distort her perceptions. It also makes her attuned to the feelings and inner experiences of her clients. This introspection, meaning "to look inside," is psychoanalytic thinking.

Regarding the subtitle of the book, according to purists the word should be "psychodynamic." But I keep the word "psychoanaly-sis" because "psychodynamics" is less specific, and includes non-Freudians like Jung, Adler, and others. On the other hand, some use the terms "psychodynamic" and "neo-Freudian" interchangeably. For reasons of clarity I prefer to concentrate mainly on Freud and to keep the original designation of the system started by him.

In the following chapters of Part One you will find practical aspects of psychoanalytic thinking and application. Part Two touches on more detailed points useful to clarify what is discussed in the first part. You'll realize that you don't need to be a psychoanalyst in order to enrich your mental-health work with the use of the psychoanalytic approach. To repeat, this book does not encourage you to practice psychoanalysis in the strict sense, or what I am calling second-level analysis. By psychoanalytic use, I mean the application of different concepts of psychoanalysis in detail both to yourself and in your mental health practice. In this way I hope you will fully realize the value of this method in your work, and learn how to use these con-cepts for the benefit of your clients.

In addition to understanding how to use any approach to psy-chological healing, another important point is to know with whom to use it and when to use it. In most cases clients will seek your help as a clinician when they have concrete problems with anger control, communication, depression, or anxiety. Or they may experience dissatisfaction with either relationships or work, or suffer from stress, phobias, or sexual difficulties, and many other such psychological issues they consider merely behavioral. The general rule is that, yes, we respond to the presenting problem with techniques directly aimed at behavioral change and not infrequently require medical opinion depending on the nature of the complaint. In a large number of cases we help people change by means of this approach.

But there are also many clients who either do not improve in a reasonable period of time or admit that they have had, often many times, the same type of issue in the past. When this happens, thinking psychoanalytically is in order. In other words, when the psychological symptom is stubborn or not new and recent, proving itself to be more than just an acquired habit, and has become almost a trait or characteristic of the client's personality, then we have psychoanalysis to fall back on. In many of these cases, even clients say things like, "That's the way I am and I want to change but I can't," or "I hate it but that's my personality all over again." These patients, without realizing it, are referring to their personality development that it is the province of psychoanalysis to understand, and they are asking us to help them in that area. Mental health practitioners must be equipped to recognize this unconscious request and deal with it if they want the client to get well, not just to feel good, or if they would rather be professionals, not simply technicians. To help people change, the clinician must know how to listen to the client's unconscious and symptom-metaphorical request for help. To consider the symptom as an isolated reality deprives the patient of the help she needs. If we understand the symptom as a metaphorical language that is speaking about the patient's inner pain and anxiety, we can assist her in an effective way. Only at this level can we connect intersubjectively with those who come to us for help.

Psychoanalytic counseling and psychotherapy

The depiction of psychoanalysis as a process in which the patient is told to remember her childhood in order to establish the link between the symptoms that bring her to therapy and her early experiences is a caricature; that is not how it's done. The point is not for her to try to remember childhood events but that she become aware of the *hidden relationship* between the symptoms and earlier experiences.

Therefore, to help the patient achieve insight, you don't ask direct questions about her childhood but you observe, listen to, study, and analyze the client. It usually takes some time before you can "interpret" effectively. Chapter 13 will discuss interpretation. To summarize here, interpretation happens when you ask (1) if she has any explanation for what happens to her or why she has the symptoms or the patterns of behavior that bother her. If the client does not have an explanation, you may (2) encourage her to think about it or to pay attention to her transference and dreams, "the forgotten language" of the unconscious (Fromm 1951). (3) Next, you may ask if her reactions, resistance, body language, and other behaviors in the session itself, when she focuses on a particular point, might not be related to some incident or person in her early years. If she accepts this possibility, (4) you help the patient recognize the validity of this link, to elaborate on it and to realize that she does not have to act and react this way. Now she can have new and different reactions and even perceptions. In other words, the client has insight leading to change when she realizes that what happens in the therapy session or the topics she is talking about have some connection with incidents or people from her early developmental years.

Take the 45-year-old woman experiencing compulsive spending who, without awareness of her grimace, frowns when she says the word "money." She had forgotten that, when she was around 8 or 9, her stepmother punished her severely when the patient was caught with any money at all. At other times the behavior leading to the origin of the problem is more mysterious, as with the big, strong construction worker, age 39, who violently rubbed his right thumb and index finger together every time he made eye contact with the analyst. He did not know why he did this. Invited to rub purposely and to let any memories, images, or feelings come to awareness, he discovered its connection with a repressed incident of sexual abuse at age 15. Lastly, the *patterns of behavior*, compulsive or not, often lead to events of the past that were never fully resolved. A case in point is the executive, aged 55, who, in spite of his success and financial comfort, practically always overreacts with anger when he encounters what he calls waste—discarded pages not fully typed, lights on, faucets dripping, and other such minor instances. In analysis he recognized that, at 11, being the oldest of four siblings when his father died, he took it upon himself to make sure that everything was "as it should be" in the house. He felt responsible for neatness and economical use of the household resources, and for teaching, correcting, and controlling his younger siblings in this respect. The forgotten unconscious link between now and then appeared several decades later in therapy.

From the above you see that psychoanalytic counseling and therapy is not an esoteric practice but rather a particular attitude or way of perceiving, handling, and understanding the client's problems. Symptoms are never considered to exist in a vacuum. So, you assume they are not and proceed to investigate possible connections. However, this attitude about the symptom not being the whole story does not mean that you can know the meaning of the symptom or its origin. What you can know is that the metaphor-symptom is often an ineffective attempt to cope with something that causes inner pain and anxiety. Because this is the case, you have an obligation—as a therapist whose mission is to help the patient not merely to feel better but to get well and grow as a human being—to inquire into the possibility of the symptom being a metaphor. By this I mean that the symptom may be an attempt to handle a repressed conflict of the past that has become too painful, too embarrassing, or too scary, and, because it is repressed, is still bothering the person—but it is not resolved. Until it is resolved, it will continue to be a source of anxiety. How to clinically handle this in order to find out what the connection is will be explained later. As a foretaste, I can state that this is where free association has its place and interpretation steps in.

The "analysis" part of this approach is the work of the clinician who observes carefully and caringly the client's patterns of behavior and speech, of her reactions, choices, and thinking style in the session. Because of this methodical observation the clinician becomes, in fact, an analyst. Based on this observation he can guide the client to the unconscious relationship the current behavior has with the past. It is this, eventually, that makes her believe that she can change, because she realizes that she is out of step with the way she is currently living; she is still acting as if she were in the same circumstances that she was then. Many of the behaviors people used in the past were practical then, but are not necessary or helpful and convenient in the present. An oversimplified example of the original practical function of the symptom might be the adult who is not feeling well most of the time, even though there is no medical reason for his condition. His mother always treated him with great attention and love when he was sick as a child. He is not aware of his hoping that those currently around him will react now the way his mother did.

As a psychoanalytic clinician you must become inquisitive and curious about the client's symptoms or patterns of behavior but without being intrusive. The best method is to ask tentative questions (Could it be that this has something to do with that?) and not to insist if the client does not seem to respond. Be patient and hopeful because the unconscious is always at work and will show itself again and again until the patient pays attention to it. Of course, when you experience this type of resistance, you invite the client to pay attention to her reactions in and out of the session, to transference and to dreams. For this you use some of the techniques described in Chapter 8 that help activate the patient's imagination and fantasy.

The medical and the psychological models

To recapitulate, let us take a close look at our working model. With the current popularity of psychotropic medications (Kramer [1993] even mentions "cosmetic psychopharmacology" as a benefit experienced with Prozac) many clinicians tend to quickly consider drugs as a solution to the stubborn symptom. We'll touch on this issue again, but here I want to remark that in most cases medications do not cure emotional and psychological problems. Often, however, they are an important help so the patient can become introspective once the severity of the symptoms is diminished. My hope is that in stubborn clinical cases mental health professionals also consider psychoanalysis, not simply drugs, for the benefit of clients. I believe that, as healers, we intend to help people heal. Of course, the current cultural trend is to agree with Kramer in *Listening to Prozac* and books like it, which claim that pharmacology will make people more "better than well."

The last point of this chapter is related to the above. "The quick fix" is a common element of American values and beliefs and, if we are not careful, it will affect us as psychotherapists. It is worth taking a moment to reflect on this danger for us as professionals. We are the shortcut culture. This might be related to the materialistic, capitalistic, economic system with its belief that "time is money" and that we are entitled to what we want without waiting for it; when something does not work well, throw it out and get a better, newer, more expensive model. The shortcut value is embedded in the English language where many words can be used both as a noun and as a verb, as in *the man mans the manhole*. We also have the largest number of monosyllabic words—more than any other language in the Occidental world. Entire long sentences can be made with monosyllables, as in *long books can be made up of short words with ease, taste, and good sense*. English shortens things, too. (He says, "My name is Peter" but his new acquaintance responds, "Hi, Pete.") Names, diseases, organizations, and titles are referred to with acronyms. Speed is favored in computer and telephone communication, in cooking, in transportation, in conversation, and in writing. It's not surprising that this type of culture would expect the same shortcut approach to solving problems, any type of problems. We invented short-term therapy and managed care (with just a few sessions per patient no matter what the problem is). America is one of the biggest (and richest!) pharmacology markets because we welcome the quick fix. And this powerful industry has succeeded in becoming a gigantic component of the American military-industrial complex. We must realize its power in order to defend ourselves from the quick-fix mentality in our work with clients.

Because of this cultural bias, psychoanalysis becomes a misfit in the shortcut culture and, due to this, many mental health practitioners, and their patients as a consequence, are being shortchanged without realizing it. Both are deceived by believing that the symptom is the whole story. This book is opposed to the quick fix, as you realize. You will have an informed choice to decide for yourself whether you want to avail yourself of this tool to help people. Moreover, learning what I call the Western Zen of psychoanalysis will enrich you as a person, even though you do not see yourself at this point using it in your mental health practice. This perception may change, thanks to what you find in these pages.

Chapter 2
TOOLS FOR KNOWING AND DOING

The concepts of psychoanalysis we shall deal with here are practical for clinical, applied, therapeutic uses. Theoretical speculations and controversial issues can be found elsewhere (see Suggested Readings, at the end of the book). This is a book for those who want to learn how to utilize these basic concepts for their personal enrichment and the benefit of their clients.

Among the many and often confusing concepts of psychoanalysis, one is fundamental to the understanding of the whole system. This is the existence of the unconscious, which, in a true sense, embraces everything else. Another basic complex of concepts has to do with anxiety and a common product of it, the urge to reenact. Anxiety is expressed in innumerable forms as the background of neurosis, but also often as the motivation for change, for therapy and healing. Drives are another fundamental psychoanalytical concept, with the primary psychic dynamics being libido and Eros. The well-known tripartite composition of the human psyche—ego, id, and superego—is a heuristic means of explaining the dynamics of the human psyche. We should also include in the list of essential concepts the generally known stages of development, which are, basically, oral, anal, phallic, latency, and genital, with the personality types that spring from these. As part of the book's overview, we shall review very briefly also some of the most important versions of psychoanalysis, which include Freudian, ego, object-relations, self, and relational analysis, all of which are branches of the same original tree.

The unconscious
Before tackling any other concept related to psychoanalysis, it is necessary to concentrate on the unconscious itself. The original term used by Freud was *das Unbewusst*, meaning "that which is unknown." Because the unconscious is made up of data that have been accumulated since we started our existence, most of it is unknown to our conscious self. It must be emphasized that the unconscious can operate for our benefit or for our misfortune. It depends on the values and beliefs that are part of our unconscious. Some of these may come from very early in life; others have been acquired throughout life in different types of experiences, positive and negative, real and imagined (like those coming from reading a book or watching a movie). Therefore, the unconscious is a basic reality of human existence.

To avoid confusion, it is good to remember that the word "unconscious" is used as both a noun and an adjective (my unconscious does unconscious things). As a noun, we are referring to something that is evident only through its manifestations: mistakes like misplacing your keys when you are in a hurry to get going, or surprises when you suddenly remember something important. The idea that the unconscious is always ready to trick us and hurt us is as absurd as believing that the unconscious will always come to our rescue no matter how foolish our conscious choices might be.

Even though Freud appears to have taken it for granted and did not mention it clearly anywhere, his concept of the unconscious seems to include not merely mental, emotional, and behavioral manifestations but also physiological and biological ones—everything in our psyche that is "unknown" to the conscious self. The unconscious may be responsible for a burst of anger that seems to come out of nowhere. This can be considered a negative manifestation but it may be a protective reaction to avoid a painful situation. Defense mechanisms, to be discussed later, are just that. The same unconscious moves you to do what is right for your health or for your sanity, even when you hadn't noticed what you were doing. And when, without thinking, you do what you have to do to protect your life, you are again operating under the influence of the unconscious. Finally, as stated a few lines earlier, the same faculty is also responsible for all the highly complicated biological functions that keep you alive, from regulating your blood pressure and heartbeat, to keeping the right amount of sugar in the blood, to producing bone marrow, red blood cells, and so on. In practice, the importance of the unconscious is summarized in the idea used many times by Milton Erickson (Rossi 1980): that in the unconscious you have much more information and data than in your conscious mind. His down-to-earth advice was to trust your unconscious. From the psychoanalytic point of view, to trust the unconscious means that you have to recognize the inner wisdom accumulated since your very first experiences in life. It does not mean that you are exempt from using your rational judgment and intelligence, expecting the unconscious to make the right decisions.

The unconscious, among other functions, has filed away every experience, good and bad, that you have had in your entire life. Learning from experience applies here: because of what has happened to you, you try to avoid the painful things and to repeat the enjoyable ones. Many manifestations of the unconscious happen every day, such as dreams, transference, and important defense mechanisms. Dreams are expressions of the unconscious in its language of symbols and metaphors. In that language they tell us things that our conscious mind does not know. They are a good example of experiential thinking, as opposed to the rational, logical, thinking so much encouraged by our culture.

Transference, as Chapter 6 will discuss in greater detail, is a current unconscious reaction to someone as if she or he were someone else from our early history. It is another urge to reenact, as described in the previous chapter. The way one reacts to the transference someone else is experiencing with us, is countertransference, as it is found in psychotherapy; it is also related to projective identification, another analytical concept. But it should be noted that these two manifestations of the unconscious, transference and countertransference, happen in most situations and encounters, not merely in the therapy relationship. My encounter with John, the dental hygienist I described in the first chapter, was transference, because I transferred onto John my perception, false and outdated, of the dangerous big guy.

Finally, defense mechanisms, to be explained in Chapter 5, are unconscious ways of coping with difficult contingencies that produce anxiety. Regression, one of the common defense mechanisms, is usually part of transference because one reacts to a friend, boss, or spouse as if he or she were an important figure from one's past who elicited strong emotions. To put it in other words, when an event or person unconsciously reminds one of something in one's history, the reminiscence now brings back emotions similar to the ones experienced then.

Id, ego, and superego

These three aspects of personality are called *structures*. For some, like Kernberg (1980), they are thought to originate in internal objects or representations, while Freud felt they came from the psychic drives or instincts. In initially describing the unconscious, and years later the parts of the personality, Freud expressed what every moderately introspective individual has noted and experienced. What I call "myself" or "I" has different aspects depending on situations and circumstances. The English translators of Freud made his original nomenclature more complicated than it was. Freud referred to the I or "*das ich*," not to the ego; to the it or "*das es*," not to the id; and to what was translated as superego as "*das Überich*" or "that which is above the I" or "the I that is, or stands, on top." I call it the "I above," but not in this book. To avoid confusion, I use the traditional, though deficient, designations of id, ego, and superego. Freud was proposing to describe, in understandable terms, our mostly conscious self or the *I*, our impulsive self or the *It*, and the *superego* as our superior (spiritual?) self that includes our conscience, or what we would call our soul or higher self as Chapter 7 discusses. Just by listing these structures, or "parts," we understand that the id and the superego are antagonistic to each other and are engaged in a constant struggle for control of the ego, the individual. We also realize that the ego is like a mediator between the other two parts. These three parts refer to our experience of doing what is expected and accepted—the ego—or wanting and doing what comes from our impulsive desires, irrespective of our own good judgment—the id—and of knowing what we must or should do, not to mention our feeling bad about things we have done or did not do when we should have done them—the superego. Developmentally, the id comes first; little children are all id, and the superego (true sense of right and wrong) appears last, at about seven or eight. The ego evolves, first in a rudimentary manner, from the early experiences and from the choices the child makes between id and superego tendencies.

We can think of simple examples of these three aspects of our self as adults. When a normal person engages in impulsive shopping, reckless driving, excessive drinking or eating, his id is active and has taken over. When a woman takes care of her small children without the help of a partner and with a limited budget, she is manifesting or acting on the influence of the ego. And when a person deprives himself of sleep to assist someone in need, or another feels bad because she missed the chance to console a relative who was upset about an accident, they are revealing the superego. Goodness comes normally from the superego and it also explains the most heroic and generous actions of humans. The superego is also unconscious in many of its manifestations.

As a clinician, you become more helpful to clients if you recognize and use these different aspects of the individual's personality. How? By honestly sharing with the patient what you notice about the client from what she is saying and from the way she is acting. It's not that you assert, "This is the way it is," but rather pose it as a question: "I notice this; what do you think?" For instance, in some cases she acts conscientiously and in others quite irresponsibly; and that there seems to be a pattern governing each type of behavior. "Patterns of behavior" means responding in similar ways, or acting or reacting the same way in different situations, and these patterns often manifest personality traits and even the urge to reenact. For example, a person who engages in three or four things at once may also find it difficult or impossible to pay attention to any single topic in a regular conversation. His mind is constantly jumping from one thing to another because of reasons that only the client can discover through self-introspection. Is it fear of facing painful memories? Looking for new satisfactions, the desire for which may pop up when she is not ready for them? Dissatisfaction with what she has and expecting always something new and better? Some biological or medical explanation? You simply present these questions to the client as invitations to introspection, to look into the possibilities. Once the client accepts at least the possibility of there being a valid explanation for her "habit," she is in psychoanalytic territory and will find the reason for her repeated behavior in different circumstances. This, in turn, as we said earlier, frees her not to have to act as she did before.

Thanks to this approach, the client starts to view her life as congruent: it makes sense. Things that happen in one's life are connected to other pieces of the person's history. Congruency is not necessarily healthy; it is often neurotic as in the example above. (Psychotic acts may also follow patterns, like the extreme cases we hear about once in a while, such as the murder of young children by sexual predators.) The therapeutic work is thus lined up before the client's eyes so she can move, with the help of psychoanalytic therapy towards a mentally healthier life.

There are many ways of using the constructs of id, ego, and superego in clinical practice. You can help yourself and your clients by acknowledging that many of your thoughts, feelings, and behaviors during the session come from your unconscious. For instance, when in the psychotherapy session you experience a memory, a reaction, a sudden feeling, or notice some quasi-instinctive behavior triggered by something that is happening in the session (countertransference), you'll benefit, after the session, by investigating how the thought, feeling, or behavior can be connected or related to other things in your life and previous experience, such as people, events, ordinary moments or special occasions. To find out if there is some unconscious reality in a particular case, when the client is gone, you use some of the many "psychoanalytical questions." For instance:

• Did I ever experience this type of reaction in similar circumstances? (If I can't make a connection, then free association is called for; relaxing myself, I let any thoughts and mental images pass through my mind, allowing them to branch off in other directions. I'll discover meaning in what happens inside of me.)

• What were the surroundings then and who were the people involved?

• Are there similarities between the situation (and its details) then and now?

• What are the differences between then and now?

• Does this elicit in me feelings I have had before in my life?

• Can I identify my basic feelings in this situation? (Fear, annoyance, anger, expectation, etc.)

• Are these feelings familiar to me? Do they bring up memories of something else? And so on.

The same method, obviously, is used with a patient. You may identify the id and the superego in your personality (or as parts of your personality) without your understanding the origin of what is happening. And the ego, mostly, and not always consciously, decides what you choose to do, although what initially took effort may have become a habit and now you do it "without thinking." Good manners and courtesy are examples, as well as the fluent speaking of a new language. But often people do things consciously and voluntarily without realizing the influence of the id (the callous criminal) or of the superego (the Mother Theresa [MT] type), which operate unconsciously. The lack of awareness of the unconscious dynamics of our actions often leads us to make mistakes or to engage in self-defeating or destructive behavior. The callous criminal may become too confident in his work. The MT type may end up being an enabler and a martyr. It's impossible to avoid all mistakes, but when we learn to consider the unconscious, we end up making fewer mistakes because we have the tools to examine our actions under the light of psychic dynamics that are, otherwise, hidden.

In sum, what you believe you are doing consciously (ego acts) may be influenced by the id or the superego. For your clinical practice, the Freudian teaching on the different parts in one's personality can take very useful forms. The client can be introduced to the fact that "I" is not a simple and constant concept. When someone says that she is afraid of intimacy, for instance, the clinician can encourage her to figure out "What part in her" is saying that. The I that has been hurt and disappointed in previous relations may be very afraid of intimacy. But another part in her personality, the one who wants to share her life with another, the one who wants to trust another and to feel comfortable with another, may be saying something different: "I know there is the risk of being hurt but with this person whom I have known for a while, the risk is worth taking." The patient can concentrate on one or another part. She may be helped to listen to both "sides" and come to a decision that is prudent and fair. Otherwise, decisions may be made out of blind fear coming from the personality part that was hurt, perhaps the id in some action, or maybe from a neurotic superego that believes she is not worthy of happiness.

How can you do this in clinical practice? There are several approaches, with a popular and well-researched one being that of ego states therapy (Watkins and Watkins 1997). What I call "activation of personality parts" modifies it slightly, emphasizing experiential imagination or *vivencia* (Araoz and Goldin 2004). For example, when the client makes a statement about herself that the clinician considers unfair to the client ("I can't let myself trust him"), the reply may state something like, "I wonder if every part of your personality agrees with this statement. Perhaps there is a soft voice in you that is not in agreement. Can you listen to that other part?"

If this is not enough to help the client recognize the personality parts, you may add, "People often say, 'Part of me wants or likes something but another part does not.' You may now check this in yourself, remembering that the two opposite 'parts' are both you." In some cases, you may even help the client designate each part with a name or nickname, like the smart part and the stupid part in one's personality, or the honest part and the wiseguy part. Let the client find a designating name for each. In general, you can always ask, "What part in you is feeling (thinking, speaking, planning) that?" and "What is another part in you feeling (thinking, speaking, planning)?"

This type of intervention is psychoanalytic and it teaches the client to be more careful and reflective, so that he does not miss the true inner conflict between aspects of one's personality (ego, id, superego) that often complicates perceptions, desires, decisions, expectations, and actions. This in itself moves the superficial approach of staying with the symptom to a deeper level. The man who complains, for instance, about always being late may realize that a personality part in him uses lateness to be noticed, or to rebel because he "is not like all the others," or out of anger, or . . . There are many other possibilities.

Notice that without this awareness, he may still unsuccessfully try cognitive-behavioral methods to avoid being late. Often therapy fails to help the client because it lingers on the superficial level of the symptom, refusing to go deeper into the personality of the client with its different parts.

Personality types

Freud's classification of personality types is very broad and, as such, is not to be used as scientific evidence of personality differences. But, given the popularity of these terms, it is important to know what they originally meant. The three interacting parts of our psyche lead us to begin to understand what happens when, as Freud taught originally, the ego of an individual does not develop naturally. In normal development all persons go through three or four immature stages, depending on the main anatomical center where vital energy is experienced; these are the oral, anal, phallic, and genital. At the height of the phallic phase comes the Oedipus complex, thanks to which eventually the superego is consolidated.

There is also the latency stage, between the phallic and genital stages, which is a period of learning and acquiring social, physical, and cognitive skills. It is a period of integration among the drives and defense mechanisms. When the ego is stuck (fixated, in technical jargon) in one of these stages without advancing to the next one, as happens in healthy development, the person is said to have one of the personality types that constitute abnormality or psychopathology, as Freud called it. The oral type is passive-dependent with others, continuing to seek sustenance from others, as he did in infancy from his mother. When he gets this psychic "food" he is happy, confident, and positive. Otherwise he is annoyed, negative, and pessimistic. If he does not get this emotional sustenance from people, he finds it in things such as food or drugs, including alcohol, caffeine, and others. The anal type, reflecting what her early toilet-training experiences were, is either very methodical and parsimonious, demanding the same from those around her, or sloppy and wasteful, annoying others she comes in contact with. The phallic type shows in adulthood as adolescent immaturity with sexual conflicts that are often dramatic and irrational. The Oedipus complex defines later problems with intimacy and commitment in relating to a special person as a love partner. Being stuck in the latency period, which is characterized by interest in the outside world as I mentioned above, produces a very routinized and limited adult whose main concerns are cognitive, physical, and social enrichment. Finally, the genital type is the normal, mentally healthy adult.

In spite of the popularity and attraction of these personality types, they have to be taken as merely one method of understanding the real differences of people as compared with their peers. Nowadays this Freudian typology is deemed rather primitive, too simple and biased, as it was based on his model of human development centered on the pleasure principle. In modern developmental psychology, the preferred language is to talk about birth to around age 2 as infancy (oral); the ages from about 2 to 4 as early childhood (anal), overlapping from about 3 to 7 with the phallic stage, with the oedipal resolution at its peak; and approximately from 7 to 12 as childhood (latency), and about 12 to 18 as adolescence (genital). Within the original Freudian categories, several of his followers added subcategories and other symbolic names like anal retentive or anal explosive, phallic narcissist or adult phallic narcissist. Others, like Kernberg (1976), emphasize the early stages as responsible for structure formation or, inversely, that the formation of the id, ego, and superego itself goes through developmental stages (for him, five stages, from the first month of life to later childhood) in order to establish *identity formation*. But the current preference seems to be to use simpler language that avoids the focus on sexual development as primary.

Inner drives

For many years Freud understood human intentionality and behavior as being motivated by or coming from the pleasure principle. Much later in his life he discovered the death instinct. Much has been said about the dual-drive theory. Here, as one of the important tools of knowing and doing, is a simplified description of this concept. Humans do things moved either by a drive to love and life and to build (Eros), or by the drive of aggression and death, to destroy (Thanatos). Most therapists are comfortable with Eros and try to foster it in their clients but Thanatos makes them uncomfortable. This is due to something Meadow (2003) explains, that "Clinical experience did not bear out the equating of the death drive with aggression. All we can see . . . are tendencies to move between tension increase and tension decrease" (p. 29). This approach–avoidance rhythm, so common in human behavior, is a focus of analysis because when the two drives do not "work cooperatively in living acts" (p. 30), they are part of the client's psychopathology.

As a practical rule of thumb, one can notice behavioral and verbal patterns of the patient that are self-enhancing and constructive and those that are the opposite. Merely to point them out to the client ("Check that; it looks to me that it was unfair to you to act that way," or "How does it feel to have done such an exceptional thing for yourself?" or any other indirect way of pointing to the appearance of one or the other basic drives) is beneficial to her mental health because it starts to motivate the client to increase Eros and diminish Thanatos. Freud's "Beyond the Pleasure Principle" (1920), especially Chapters 5 to 7, is very enlightening in this respect.

* * *

Awakening an awareness of the psychoanalytic approach to the real understanding and handling of human difficulties and problems has the advantage of getting the patient interested and motivated in his self-knowledge, government, and improvement. Clients with these attitudes are willing to work, value their therapy sessions, and cooperate with their clinician because they learn to trust the method that helps them be well, happier, and more in control. Satisfied patients are the strong evidence that makes psychoanalysis valid and legitimate. Frattaroli (2001) makes a sober and excellent argument in favor of psychoanalysis as the "scientific" tool to study subjectivity. While I don't want to repeat it, here, I merely ask you to consider this as seriously as you can. The main aim of science is to know the truth about things. In order to attain this goal, science applies diverse methods and tools. These techniques serve a precise purpose;

astronomy uses different methods and instruments than oceanography or biology or any other science, but they all go after the truth of what is. We claim that to find the truth of subjectivity, to understand what it is, psychoanalysis is the method to use. You may start right now to think psychoanalytically about your actions and feelings. This will make it natural and easy for you to lead your clients in this direction of lasting positive results. On the other hand, for this type of therapy, trust in the therapist is still the main variable to explain success. The current heavy emphasis on evidence-based practice, encouraged by managed care in order to shorten treatment to a minimum, does not apply to a form of therapy that is trust-based. Therefore, your psychoanalytic thinking about yourself will make you sensitive to your clients in a new way and will allow them to truly trust you.

This chapter is an introduction to the richness of psychoanalysis. However, not all aspects of it are essential to your clinical work as that of a non-psychoanalyst who wants to work psychodynamically. To start working with unconscious material, there are many refined theories and concepts that you can wait to learn later, after you have become both familiar with the hidden levels of human behavior and adept at dealing with the area of psychodynamics or depth psychology in human conduct. Among the theories on the waiting list, you may have, for instance, the Oedipus and Electra complexes, narcissism, and the castration anxiety and complex, just to mention a few. And there are also many technical terms like "cathexis" (a word not used by Freud but by his English translators), or "anagogic" among the different forms of interpretation, or perhaps even "anaclitic," to mean erotic attraction to someone because of some resemblance to positive figures of childhood. But these are all terms that you don't need in the beginning in order to make use of unconscious elements in your mental health work. Finally, specific ways of applying psychoanalysis, such as the ones to be discussed in the next chapter, can be added to the waiting list.

Please note that I insist on the fact that you don't need these concepts and terms to start working psychoanalytically. This does not mean that the things you don't need at the start are useless or frivolous. As suggested in the Introduction, basic math is sufficient and effective to pay your bills and balance the checkbook, without the need for algebra or advanced calculus. As you progress, you will learn as much as you can, and discover the meaning, applicability, and clinical value of these terms and concepts and many more. This book is intended to open new doors in your development as a psychotherapist. If you begin with the premise that the unconscious is an inevitable aspect of our human nature, you will want to know more about it. But this "knowing" is much more than rational, intellectual knowledge. It is *experiential* knowing, and your own experience of being in psychoanalysis is an essential part of it.

Chapter 3
BRANCHES FROM THE ORIGINAL TRUNK

Psychoanalysis, because it is rooted in the unconscious (what is not known), has been a living system from the very beginning. Freud himself made significant changes to his theories over his long career, and after him his followers refined, unfolded, and complemented many aspects of the original psychoanalytic product. Again it must be stressed that much as Freud deserves credit, respect, admiration, and thanks for his work, he was just the pioneer of the unconscious and did not say, much less claim to have said, the last word about psychoanalysis. In both its theory and applications psychoanalysis is still changing, growing, and improving. Moreover, it is important to realize that psychoanalysis today (both theoretically and especially in its practice) is very different from what it was when Freud started it, or even from what it was thirty years ago. Personally, had I not kept in touch with the modern developments of the field, what I learned in the late 1960s would now be mostly incomplete and out of date. In sum, when someone identifies herself as a psychoanalyst, it might be helpful for you to find out what school of thought or what model or school she follows, just as when someone says she is a physician and you want to know what her specialty is. The subsequent brief descriptions of some of the branches of the main tree may help you to recognize the differences among some of the well-established and popular psychoanalytic models. Of course, to really know any of these schools you have to study the original writings and significant commentaries.

Ego psychology

Anna Freud, three years before her father's death in 1939, published a landmark book that launched ego psychology as the first direct development of Freud's system. The father's emphasis on the struggle of our inner forces for control allows us to call his theory an "id psychology." Whereas originally the ego was seen as an arbitrator between the id and the superego, Freud's daughter viewed the ego as having its independent energy and purpose, especially in its movement to establish useful relations with the outside world, including others (that is, psychosocial development), in areas like competence in decision-making and in moral choices. In order to accomplish this, the ego, with the help of the unconscious, uses healthy and normal defense mechanisms that are essentially adaptive and self-protective. There is no official list of defenses because many ego psychologists have added to Anna Freud's (1936) original list and have found more. Even nonprofessionals use "defense mechanism language" when they discuss denial, repression, magical thinking, identification, regression, projection, and the like. Only the misuse of these defense mechanisms is neurotic, self-defeating, and counterproductive. For example, we may say of someone that her defenses are up, or that he has built up a thick wall of defenses around himself. People who are trapped in their defense system limit their capabilities, weaken their ego, and become unhappy and less productive. And notice in passing the relationship of Anna's defense mechanisms to her father's repetition compulsion; we tend to repeat or reenact the original ways we learned (defenses) to cope with anxiety, even though they may have lost their usefulness. We'll come back to these psychic defenses when we deal with anxiety in Chapter 4.

Therefore, the ego's function is not merely to control the contradictory demands of the id and the superego but to develop its own capabilities (ego strength). Erik Erikson (1950) was one of the many ego psychologists who stressed the need to develop a healthy ego. Moreover, although Freud thought the personality was basically complete by adolescence, ego psychologists found in Erikson the theoretician who recognized, with his eight stages of development, the lifelong formation process of human personality. More recently, Levinson (1978, 1996) expanded on Erikson's work and enriched earlier information on human development.

What does ego psychology add to psychoanalytic thinking? The emphasis on defense mechanisms helps clinicians to make people aware of their interactive and self-reference styles (the way one thinks of and feels about himself). If the client is using self-defeating defenses, the mental health practitioner may suggest trying other defenses. Some ego psychologists refer to "analysis of defense mechanisms." Here is an example. A math professor was a good painter and depended on his academic income to pursue his painting career. In his dedication to art he neglected his teaching obligations, to the point that he lost his academic position and with it his ability to afford the costs of being a professional artist. His wife saw the shift in professional interests and talked to him many times in the two years before he lost his job. He always reassured her that he could manage both occupations. You figure out, as an exercise now, what type of defenses (more than one) the math professor was using against his better interests.

Ego psychology also helps the clinician to concretely support clients in their ongoing personality development. The emphasis on healthy stages of human growth teaches us that people can catch up on lost benefits of previous developmental stages, as shown by Levinson's research, mentioned above.

Finally, ego strength gives support to the importance of self-esteem and respect as a vital element of subjective well-being and satisfaction, a view popular since at least the early 2000s (Seligman 2000). The clinician would do well to monitor how the client views herself and what sort of self-talk she engages in. Self-talk, and the mental images that it triggers, activates feelings that strengthen or weaken the ego (Araoz and Sutton 2003).

Object relations
In the 1930s and '40s a new emphasis started to grow in psychoanalytical thinking in part as a development of ego psychology. The organizing principle of the human psyche was seen as the relation of the individual with others. However, the object relations view holds that one's perception changes "others" and often distorts them in one's own mind. This representation of the other in one's mind is called the object. Thus, the strange name of this new psychoanalytical development comes from the fact that we relate, not to real people, but to perceived objects. Object relations theory comes from the direct study of infants and children, initially stressed by Melanie Klein (1932). Her findings made the researchers realize that in early infancy babies perceive all people around them as mere objects to satisfy their needs, and that growing up to be autonomous requires the change from taking to giving, as Fairbairn (1954) puts it. He and many others, like Kernberg (1975, 1980), concentrate on the first three years of life and study how humans become individuals by developing their conflict-free ego. The mechanism of mental representation starts in the very early interactions, especially with the mother. In this sense object relations thought emphasizes the

mother's role in the development of human personality, correcting Freud's overemphasis on the father. Other luminaries stressed the importance of play in early development (see Winnicott 1971).

What does object relations theory add to psychoanalytical thinking? I see it as a concrete tool to test reality by accepting others as imperfect and also to be realistic in our expectations of them. In particular, the importance of a nurturing mother in the first months and years of a child's life is highlighted in this approach, giving women the greatest importance in the emotional rearing of the infant, something that had not been realized before the arrival of object relations. A corollary of this, for both men and women, is to be aware of object relations in intersexual relations, especially in courtship and marriage. Among many possibilities, the man may see the woman as the source and cause of his happiness, while she may react to him as the normal mother reacts to her baby. Finally, guided by this new thinking, we become aware of the danger of negative self-hypnosis, as I called it (Araoz 1981) in agreement with Kernberg's (1980) and Kohut's (1971) insights. The former emphasized that among the most serious distortions of object relations are, first, not to distinguish clearly between the self and others, and also to confuse one's inner perceptions with external stimuli. Because of these two elements, among others, we can get into a negative self-hypnotic state that distorts reality. In clinical practice, I often find it helpful to assist the patient to double-check his perception on the basis of the facts that distress him and also to pay attention to overidentification with others.

Self psychology

When it comes to psychoanalytic systems, ego and self are different. Self psychology is an offshoot of object relations, as St. Clair (1996) indicates. It too focuses on the early relationships, and stresses the inner representation of one's own self, not merely that of others. Self, as used here, refers to the habitual, most-of-the-time subjective state of well-being, including one's general mood, sense of independence, and autonomy, as well as the level one maintains between tension and relaxation. Kohut (1977) analyzes the self based on the two early emotional needs of infancy. One is to have the parents accurately notice and reinforce the behavior and experiences of the infant to make him or her feel important (*mirroring*). The other is idealization, the need of the infant to view his or her parents as perfect and to see him- or herself as part of them (*the grandiose self*). These immature needs have to contribute to the formation, throughout one's life, of a cohesive self with a healthy superego that includes an *ego ideal*. The opposite of the cohesive self is the defective self. Narcissistic disorders, unhealthy relationships, general personality insecurity, and other mental health problems are understood as results of the defective self. As an historical detail it must be noted that Winnicott (1965) had earlier redefined Kleinian concepts and explicated ideas later taken up by self-psychologists (1971), enriching the understanding of the self.

Obviously, then, self psychology's contribution to psychoanalytic thinking consists of a concrete understanding of what the mature self is all about. It also offers a plan of action to achieve the elusive cohesive self by relating it to the early developmental stages and by clarifying Freud's reality principle in very practical ways. In clinical work, therefore, it is important and useful to encourage the patient to recognize the impact that his parents had on his personality, that is, on his self. Often in psychotherapy the client learns to accept the shortcomings of his parents and recognizes that, as long as there is insight and awareness, there is the possibility of freeing oneself from the desire for "perfect parents" so that one can, as an adult, make up for what was lacking in the early years.

Relational psychoanalysis

This model, often present in contemporary psychoanalysis, is also closely linked to object relations and pays close attention to mental representations of early interactions with their three elements: self, other, and the interaction itself. All mental representations of important early interactions color and give shape to subsequent experiences. But each new experience influences and modifies the previous mental representations. What we perceive is a function of our basic needs for security and for excitement. But because during our development from birth to death our needs change, we need flexibility and freedom to alter our interactions. In order to succeed we have to find a way to modify our mental representations. For instance, healthy growth moves from absolute dependence to mature dependence, as Fairbairn (1952) puts it, combining independence and intimacy, and to interdependence, as others like Russianoff (1982) have called it.

If the therapist misses these psychodynamics, the patient may never connect her current interpersonal style with the original influences that shaped it. Yes, she may be able to modify it slightly, but will revert again and again to the early representations. In this therapy model, initial goals often change or are modified because in order to understand current interactions one must explore and study the nature of early relationships. This requires an openness to exploration and a readiness to find the unexpected. The mental health professional, especially when working with couples, may find this psychoanalytical model useful. This approach, more than others, liberates the client from stereotyped and archaic ways of relating, giving him new possibilities that enrich his life. Mature dependence is truly interdependence and the clinician using this model helps clients to develop their mature dependence so they can give more of themselves in relationships, while expecting less from the others for their own happiness. The relational school stresses the therapeutic value of the genuine relationship between clinician and client in analysis (see Mitchell 2000).

Modern psychoanalysis

This school is also called "new psychoanalysis" (Meadow 2003), and although its theorists claim to go back to Freud's original meaning, it also is an effort to avoid complicated jargon. Its proponents criticize many of the modern authors who use such terminology, and instead zero-in on the essentials for clinical practice. Thus, they use the dual-drive theory of Freud's late writings, namely Eros and Thanatos, finding these elements in every human conflict. One of the justifications for their approach, among others, is that—together with the need for attachment—many who had deficient emotional experiences early in life feel the drive to detach and destroy.

One merit of modern psychoanalysis (Spotnitz 1976, 1985) is that its practitioners have accepted very disturbed clients, such as patients diagnosed as psychotic or schizophrenic, and by applying psychoanalytic principles and techniques have been able to help them to grow as human beings. The emotional connection of the therapist with the patient is emphasized and used throughout treatment. Because of this orientation, unlike other forms of analysis, they always concentrate on primitive, preverbal (preoedipal) defenses, including somatization or projective identification, among others, that may be at work unconsciously.

Jungian psychology

We shall discuss Jung again in Chapter 15. Carl G. Jung (1959) was originally very close to Freud as a young psychiatrist, and had been chosen by Freud to be his successor. But on a voyage they took together to lecture in the United States, when the disciple spoke publicly about disagreements with the teachings of the master, their contentious and tense relationship came to an end. Thus in 1913 he became one of the most important disciples to break away from Freud's theories, though not from psychoanalysis, for which he preferred the label *analytical psychology*. For instance, Jung's balance of personality preferences has been presented as more accessible and easier to understand than Freud's theories; moreover, Jung's basic ideas have been made popular through the Myers-Briggs Type Indicator (Myers and Myers 1993), widely used in training institutions and generally in the corporate world to identify the personality preferences of individuals. For Jung, libido is a fundamental life force, including deep-seated personality attitudes toward life and death. He analyzes the major personality functions or the ways we perceive the world and make decisions about events, people, and possibilities of the past, present, and future. Those who have a balance between these functions are healthy and therapy aims at this goal of parity. These functions include extraversion/introversion (contact with the world around and introspection), sensation/intuition (an equivalence between the evidence of the senses and one's gut feeling), thinking/feeling (in judgments and decisions), and judging/perceiving (a regular evenness between order and planning and spontaneity and risk-taking). In most people there is an imbalance between these functions. Hence the need for analysis that emphasizes the intellectual and spiritual aspects of human personality, not the primitive drives (pleasure and aggression).

Jung held that we have both an individual/personal as well as a collective unconscious that connects us to the rest of mankind through the centuries with the archetypes. He spoke of our *persona*, with its animus and anima (the feminine and masculine in every person), and finally of our *shadow* or darker self.

From a clinical perspective, the emphasis on personality functions can be very useful when working with couples, families, and groups, so that the differences between two people who work or live together can be respected as "different" rather than only oppositional. This change in perception helps the client adapt better to the other person and to benefit by learning from the other about responses that may enrich him. In a couple in which the wife is much more perceptive than her judging husband, both can attain the healthy balance as each comes to learn the ways of the other: he becomes more spontaneous, she more organized.

Others

The list of psychoanalytical schools of thought is much longer and includes the Adlerians, whose founder Alfred Adler also parted with Freud but not with the basic ideas of unconscious dynamics set out in his theory. Others who strongly proclaimed their anti-Freudian stance are still working in the territory of the unconscious, like Fritz Perls with his gestalt therapy, with the many techniques he developed to help patients become aware of inner realities that affect their quality of living.

The simple rule of thumb is easy: Any system or method that recognizes the importance of unconscious dynamics in human behavior and focuses clinically on them is essentially psychoanalytic, no matter what name it uses or what claims it may make against Freud.

* * *

As a non-psychoanalyst, you don't have to be an expert in any of these models of psychoanalysis but you must realize that the practice of psychoanalysis is far from uniform. The one common element is the unconscious and its psychodynamics. This means that all those who identify themselves as psychoanalysts consider the unconscious and work with it. Those who work with the behavioral symptoms, with erroneous beliefs, and, in general, with distorted cognitions are non-psychodynamic in theory and practice. In utilizing psychoanalysis, you always look for the inner dynamics that produce or maintain the symptoms. You know that to remove the symptom effectively you must help the patient look for the possibility that it (the presenting problem, what bothers him, the symptom) might be connected to individual psychological needs, usually neurotic, rooted in the makeup of his personality as it was influenced by early experiences. Santayana summed it up well, even though he was not a psychoanalyst: "If we ignore the past, we are bound to repeat it." The patient's personality, like our own, is the result of his entire past. As a consequence, to focus on the symptom without considering its roots and genesis will provide only short-term benefits because the cause and core of the symptom remains untouched. On the other hand, by directing the client to examine the dynamics of her early development you help her separate herself from early "learnings" that have become useless or damaging in the present and allow her to face her freedom with the opportunity to act differently.

Regarding personality, the authors of the *DSM-IV-TR* (2000) had the good idea of grouping personality disorders into three "clusters," following the main manifestations of the different types listed as personality disorders. For Cluster A comprising paranoid, schizoid, and schizotypal types, the common trait is bizarre thinking and behavior. Cluster B, with the antisocial, borderline, and histrionic personality types, shows extreme self-absorption. Lastly, wimpiness or psychological ineffectualness are the common traits of Cluster C, encompassing the narcissistic, avoidant, dependent, and obsessive-compulsive personality types. These are helpful guidelines to consult when considering the possibility that negative psychodynamics are at work.

For example, if a patient repeatedly finds herself in serious interpersonal difficulties, in order to really help her (not merely to assist her in resolving the current difficulty with succinct behavioral formulas), we may consider the possibility of Cluster B problems and explore it. If another client constantly fails in every endeavor she starts, most of them good ideas, we might help her investigate whether Cluster C elements make up her personality. Again, if the person we are dealing with comes up regularly with strange methods of behavior in conducting himself and resolving his difficulties, or is acting in ways that are noticeably different from the cultural and age-appropriate norms, we should think of Cluster A. Thus, the closest the *DSM* comes to psychoanalytical thinking, aside from Axis III, dealing with the stressor that produces anxiety, is in the section on personality disorders, indexed in Axis II for adults (see McWilliams 1994).

Briefly stated, the clinician will often notice that the particular problem the individual complains about is connected with the client's personality makeup, fitting at least one of the *DSM* "clusters." Traits of two clusters may be present. Even so, the cluster idea is a handy tool that helps one to proceed to the area that gives meaning to "the presenting problem." And its use with the later developments of psychoanalysis offers an opportunity for the clinician to be more effective with clients.

Chapter 4
STRESS AND PSYCHOANALYSIS

Freud, even before his interest in psychodynamics, was curious about the relation between body and mind. Studying human behavior and subjectivity, he realized, as Hall (1954) explains, that most "mental processes are essentially and basically unconscious" and "that those [processes] that are conscious are the exception, merely isolated acts but, and none the less, parts of the whole psychic entity" (p. 56). So, initially, he made the broad distinction between conscious and unconscious, though later he developed it by introducing the three-part organization of the personality that we discussed in the second chapter. Most of the qualities he had attributed to the unconscious were later included in the domain of the id. Freud explained that all mental activities begin at the unconscious level, and that only by reference to the unconscious (the larger psychic system) can conscious processes be understood and explained.

Perhaps you remember an analogy from your first psychology class that compared the mind with an iceberg, with most of it underwater (the unconscious) and only a small fraction of its mass visible (the conscious). Freud, through the creation of psychoanalysis, tried to find out how a particular "visible" symptom fit into the larger psychic system, one that was not directly evident and that showed itself only behaviorally. He tried to uncover the unconscious meaning of the symptom, knowing that it is impossible to completely objectify subjectivity. This, by the way, is an important point nowadays, as one confronts the assertion that only objectively validated procedures should be used in psychotherapy. However, because of his interest in subjectivity, Freud's method was focused on the individual, whom he tried to observe with an open mind and without preconceived assumptions in order to find the connections of the known and evident with the unknown or unconscious. This still stands as one of the few methods available to study subjectivity. Stated differently, in this view all symptoms and neurotic behavior are ineffective attempts at expressing and resolving inner conflicts, that is to say, unconscious issues that still remain from previous experiences, mainly those of our early development.

And here lies one of the points of controversy between psychoanalysis and the cognitive-behavioral approaches to human problems, as I intimated before. Initially, Freud considered that once the origin and meaning of the symptoms were found and understood, that is, how the symptoms were part of the larger psychic system with its id instinctual impulses, there was no longer a need for the symptoms and the person became well. This theory arose from the fact that Freud took the universally natural process of homeostasis as also applying to the human psyche. Natural systems correct themselves; they modify themselves in order to reestablish equilibrium. So too in our psyche, Freud thought, viewing the symptom as an attempt to restore normal functioning or homeostasis. It is a sign that an attempt at healing is at work, yet the symptom is a mistake (neurosis) because it is not producing the desired effect of establishing healthy psychic balance.

Freud's early thinking, very briefly, can be outlined thus: a mental maneuver from one's early learning is used unconsciously to cope with or handle anxiety. But it does not work; anxiety continues. Why that should be the case was the big question. Psychoanalysis came along to explain the mistaken origin of the symptom but at first expected that, once its cause was elucidated, the symptom would disappear. However, the human psyche is more complicated, as Freud soon realized. A combination of two elements, according to this thinking, explains the symptom. One is from the past, namely, its origin in early life. The other element is its status in the present, or the function the symptom serves now. This function of the symptom is directly related to anxiety, consciously felt but not understood, caused by "loose ends" from the past still awaiting resolution to a greater or lesser degree. Therefore, in one form or another, the symptom develops in an attempt to cope with anxiety and hopefully to ward it off. Neurosis is a pseudo-homeostasis.

Anxiety

Because of its powerful effect, anxiety is also the common motivator, in one form or another, for getting well. After the individual has unconsciously developed neurotic symptoms to avoid or diminish the painful experience of being anxious, and after having discovered that they do not do the trick, and after perhaps having tried other means of getting rid of the anxiety, the patient turns to psychodynamic psychotherapy in order to find the right way to resolve it. At that point, it is hoped, the entire and long unconscious process is slowly brought to consciousness and understood, allowing the patient to freely choose more productive ways to live. In other words, anxiety does not arise from the symptoms; they are only the misguided attempts at ending anxiety. As a matter of fact, because anxiety is still experienced along with the neurotic symptoms, it shows that they do not work to reduce or end the anxiety. But, and I have to insist on it, this whole process is unconscious.

Freud's first theory of anxiety was rooted in physiology. Libido, considered as allied with the pleasure principle, was the only drive. Therefore, if libido was not satisfied, anxiety was the result. Later, in 1926, in his paper "Inhibitions, Symptoms, and Anxiety," Freud emphasized the psychological view: anxiety comes from the anticipation of danger, from a threat to the individual; hence, he distinguished two types of anxiety, one arising from physiological sources, the other of psychic origin. The first is elicited as a response to a real external danger and may be very adaptive, while the second is a response to anticipated danger (*signal anxiety*), which means that the ego produces defensive thoughts and behaviors, the extreme expression of them being a panic attack and/or a traumatic state. Worrying about a suspected illness, for instance, especially when it starts affecting areas of your normal functioning like sleep and food intake or digestion, is a familiar expression of signal anxiety.

Because anxiety can do so much harm to the entire human system—mind and body—its treatment is always considered a priority. In the 1950s, mental hygiene was commonly accepted as a preventive measure against anxiety. The term is rarely used today, but the concept of checking our inner self (thoughts, wishes, reactions, judgments, and feelings in general), much advocated by self-help theories, is centered on the experience of anxiety as a negative and self-limiting psychic experience. As physical hygiene benefits the body, mental hygiene keeps the thinking/feeling apparatus functioning to our advantage. Therefore, mental hygiene is proactive, encouraging the cultivation of optimistic and constructive attitudes, not waiting till worry and anxiety take over in order to react against self-defeating thoughts. I'll come back to this in Chapter 15.

From quick fix to introspection and self-transformation

Myriam is a case in point. At 42, she was a top executive in a relatively large public relations firm, where over 50 percent of the employees were black. Though her skin color was very light, she considered herself African American. However, she did not get along well with people of darker skin. She rationalized it by believing that it had nothing to do with skin color but simply with qualifications and competence. However, so many complaints were lodged with respect to her management style with the darker employees that her boss spoke to her very sternly and ordered her to change. She decided to seek therapeutic counseling, presenting the problem of anxiety arising from her boss's admonition and from her need to learn quickly how to improve her interpersonal relations. All she wanted was "to learn new ways of dealing better with my subordinates." The quick-fix wish was soon modified. It soon emerged that with some (all of lighter skin color) she did very well and with others (all dark-skinned people) very poorly. She first denied that there was any difference in her management style. When asked psychoanalytical questions, as explained in Chapter 2, Myriam found the answer to her interpersonal difficulties in her upbringing. She was the third child of a five-sibling family, the only girl among four boys who all treated her as "inferior and dumb." She also had the lightest skin color in the family, because of which her brothers teased her as if to suggest she had not been a legitimate child. The remarkable thing in this story is that she had put this out of her mind in such a way (through defense mechanisms of denial and repression) that when she "rediscovered" what had happened during the first 18 or so years of her life she was surprised; she kept saying, "I can't believe I didn't realize this." In the eight sessions of "psychoanalytical counseling," as she insisted on calling it, she did not learn concrete rules and formulas to handle dark-skinned people with respect and patience as she had expressed the desire to do when she started therapy, but she increased her self knowledge and resolved her repressed identity conflict that had bothered her all her life. She stopped depending on her brothers' early assessment of her ethnicity and legitimacy and used her current, mature, judgment to decide who she was and what she was. She made the important distinction between her brothers, who were truly unfair and mean to her in the past, and the current black people, who were no threat to her as her brothers had been when she was a child and adolescent. Myriam learned to use introspection in order to understand her perceptions and reactions. About six months later, she came back "to finish the job I started with you." She had gotten a good promotion and explained that she had no problems dealing with her subordinates now, no matter how dark they were, but that she wanted to do more "tying-up" work in order to have better control of her life. She had met a new man in her life, a "dark chocolate" person who she thought was "the right one" and she wanted to make sure that none of her past issues would create problems. Because of her first psychoanalytic experience, she was able to establish clear distinctions in her mind between real and imagined danger. Her original anxiety was now under control and she felt free to decide on her future with a realistically optimistic attitude.

Anxiety is everywhere

In practice, I use anxiety and stress as synonyms, because the roots of both words express a feeling of being constricted and pressed on all sides, as when things are closing in on a person. According to Freud's refined theory of anxiety, normal or healthy psychic functioning means that everything is balanced and coordinated, producing inner peace and contentment. When this peaceful state is disrupted by external factors or by negative feelings triggered by internal factors, we experience anxiety. Anxiety can be useful or it can be damaging, as Selye's (1956) research demonstrated and for which he obtained the Nobel Prize. We have to remember that both types are always a consciously felt experience: we are aware that we are anxious. Often we don't know why we are anxious, a state that is a sign of neurotic anxiety requiring psychoanalytical work. There is also moral anxiety, which has a connection with neurotic anxiety in that it does not come directly from the outside, although, as the term implies, it is experienced as guilt and shame. To summarize, all types of anxiety are subjectively painful and uncomfortable, although the source of the anxiety is different for each.

The common, subjective experience of any anxiety is fear. However, Freud avoided that word, no doubt because fear usually refers to things outside oneself, as is the case with the anxiety that is a response to concrete, external, realities. This is what Freud had called *reality anxiety*, whether fear of germs, traffic, or terrorism, it is an ego function. Neurotic anxiety, however, has a different source, in inner conflict related to id functions, and arising from uncontrollable desires, impulses, and drives, often sexual, violent, "irrational," or self-damaging. Lastly, in moral anxiety the origin lies in one's conscience and sense of duty or propriety, caring, sacrifice, and selflessness; these are superego reactions.

The problem lies in the fact that often we do not identify the source of the anxiety, and that the subjective experience of it may come from a combination of all three sources. Thus a grandmother may believe that she refuses to babysit her grandchild because it is inconvenient, realistically, to drive for hours to her son's home. And neurotically, she might also be afraid of not being able to do a good job at it because of her age, or that she might do something that may harm the child. She may also feel angry at her son for some past disagreement or disappointment and, at the same time, ashamed and guilty for having these feelings and for refusing to babysit, an example of moral anxiety.

Anxiety is a signal of danger for the ego. In healthy cases, the person takes the necessary ego measures to face the issue or remedy the situation and therefore the initial anxiety disappears. This is especially so in reality anxiety. However, in neurotic cases, the anxiety is increased by negative thinking and worrying, while nothing constructive is done to resolve it. For instance, two middle-aged men diagnosed with colon cancer realistically feel great anxiety. One takes the necessary steps to obtain treatment. His experience of anxiety and the results of his reaction are very different from those of the second man, who worries but neglects treatment or tries to forget about the diagnosis, or starts to convince himself that the physician did not know what he was talking about and so on, but does not seek a second medical opinion.

Therefore, anxiety, painful as it is, fulfills a beneficial function, alerting us of dangers. The difficulty is that, unlike the above example of the two men with colon cancer, often we perceive something as a danger when it is not. This is what the worrying type of person does, when he allows negative thoughts of possible danger to grow in his mind without realistic foundation. An example of this is the parent of a teenager who thinks of the worst possible scenario when the adolescent is just a few minutes late from an errand or a date. This worrying happens either because of our own misunderstanding of the situation, as with the person who has chronic lymphocytic leukemia and over-reacts as if it were full-blown leukemia, when the chronic type may take decades before it becomes acute, or it may be a response to external factors, like official announcements of serious danger, as we had in the United States after the tragedy of September 2001. The fear of danger that is not realistic and imminent is a frequent source of anxiety.

And the person who often falls into this error of perceiving calamity where there is none is probably suffering from neurotic anxiety. Anxiety that is not managed, whether by avoiding appropriate action or by trying to ignore it while pushing it out of awareness, is typical of neurosis and poor mental health, because the attempt to ignore anxiety takes up more and more of a person's life.

Anxiety is always unpleasant because it has to do with one's identity, one's worth, one's faith in oneself. In other words, I am anxious because I feel insecure about myself. This is the reason why humans develop many different symptoms in an unconscious effort to get rid of anxiety. In psychoanalytic terms, we find that the id tries to get rid of stress by building defensive mechanisms against it, perhaps in the form of drug abuse, and especially alcohol, fanatic religious practices, excessive physical exercise or sleep, promiscuity, workaholism, and so on. Every time you find any of these symptoms, you can be sure that there is anxiety. Even if one symptom is conquered and disappears, as long as the anxiety has not been dealt with in a constructive manner other symptoms will emerge in an effort to cope with the original anxiety. This is the meaning of the term *symptom substitution*. For instance, experience teaches us to beware of the "dry drunks," the person who after having been a chronic alcoholic stops drinking without treatment or insight into the personality traits that made him depend on alcohol to begin with. In most cases, alcoholism is not just a bad habit but the behavioral expression of a personality disorder, what psychoanalysis calls *character disorder*.

One of the most constructive measures to take, besides one's own attempts at managing high anxiety, is to enter psychodynamic therapy. In this sense, anxiety becomes the motivation to grow and get well. But dealing with anxiety is no simple matter, as we have been discussing in this chapter. Because we are thinking organisms, anxiety is part of human life: we want to know and at the same time are afraid of the consequences of knowing the truth; our wishes turn to disappointments; our possessions become burdens but we can't let go of them. We are not satisfied: when young we dream of being older, then we try not to be old. Basically, anxiety accompanies the struggle between the flesh and the spirit, between being and having, between light and darkness, and between the truth and falsehood. All this points to our human need for transcendence and spirituality. Purely material things, immediate satisfaction of wishes, happiness based on lack of thought, denial of reality and self-deception, cannot satisfy and fulfill our soul. We are ever restless until we find the spiritual fulfillment that the material world, with all its comforts and riches, does not and cannot provide. The basic tendency of humans, as for all living organisms, as Thalheimer (1972) explains, is to remain in a state of adequate vitalizing stimulation, diminishing it when it is excessive and increasing it when it is too weak. Neurotic symptoms, with their accompanying anxiety, do not work as a type of vitalizing stimulation. Psychoanalysis helps the patient find the adequate level of vitalizing stimulation that eliminates anxiety.

Anxiety as part of human existence

Existential psychotherapy, another outgrowth of psychoanalysis, addresses itself to our *existential anxiety*, which arises from our human limitations and many frustrations, from the frailty of our physical selves, and ultimately from our mortality. All anxiety is ultimately existential anxiety. Freud's encapsulated statement about replacing the id with the ego is another way of emphasizing the need to become aware of the unconscious causes of our anxiety in order to find and enjoy the adequate vitalizing stimulation of living.

We can help patients, first, to recognize anxiety, and then to question themselves about it. This starts introspection, which is the means to acknowledge the unique connections between the current problem and previous experiences, as well as the similarity of the present symptom with past details of one's history. Also, thanks to introspection, one discovers the beliefs that color perceptions and reactions, desires and expectations, attitudes and actions. This activity of becoming truthful with one's innermost self makes it possible to put into words, ideally with the help of a trained professional, the discoveries made during the introspection. Ultimately, while experiencing resistance to insight and change (which are always to be expected), including the inevitable transference projections (which often can be seen as resistance through regression, projection, and idealization), we are able to guide the client to activate ego resources (realistic means) to find satisfaction in life as well as productive ways to handle difficulties, and to enjoy doing so. This is the final goal of psychoanalysis: to empower the patient so she can continue to grow as a complete person in her society.

Because anxiety and stress constitute such basic elements in psychotherapy generally, the introduction of the following case, which triggered anxiety in me, may serve as an illustration. The complete case presentation is in Chapter 11 of this book.

Titus, in his mid-fifties, divorced, with no children and well off, started by telling me that he was "afraid of going crazy." He had everything that he ever wanted: the woman he was dating, whom he "had conquered" after several years of trying; his three houses (a primary residence in the suburbs, his apartment in New York City, and his chalet in the French Riviera); and the toys that he had compulsively accumulated since he had become a highly successful defense attorney—very expensive cars and motorcycles, a transatlantic yacht with a crew of five, a private plane, jewelry, the best wines and whiskeys, reserved tables at the most prestigious restaurants in several American and European cities, membership in the most famous golf and tennis clubs in the world, and the most elegant custom-made clothes. But he was miserable. Working hard and successfully and playing harder, he found no joy in anything; even the food did not taste good anymore. He had been checked by several top specialists and no one found any disease. As a matter of fact, he was in better health than most people his age. A couple of the physicians had wanted to prescribe psychotropic drugs but he refused initially and then took them for a few months. "They didn't work," he complained, and repeated, "I'm desperate and you have to help me. This is a matter of life and death."

My own anxiety came up with the urgent question, "What if he is suicidal?" I dismissed the inquiry about his sanity. He was obviously not psychotic. My anxiety was really about my reaction to his situation, which I didn't realize right away. Somehow, his plea made me uncomfortable. "What if I cannot help him?" My countertransference was evident and complicated. Without full awareness, I was saying to myself that I could be very happy with much less than one-tenth of what he had. This produced my anxiety because, as a professional, I knew better than to be distracted by the yacht with a crew of five, the charming French chalet, or the fancy cars and motorcycles. The fact that I was distracted and relegating Titus to the background triggered my anxiety, and I felt shame, surprise, and discomfort about my professional self-image and self-expectations, further distracting me from the person, Titus. However, by questioning (not dismissing) my anxiety, I moved to introspection and ultimately to self-awareness.

I use this case as an example of my own anxiety, since many clinical reports detail patients' anxiety and keep silent about that of the practitioners. Thus, as in the case of a patient's anxiety, my "professional" anxiety was the initial motivation for change, leading me to self-questioning and, in turn, to introspection. I first felt threatened by Titus's abundance of goods. When I questioned my anxiety, I was already becoming introspective. First, I noticed—with embarrassment and shame—a sense of failure for not having the things that many consider a sure sign of success. Then I realized that my riches were much more personal: satisfaction, service, honor, genuineness, and reverence for others and from them to me. All the material goods this man had would be a painful burden to me. The client too, by the same means of introspection, starts experiencing diverse feelings, discovering connections and links between the current event and other ones in his life, recognizing attitudes and values he was not fully aware of. This introspection is what Frattaroli (2001, pp. 19, 65–66) calls "listening to the soul." And as you will read in the chapter about Titus, by putting one's introspection into words in psychotherapy, one allows oneself to grow as a person, to know oneself better, and consequently to have wider options in choosing the way one's life will go. The patient gains in decisions he can make about his life.

Note the tremendous difference between this approach, which is the core of psychoanalysis, and modern pharmacological psychiatry. Nowadays, anxious patients are prescribed antianxiety medication, which stops the above process of introspection dead. The psychotherapy model does not consider this approach as the cure. We see medication as a powerful facilitating agent for introspection. We don't see the cure of anxiety without self-questioning, or introspection, or talking about it, or without the benefits from the painful experience of anxiety. Without thought or introspection humans become robotic.

Cognitive-behavioral therapy (CBT) keeps its focus on the symptom as if it were the whole story. It is true that many people do change with CBT but often without ever knowing the inner forces (psychodynamics) that explain the presence of the very symptoms they want to get rid of. For us, uncovering and knowing the psychic roots of our symptoms is true mental hygiene and not merely an intellectual exercise. To recognize what is underneath the symptom teaches self-understanding; with it we stand underneath what is evident, or we look from within (introspection) and experience ourselves differently than before. Because we humans think, we benefit from changing through understanding rather than from change brought about by external factors like medication. Philosophers like Watzlawick, et al. (1974) refer to first-order and second-order change. The first type of change of behavior happens within one system (the person) but without changing the larger system, as happens with the person who changes his way of treating a particular minority well because he can be fined if he does not do so, rather than from an inner conviction. Dry alcoholism, mentioned earlier, is another example of first-order change. Second-order change, on the other hand, alters the system itself; here, I treat a particular minority well because of respect for them as fellow human beings. The alcoholic realizes that drinking is a symptom of his anxiety and she stops drinking, not as an end in itself but as a way of improving personality deficiencies.

Second-order change is what was meant by "personality restructuring" in the era when traditional psychoanalysts explained the generic goal of their therapeutic method. It is not that the psychoanalyst restructures the personality of a client, but that through the three initial steps (to acknowledge, to question, to introspect), as described above, the patient himself restructures his personality. Therefore, the restructuring of personality is the result and lasting outcome of the psychoanalytical method; it is the second-order change the patient has experienced. The frequent comment of psychoanalytic patients, "Now I know what makes me tick; I understand myself," reflects this. By changing their behavior and attitude toward the symptom that bothered them, they have recognized important aspects of themselves as unique individuals. The unconscious becomes conscious, giving a person insights and awareness about oneself, with new opportunities and a larger range of choices. As a corollary observation, it is refreshing to remember Racker's (1968) wisdom, as in his comment that if we don't see positive results from psychoanalysis, we can't be too quick to blame the patient; we must look at ourselves and at what we are doing. This advice is useful for any method we employ in trying to help people improve their lives, but especially so when the clinician finds himself reluctant to apply psychoanalysis to a relatively unsophisticated patient who could benefit from it.

Anxiety can be the springboard for change, as I keep repeating. People think of changing when they are dissatisfied with something in their current condition and lifestyle. In this sense anxiety is the signal of danger to the ego. And, as even the *DSM* (Axis IV) acknowledges, stress is a component of every emotional, mental, and social problem. Phobias, as well as panic disorders, are forms of anxiety. Adaptation difficulties, crippling depressive moods, sexual functioning problems, and relationship difficulties, just to list a few examples, all elicit anxiety. The same is true, as we indicated before, of general life dissatisfaction, over-worry, paranoid thinking, general negativism after a sickness or following an accident involving the individual client, or a tragedy affecting others close to the client. From the anxiety perspective, it is true to say that all patients who come to us suffer from a form of anxiety or that the diagnosis of anxiety is always understood and taken for granted as underlying any differential psychiatric diagnosis.

A practical way of going about it

You may now start using the method described above. With a patient who is not very sophisticated or introspective, you can simply point out that whatever has happened (her presenting problem) has changed her. Her problem has produced changes in her thinking (lack of concentration, memory problems), in her feelings (moodiness, depression, irritability), even in her body (sleep patterns, eating habits and weight alterations, perhaps even some symptomatology like digestive difficulties, skin reactions, aches and pains, and other changes). Then, you suggest that it might be interesting to find out if these recent changes have anything to do with the problem. Even people without much awareness of inner processes (psychodynamics) are curious about this possible connection. Only then do you mention anxiety. To help the client find out if it is anxiety, you follow the initial three steps mentioned above (acknowledge the changes in one's life that have produced anxiety, question yourself about them, look into them introspectively to find possible connections between them and other "pieces" of one's life). Very often these same unsophisticated people are very grateful for having understood the reason by just "talking" about one's problem and become motivated to try this method. By using this approach ("This problem has affected my health in the general sense of how my body functions") psychoanalysis can also help those who are less comfortable with the mind–body interaction. If we try, we'll be surprised at the number of people who are interested in knowing the hidden things about themselves. Horoscopes, psychics, popularized personality tests, handwriting analysis, and such are so popular because people, typically, are curious about themselves and their inner dynamics.

Well employed, psychoanalysis goes to the point to help the client, without taking shortcuts, yet also respects the psychological mode and tempo of the individual patient. You may start by asking the patient to tell you what mental images come to mind when she thinks of her problem. Let's assume the problem is that Tina, who at 61 and still very involved in living, feels very lonely without a mate, and, after having done many things to find the right person, she now fears that she'll never attain what she wants. Let's say that the image that came to her mind when you invited her to allow any image to appear, was of her in her darkened living room, wanting to go to the kitchen but unable to do so. Still using her imagination, you may suggest that she visualize herself getting up, preparing a cup of tea, and going back to the living room to call one of her friends on the phone. You may ask what she's talking about with her friend, and so on. After this practice, you help her recognize the importance of the images she harbors in her mind to the way she feels; negative images produce anxiety and the opposite type make her feel better. Then you help her find some meaning in the image she offered and, if the meaning is negative, you assist her in finding something more positive, recognizing that in most cases the negative meaning comes from events, people, or beliefs experienced earlier in their life, and that she can look for other such things that may provide a more constructive meaning for her.

If no mental images come up spontaneously, however, you can ask her to think of a comparison of her problem with a specific natural phenomenon or event. For instance, the images that came to me about this case were a heavy rain, a very tall mountain facing Tina's house, and quicksand between the house and the mountain. But these are my images and I am silent about them; I cannot impose them on the patient because I am there to help her discover the meaning of her own experience, represented by her imagery. Of course, I could spend some time analyzing my images afterward, the way I might work with a dream. Whatever images come up for the client, you help her question the meaning of the mental images. If, for instance, Tina offers the comparison of a big lake she has to cross with a flimsy rowboat, you may respond, first, by asking her to put herself into the image as if she were dreaming it and to pay attention to as many details as possible. Then, without rushing, giving her plenty of time, you may continue with something similar to the following: "In your mind's eye, you saw a big lake, rather than any other natural thing. Stay with your feelings about this big lake, picking out all the details that you can." Then, after a moment of quiet to encourage her reflection, "Can you find any meaning in this image of a big lake? Where does the image of the big lake come from? What's the link between your problem and the lake?" (The same about the flimsy rowboat.) And when the patient mentions the lake, you yourself may get very different images that you may want to analyze by yourself later, but that you do not superimpose on those of the client. The theory is that these images (both yours and the patient's), are similar to those of dreams, and so are unconscious choices, representing the manner in which the person experiences her problem. Chapter 8 will delve in greater detail into the therapeutic use of imagery in psychoanalysis.

As you notice, your questions invite introspection. And because you, the clinician, ask the questions, the patient finds it easy to start talking about herself, using your questions as a handle. Once the first three steps are taken (awareness of anxiety, self-questioning, and introspection), psychoanalysis is on its way. This means that the client is ready now to discover her own unique psychodynamics and to work on them. To emphasize the concept again, psychodynamics are the connections between current attitudes and behavior and past influences, events, experiences, early values, and beliefs that are still active, or "on." Working on the psychodynamics means that the patient can start making the differentiations needed to separate old from new, useful from habitual, positive from negative, self-limiting from ego-enhancing. This is the task of psychodynamic counseling or psychotherapy that the nonanalytical approaches ignore and miss.

Another important aspect of anxiety is that if the individual has not worked on his psychodynamics, the anxiety is not resolved and we find the repetition compulsion or urge to reenact, as experienced in transference, discussed in Chapter 6. The need for the clinician to have had this type of psychotherapy himself is based on the fact that if loose ends from his past are still bothering him, producing anxiety without his realizing it (unconsciously), these may, at best, distract him from the work with the client and, at worst may cause him to misdirect the client, damaging or hurting her. On the client's side, with the passing of time she may have learned to repress those loose ends so that they do not bother her all the time. But the repressed anxiety is triggered again and again by unexpected events. In other words, her unconscious maneuvers to keep this under control result in different symptoms or manifestations of her anxiety. A fairly effective portrayal of this aspect of anxiety is Clint Eastwood's (2003) movie *Mystic River*, the story of a murder in South Boston that has twenty-five-year-old roots connected with a cruel incident of sexual abuse. The man who was abused as a teenager, played by Tim Robbins, had carried his anxiety fairly well for a long time until a vivid reminder of his dark moment triggers strongly repressed feelings, leading to his death at the hands of one of his two former childhood friends. Eastwood's insight and understanding of long-standing anxiety and its possible damaging effects in a person's life supports the superb acting.

Any clinician who wants to do more than merely remove the symptom, needs to pay attention to the anxiety level of the client, and to observe what links the patient recognizes between this and other things in her life, and so on, as discussed above. The most effective way of dealing with anxiety is indirectly, by helping clients to discover the symbolic and metaphorical aspects of the symptoms. One can choose different methods to really learn about anxiety and its behavioral manifestations. For example, take any one of the five clinical case studies found in Breuer and Freud's *Studies on Hysteria* (1895) and read it carefully, paying special attention to the manifestations of anxiety and how it was handled clinically by the therapist. You may want to fantasize how to apply what you have learned to one of your real patients.

Another practice is to pick a character in a good novel or movie, as we have just done, and try to understand the underlying anxiety of the behavioral manifestations, especially the interactions with significant people in the character's life.

However, the most practical way, and a benefit that comes from one's own analysis, is to keep yourself aware of the dynamics that influence your behavior, the psychic forces in you that trigger strong feelings, and your subsequent behavioral reactions in diverse situations and with different people.

Chapter 5
DEFENSES AGAINST ANXIETY

Because anxiety is painful and annoying, we humans are constantly trying to minimize it, as we all know from daily experience. We hinted in the section on ego psychology, in Chapter 3, that besides taking effective and realistic measures to deal with anxiety and to grow in our humanity because of it, either to master it and resolve it or to avoid it even before it shows up, we can also use ineffective methods, hoping to achieve the same end. Among these ineffective attempts is the misuse of defense mechanisms. But not all ego defenses are neurotic. In this chapter we shall discuss their general characteristics, as well as their unconscious use (which is most of the time neurotic), and finally the healthy aspects of the same psychic activity.

The nature of defense mechanisms
It is the ego that faces reality and at the same time it is the ego that uses defense mechanisms. Reality (something real that has happened or is happening, or thoughts of things past, present, future, or possible) often triggers anxiety and, as it grows, the person experiences

it as coming from the inner conflict between wish and duty, between selfishness and caring for others, and so on. The ego reacts (unconsciously!) to this anxiety-creating conflict in ways that were originally a part of the behavioral repertoire of infancy. The normal infant cannot cope with all the demands of her real world. Because her psychic equipment is too rudimentary and weak to cope with these demands rationally, it uses other cognitive strategies, such as denial, make-believe, dissociation and identity split, identification, projection, and many other such defenses. The greater the stress, the more defenses and the more frequently they are used. Think of the pathological extreme: children who are neglected and ignored, abused and psychologically put down, or sexually violated. Because there is no physical escape, the only way to cope is often to escape mentally by the use of defenses. At that developmental stage, these defenses were useful for survival. But often the anxiety experienced in infancy interferes with normal psychological development and these people grow up with deficiencies. This is because they did not have the proper environment to mature as human beings—and here I mean not necessarily the physical environment but most essentially the psychological one. Consequently, such a child develops with a deficit and, as he grows older, he reverts to those mental mechanisms that he had become familiar with earlier, without even realizing that he is using the same maneuvers of self-protection and defense that worked, to some extent at least, in infancy and childhood. This explains the presence of neurotic defense mechanisms in adulthood. Remember Myriam from the last chapter who, as a child, was correct in seeing her four brothers as enemies of her personhood, and who later, as an adult, continued to be overly self-protective of other people like her brothers to the point of being ineffective with them and damaging to herself. This also makes us think of how limited we can become in our behavioral repertoire if we don't make an effort to break down the invisible walls that force us to stay within the familiar patterns even if they don't work for our benefit any longer. The repetition compulsion is an indication of our lack of choice.

A clinical example

It is not clear why we use defense mechanisms so naturally in early childhood and such inquiry is beyond the scope of this book. But the practical side of defense mechanisms is something his own psychoanalysis helps the therapist handle. How do we know when a patient is shortchanging herself by resorting to neurotic defense mechanisms rather than handling anxiety constructively and in an ego-enhancing manner? Usually, we begin to notice that the client frustrates himself by the actions he takes. For example, a man like Linus, who is unsuccessful in his relationships with other people, keeps repeating his ineffective ways of relating. He tells others what to do, or he tries to control them by giving unwelcome advice. He repeatedly pushes for his way, disregarding what the other person may prefer, and he is sarcastic. Linus does not listen seriously to what the other person is telling him and then he blames anybody but himself, complaining that others are wrong, stupid, or uncooperative. Is he denying the feelings of others? Is he deceived into believing that his way is the only—or at least, the best—way? Does he perceive others always as a threat to his individuality? Is he seeing in them some figure of his past that was a negative force in his life?

These kinds of questions that the clinician asks himself about his client are also necessary for the mental health worker who wants to help the client change—we obviously mean second-order change, not just behavioral change, as explained in the previous chapter. But how does the clinician use these questions constructively to help the patient? The traditional way, still effective, is to point to patterns of behavior and to some consistency of disappointing results. When you find these two elements in the course of counseling or therapy, you then apply the same three familiar points of awareness, questioning, and introspection. With Linus, the man just mentioned, you may ask if he notices that there seems to be a pattern in his recent life. If he agrees, you can begin with the analysis of it. However, if he blames it on bad luck or any other external factor, you can ask him to make-believe that there are some things that he can do differently in order to obtain the outcomes he is after, and invite him to imagine some possibilities. If after all the expected resistance he begins to recognize some of the attitudes, expectations, or actions in general that he could change, you are helping him to move toward second-order change and lasting improvement.

This approach will be useful in order to discover the defense mechanisms Linus is using, without his full awareness, in order to avoid anxiety or to cope with it. Earlier, we saw displacement and projection, when he blamed others for his mistakes. He also uses denial, in not recognizing elements of reality, as with his impatience and inability to focus on the feelings of the other person ("I do the right thing; I know how to handle people"). Along with this, he may also use projection, by which he attributes to others his own faults and deficient ways of reacting ("*They* are impatient; *they* don't listen"), and rationalization, with which he finds logical reasons to explain away his own faults and deficiencies in dealing with others ("They have to think and I help them do so"). A form of reaction formation may also be present, as when he believes that his unacceptable behavior is acceptable, even necessary, to help others to improve and so continues to act in ineffective ways. Linus also represses the anger and frustration an overly strict upbringing may have generated in him, and he uses others, without awareness of it, as substitute targets for his repressed anger.

As we said earlier, the list of defense mechanisms is long and far from written in stone. The important thing is not so much to label a particular defense, but to recognize it as a mistaken maneuver, used ineffectively to avoid anxiety and to protect oneself from negative and painful feelings. Truly, these uncomfortable feelings are like landmarks that point us toward constructive change, inviting us ultimately to face our own inadequate personality style that we need to change. This second-order change is a real personal transformation, as we also saw in Myriam's case, and the analytical method makes it possible and smooth.

After all, defenses are necessary for development and subject formation; about this there is agreement among the different schools of thought within psychoanalysis. However, the discussion can become intricate because the language used by different theorists changes. Thus, Lacanians like Dor (1999), Verhaeghe (2004), and Nasio (1998), among others, explain castration anxiety as a defensive psychic construction (never, of course, an external reality) that accounts for the early formation of defenses and the determination of specific psychic structures, specifically the "perverse" structure which brings about two defenses, fixation and denial of reality (Dor, pp. 34, 35). Nasio (1998) gives a very clear and brief explanation of "the internal dynamics of the unconscious castration fantasy. What we find there is that the entire body, by which I mean all the libidinal tension of the fantasied [sic] body, becomes concentrated in one sole place that, in the vocabulary of medical anatomy, would be called the genital area, but that, in fantasy, is called the phallus" (p. 48). I find this quote especially helpful because it explains so well the nature of castration fear as an unconscious fantasy, even though this fear is often, in nonpsychoanalytic groups, taken literally—to become only another form of hypostasis (when a concept is made into a concrete, real thing).

Therefore, our attention to psychopathology must include the defenses the patient uses to handle anxiety. Psychopathology was Freud's general term for all the many psychic and ineffective reactions to the difficulties of living that cause anxiety, by which a person handles those difficulties poorly. Consequently, psychopathology means everything you find in the *DSM* and more. Merely from a behavioral perspective, it includes the many different shades and levels of neurosis, phobic, hysterical, and obsessional, as well as perversion and character disorders, as well as the psychoses.

On the other hand, it is always good if defense mechanisms are recognized as such. For instance, if a husband denies the alcoholism of his spouse, he may either accept the denial as the truth ("She's just stressed and needs a way of relaxing") or he may recognize his own denial as a defense mechanism and take constructive action to help his wife. In this way we can connect psychopathology with defense mechanisms. Although perhaps oversimplifying the psychic process, it may not be a mistake to say that every psychopathology uses defense mechanisms unconsciously and every neurotic (unconscious) defense mechanism fosters psychopathology. This is a segue to the next section.

Healthy defense mechanisms?

Defense mechanisms can be viewed as if they were on a continuum, with one end being positive and the other negative. I visualize the positive end as a clear color that becomes darker as it moves toward the negative side. This continuum applies both to the healthy and the neurotic, and to the conscious as well as the unconscious dimensions. Thus, *sublimation*, for instance, may be conscious and a healthy ego function. For example, the person who feels romantically or sexually attracted to someone forbidden may change his focus to other aspects or qualities of the relationship with that individual. By the way, a "forbidden" person is someone who is closely related to the other by family ties, by social or professional obligations (student, customer, patient, neighbor, etc.), or with whom circumstances such as age, geographical distance, or the like, make erotic contact at best unwise and at worst crazy. In such cases, instead of concentrating on the physical attributes and sexual attraction of the forbidden person, attention is paid to personality traits and accomplishments. This would be considered a form of healthy sublimation.

Distortion is another example of a defense mechanism that can also be used constructively. The person who is trying to get rid of extra weight, for example, may imagine chocolate chips, or raisins in a slice of bread, as sleeping cockroaches. This kind of repulsive but constructive self-deception is another conscious and healthy defense mechanism. As a matter of fact, clients often need to learn how to control irrational thoughts or expectations by devising their own defense mechanisms against them. CBT suggests mental tricks like imagining a huge stop sign when the client starts worrying, or visualizing the bad thought leaving the client's body when he exhales. These types of hypnotic techniques, as Chapter 8 will explain, fit well within the psychoanalytic frame.

The general principle is that any mental maneuver that helps to control id impulses in order to help the person stay within the ego demands of reality is healthy and ego-enhancing. In other words, the psychic dynamic that at first begins unconsciously to ward off anxiety can be self-defeating and neurotic. This is what is called traditionally a defense mechanism. But a similar mechanism can be triggered consciously as a deliberate protection against a difficult situation and it will often be a healthy activity for the ego.

Some defense mechanisms, like projective identification, for instance, may have different meanings depending on the setting the person is in. According to Ogden (1982), when it is a defense it creates distance from one's frightening feelings or aspects of the self. But when it helps to elicit feelings like one's own in another, it is a type of communication. It can also be a form of object relations that allows one to connect and be close to another person.

The problem with all these defenses is their complexity, which brings about the need for a competent analyst to help the individual sort this out for his or her benefit. Consequently, in clinical practice the analysis of defense mechanisms is a valid and practical approach. As I said before, many ego psychology practitioners work primarily with defenses. The clinician can always keep her eyes open for any indications of these psychic mechanisms. She can point them out to the client, reminding him that anxiety triggers this reaction. Then she can help him to connect with earlier experiences of avoiding anxiety, which usually include similar or identical defense mechanisms used in his family and by his parents, all expressions of the urge to reenact, as the next chapter will consider.

Among your clients who are using learned defenses, you will find that some deny the problem or crisis, some blame others, some explain things away, and so on. This concentration on defenses in the process of therapy can help the client recognize the urge to reenact the unconscious dynamic at work to cope with anxiety. Once it is discovered, it often produces a sense of liberation, opening up greater choices, as the client realizes that by reacting to anxiety the way he learned to react, he is not making any personal choice; he is not free; he is just repeating now, regardless of the circumstances, what he learned from his family (without realizing it) in his early life. In general, the more a person accepts reality (as in *reality testing*) the more indications we have of his or her emotional and developmental maturity.

The reality principle

What connects anxiety, the defense mechanisms, and psychopathology is the reality principle. You probably are clear by now that the id moves according to the pleasure principle, seeking immediate gratification without considering the consequences of its actions. That is why the id, or "inner dummy," as Weiner and Hefter (1999) describe it, can lead us to crazy, self-destructive, and irrational behavior. The ego, on the other hand, operates on the reality principle, as the well-known prayer used by Alcoholics Anonymous states— accepting the things he cannot change and accommodating to them, changing the things he can and should modify in the world around him, and especially in him, and finally having the wisdom to know the difference between the two situations.

The reality principle is so central and important because our personality has developed in response to the influence of those external events (especially the people in those events) that comprised our "reality." An important indication of good mental health is good reality testing, or the ability to differentiate what one wants from what the "reality limits" of that desire are, and to tell what is fantasy from what is real in the world in which we live. Reality testing means being able to recognize the constant possibility of being disappointed by the people and things around us. It also means that our expectations, especially of people, are not exaggerated and that our perceptions are focused on the positive and good, rather than on the opposite. For the clinician, reality testing is a way of recognizing how the client fits into this imperfect world, into his imperfect family, into his deficient work environment, into his country with all its limitations and badness. The reality principle, though a very positive concept, is tested in negative things, as you see. The possibilities of these tests are infinite. A few examples may suffice; for example, the way a person copes with disappointments and frustrations; how she deals with her expectations and hopes; how she reacts to the things beyond her control, such as unexpected events, including negative ones like sickness, death, and weather calamities; how she handles unfair treatment, or unlikable personality traits of important people in her life, and other inevitable aspects of living, such as broken dreams or getting older, with all the concomitant inconveniences these impose. We shall return to reality and ego functions in Chapter 16. However, it is necessary to stress that we often hear about the dark side of accepting reality, because it is the one that challenges our character and sanity. But there is also the other half of reality, which is glorious and full of light, and holds all the good things worth celebrating and enjoying.

Reality is one of the important sources of anxiety, true, but the main producer of anxiety is our own thinking. "There is nothing either good or bad but thinking makes it so," is the way Shakespeare put it. Clients frequently don't realize they are worrying in the neurotic mode—or, if they do, they insist that they cannot stop worrying. Many of the techniques used by CBT and similar therapy approaches help patients to stop worrying by focusing on the worrying behavior itself. Once the person can think straight, as the saying goes, psychoanalysis can assist them to recognize the repetition element in the symptom. This makes it easier for the patient to abandon the defense mechanisms learned as a child by focusing on the true, current, reality of their life situation. Then they can handle their life for what it is, not just whatever emotions it triggers in them.

With psychoanalysis, not only does the client say that she must stop the anxiety-producing worrying. She adds that her worrying comes from the way she learned to react to specific difficult things as a child. And, most important, that these difficult things are not in her life any longer. This defense mechanism was originally her way of coping with anxiety then. This reaction belongs to her past. She goes on to emphasize that things are different now because she has acquired much experience through the years; she is not the same person (psychologically) that she was then. This present reality makes her understand things differently than when she was a child. Next, she focuses on other aspects of her current life situation to find out what she can do about it without allowing the worry to control her. Finally comes reality testing, and the client is encouraged to practice it by acting differently and realizing that it is okay not to do it the same as before.

*   *   *

Anxiety always elicits some reaction, effective or not, by which we try to stop its painful influence on our mind. Because anxiety underlies every problem that clinicians deal with, mental health professionals must be experts in this area. Analytical theory is an aid to clinicians, helping them provide a lasting cure, one that helps the client learn a better way of coping with anxiety, since the one she was using did not produce the expected results. You'll often find that having helped the patient to think psychoanalytically has lasting benefits. Many past clients, in a spontaneous form of generalization, tend to apply to new situations what they have learned in therapy; they may report that they have used the same method in other areas of conflict and distress in their life. Analytical thinking has become a good habit and a good defense against unhealthy defense mechanisms.

This was the case with a woman in her early thirties who had been raised in a culture that held to the belief that women were worth nothing until they had a male child. Born in the U.S., she had been Americanized despite the strong control her parental culture had over her. She could not free herself from the imperatives that culture imposed on her. Now a doctoral student in an American university, she felt guilty and ashamed for not being married and disappointing her parents. She had become so anxious that she neglected her studies and experienced somatic reactions like absence of hunger and sleeping disorders.

The therapist helped her to identify the part of her personality that had decided to consult with the therapist as different from the part that was feeling anxious because of her transgressions against her cultural imperatives. Moreover the therapist emphasized that the first part in her had prevailed over the other, older and very strong part. Once this was accomplished it became possible to start the therapeutic process that allowed her to become an individual, different and separated from others, including her parents and family.

Chapter 6
ALWAYS TRANSFERENCE

Transference is related to other psychoanalytical concepts such as resistance, acting out, regression, idealization, projection, reality testing, the repetition compulsion, and communication and personal interaction in general. This is the reason why transference is so universal in and out of psychoanalysis and such an important aspect of it. Transference happens all the time. In psychotherapy it takes unique and special forms, as we shall see later. There is transference every time we react to other people, or even to new situations, as we did in previous experiences that are now completely forgotten. Thus, there is transference when we find someone especially attractive or repulsive. Personally, almost without exception, a person I find attractive (someone who is nice to me and I feel I can trust) is someone who, in subtle ways, embodies characteristics of people in my past, even as far away as infancy, who were good to me. On the other hand, those new people whom I find unattractive, even repulsive, ugly, dangerous and threatening, or untrustworthy, bring back, unconsciously, memories of others in the past who hurt me in one way or another. When I meet someone for the first time and immediately find him okay or not okay, I am experiencing transference. This person may be a complete stranger (a bus driver, store clerk, party guest) who, without doing anything specific, elicits in me an unconscious emotional memory. Thus, in general, a large part of falling in love is transferential, as is all irrational (meaning not based on objective facts) hatred toward another person. It must be noted that biases and prejudices against groups of people elicit transferential reactions toward members of such groups, even though we never had anything to do directly with any of them. This is how ethnic hatreds can be explained.

What happens in our relationships with others, we can also find in many other circumstances, including the phenomenon of déjà vu. The difficulty lies in explaining what an "unconscious memory" is. How can a memory exist that is not remembered? How can something in the present bring back something from the past that I don't remember at all? First, keep in mind that unconscious memory is not merely factual, as a conscious recollection is. If a normal person puts his mind to it, he can remember in detail what he did last night after dinner, before he went to bed. But memory that is unconscious refers more to the feelings and emotional reactions (good or bad) that the person experienced with someone or in a particular set of circumstances. This was the case with John, described in the first chapter. He did not simply trigger feelings of discomfort in me because he resembled someone who had made me uncomfortable. His presence itself was a symbol that elicited in me feelings that I had experienced since I was a child. A conscious memory says, "He reminds me of my uncle (or of any other particular concrete person)." An unconscious memory would say, "He brings back feelings or emotional states that I have experienced before in my life." Unconscious memories are the result of a catalyst (the current encounter or situation) that precipitates the flow of specific feelings. Simply put, conscious memory refers to facts; unconscious memory refers to feelings—and often, because of this, alters in our mind the facts of reality. You can see how easily prejudice can develop.

Objectivity

Transference is an inevitable phenomenon that should make us humans humble. We cannot be truly objective; we do not perceive what is, but always alter it with our feelings by the mere act of perceiving it. In the perception itself are subtle expectations, personal emotional connections, biases and prejudices, all barely noticeable. The concept of mental representations, as images or concepts that give us an impression of external reality, is found often in psychoanalytical writings. Even quantum physics, to paraphrase the great scientist, Niels Bohr (1927), found that what our senses perceive depends on how we observe what we are focusing on. Or as Frattaroli (2001) puts it, "What we end up defining as reality is determined by the lens through which we choose to look at reality" (p. 169). Our unconscious memories, values, expectations, fears, and biases, just to mention a few dynamics in general, get in the way and alter what is there, sometimes distorting it completely. It is as if we are wearing colored glasses, to extend Frattaroli's analogy with one verse of Ramón de Campoamor, a popular Spanish poet of the late 1800s: "Todo toma el color del cristal con que se mira" (All takes on the color of the crystal through which one looks at it).

Transference, as a practical concept, reminds us that we often don't relate to things and events or interact with people as they are. Because of this, Freud referred to *transference neurosis*, a self-damaging distortion of reality, which nevertheless many psychoanalysts make good use of in therapy to help patients recognize these distortions and correct them. To sum up, it is thanks to the phenomenon of transference that we must question our objectivity. Because we carry so much of ourselves into any situation or interaction, even when we are sure that we are being objective, we must double check and triple check before we can act safely. This observation on the difficulty of being objective also has important applications in our psychotherapy work. This topic keeps coming up because it is so important. Here we can give some thought once more to the current rage for "research validated treatment," hinted at earlier, although other descriptions are used for the same view, such as "evidence-based practice" or "science-validated interventions." Obviously we cannot accept the idea that "anything goes" in mental health practice but, unlike the situation in pharmacology, transference means that we cannot demand the same sort of relationship between intervention and outcome that is expected there. This is because in pharmacology we have chemical elements predictably affecting each other. In psychology, however, we are dealing with the living psyche of an individual, not only with her current mood and modality but with her unique personal history, values, and experiences, and this means that we cannot predict objectively and with accuracy. Because transference alters perception, it is difficult to be sure how two patients, outwardly and superficially similar (even with the same *DSM* diagnosis), will react to a specific psychotherapeutic technique. Any psychic experience (anxiety in all its forms, or depression in its many manifestations) is subjectively different regardless of the patients' similarities or whether the events seem to be the same, such as the death of someone close, a car accident, a troubling diagnosis like diabetes or leukemia, a serious reverse in financial status, and so on. Transferential dynamics make responses unpredictable and different from person to person. In pharmacology, however, the opposite happens with regularity: what is true for one person within a range (sex, age, weight, general health, etc.) is true for most. Thus, the medication that helps one person within that range will most probably help someone else within the same parameters. This is not so in psychology. Here we can only predict based on some observed patterns: the man has consistently acted this way under these circumstances, therefore it is expected that he will act thus and so under similar circumstances. There is a general emotional pattern in the trajectory of every person's life that forms his individual nature and is often referred to as personality or character. We could simplify the difference between the two approaches by stating that pharmacology follows the pattern of the medication, while psychology follows the pattern in the client.

In the direct interaction of psychodynamic psychotherapy, the mental health worker gathers information, factual and emotional, before she intervenes with any technique. Based on her observations of the patient, as if the therapy sessions were laboratory work on an experiment, the therapist can act by stressing a point, asking a question, offering her interpretations and conclusions, and so on. This process has all the hallmarks of scientific objectivity—not the obsolete nineteenth-century model, but the current one from quantum physics. This is then what allows us to assert that the method devised by Freud is valid and reliable *to study subjectivity*. To do otherwise changes the subject of study (the patient) into an object, and as I stated before, subjectivity cannot become objectified. Those who say that psychoanalysis has not been proven scientifically base their reference point on physical science (see Lothane 1996). Psychological science requires different measuring instruments than those used in the physical sciences. And just as we cannot measure distance with a cup or liquids with a speedometer, we cannot study subjectivity— love, heroism, magnanimity, and the like—by using the scientific method appropriate to a discipline like pharmacology.

Bowman (2002) considers the scientific argument a resistance (defense) against psychoanalysis and of its ideal result. What is feared by many is precisely the ability psychoanalysis offers: a way to master oneself without blindly depending on the influence of cultural imperatives of family, state, or religion.

Transference in psychotherapy

A typical aspect of transference, as already mentioned, is the unconscious inclination to react to individuals (strangers) in an emotionally personal manner. We meet someone new and transfer onto him feelings (good and bad, acceptable and shameful) that do not realistically belong with him. We do this unconsciously, that is without realizing that we do it, and in so doing we complicate our interactions with others, be they spouse or children, friends or business partners. What we transfer to people, places, or situations are aspects of ourselves, or more exactly, things that our wishes, needs, values, biases, and so on make us feel we see, sense, or feel in the other person. This way of distorting reality by demonizing or deifying people is also at work in psychotherapy, as much on the part of the clinician as of the client, although we hope that the clinician, because of his own analysis, will handle his transference constructively.

In practice we cannot ignore the fact that simply because of our position and role as clinicians we are inevitably the object of our clients' transference. They unconsciously perceive us, among other things, either as a good parent, as an all-knowing guru, or as a miracle worker (positive transference), or else as an inflexible judge, a punishing parent, or a charlatan (negative transference). When you notice this, you can ask them to use their imagination in order to set up an emotional bridge (between the current feeling and similar feelings experienced in past circumstances) (Watkins and Watkins 1997), that is, to relax, concentrate on themselves, and to accept the feeling they are experiencing toward you. Once they can stay relaxed with that feeling, without deliberately looking for connections, they can try to let the feeling go to an event or person in their own past history, perhaps by asking themselves, "When have I felt this way before toward someone else, or in a special situation?" They then allow their unconscious to make the connection. Once they connect the present reaction to you with something or someone in the past, a couple of things happen: they are able to correct their perception in the therapy situation or, at least, to become suspicious of the extra-good or extra-bad way they feel toward their clinician. The second benefit of this technique is that clients find it rather easy to recognize the same or similar transferential phenomena with other people or situations in their life. The final outcome is that they recognize events and experiences from the past as still relevant and active in their psyche.

Racker (1968) emphasized that it is easy to recognize the patient's transference in the process of clinical counseling or psychotherapy, but equally easy to ignore one's own transference, a response that has, since Freud, been called the *countertransference*. There are basically no differences in the dynamics of transferential reactions on the part of the client or the therapist. However, the consequences are very different. If the clinician unconsciously distorts the reality of the client and allows herself to feel, for instance, that he is a child in need of guidance and assistance, or a younger brother who was stubborn and unhappy, just to offer two possibilities among many, the interaction can become very nontherapeutic; the therapist will be in danger of becoming codependent with the client and an enabler of his neurosis. If that happens, the patient will not be helped at all. My suspicion is that many failures in psychotherapy (of any persuasion, by the way) happen for this reason: the therapist has not been paying attention to her countertransference. Of course, it's difficult to pay attention to countertransference if you don't believe in the unconscious.

Clearly, this again demonstrates the need for mental health clinicians to have been in personal therapy. By getting to know oneself better, one also avoids the danger of falling into situations of countertransference that will damage the therapeutic relationship. This is one of the reasons I believe that the professional training of psychotherapists is dangerously incomplete without individual or family psychodynamic therapy, even though transference is more complicated in family therapy. From both sides, transferential dynamics become part of the therapeutic process. Awareness of one's countertransference is essential in effective psychotherapy. On the other hand, positive transference and countertransference are necessary for self-discovery, integration, and healing; in other words, for successful psychotherapy. Both the patient and the analyst must arrive at a positive transference after (in many cases) having gone through numerous variations of negative transference. Positive transference on the part of the analyst means caring for the other, and genuinely respecting the patient and what she is trying to do in the psychotherapeutic interaction. It does not necessarily mean liking the other person. But so long as there is no positive regard and acceptance of the other, no healing can take place. In our terms, these are superego reactions and cannot be forced. If they are forced, they become fake feelings. Because of this, any negative transference on the part of either the clinician or the client must be acknowledged and resolved before proceeding any further. In broad terms, the effective way to resolve the negative transference is ultimately by making the separation and distinction between the two component elements of the transference, the current and the past persons, events, circumstances, and feelings. When this is successful, two main goals are achieved: first, by testing the reality of the past and current scenes, the distortions inherent in the transference are stopped. And second, an accomplishment useful in many other forms of therapy, one's knowledge, awareness, and control of oneself are enlarged. You'll see some of this in action in Chapters 9 to 11.

In the process of psychoanalytic work, transference and countertransference, its opposite, emerge naturally. Here I concentrate first on the client, who by definition is a person in need; she looks up to the therapist for help. The need of the patient may be for clarity, the solution to a problem, a change of perspective or perception; or discovering new strengths, self-knowledge, motivation, and courage; or getting help in decision-making, and so on. Because in most cases the expectation is somewhat unrealistic at the start of therapy, soon after beginning to work psychoanalytically, there is impatience, frustration, dislike of the therapist, anger, and disappointment—seldom clearly expressed verbally by the patient and often still unconscious, only showing up in her behavior. If the expected help is forthcoming, the other set of feelings aroused in this type of work must also be handled well if genuine progress is wanted. Here you'll find yourself receiving admiration and idealization, and notice the patient's desire to work harder in order to please the therapist, fantasies of friendship or romantic/sexual involvement, and the like. As I just said, the client is a person in need, hurting emotionally, and because of that unique mental status, the patient's expectations of psychotherapy are often not completely realistic. She may want a quick fix or a nonexpensive cure. She does not want to inconvenience herself traveling forty-five minutes to the office every week or to do it early in the morning or late at night. As we all know, clients who seek professional counseling or psychotherapy often unconsciously resent doing it, and as a result create difficulties with such things as appointments and/or payment; they may also misunderstand or forget topics mentioned earlier.

This is part of the transferential dynamics and requires tactful handling. The first rule is not to show annoyance. Indeed, you do know better and can expect this to happen. The second rule is to be accommodating but not to the extent that you really inconvenience yourself. The third rule is to mention your fee and the length of the session when you (or your secretary) make the first appointment. I remember a couple, many years ago, who insisted on seeing me on a day and hour that was very inconvenient for me. In a moment of weakness, I gave in. A few hours before the appointment, I got a telephone message saying that "something" had come up and they could not make it but that they would be in my office at the same time of the same day the following week. The message added, "We hope that we can pay half of the fee when we see you and owe you the other half." I was grateful that they called (others, as you know, just don't show up), but what about the inconvenience? I had changed my schedule to fit them in. I called them back to inform them, respectfully and firmly, that I was unable to see them on the only day and hour they wanted and that my entire fee for a session is paid as the mental health service is rendered and received. As you can guess, I never heard from them again. But I learned to pay attention to transferential issues, even over the phone and before having met patients.

This simple example, as with so many things that happen every day, shows the transference dynamics. On their part, it was obvious that they saw "the therapist" under the distortion of a never-says-no mother. On my part I realized after psychoanalyzing my behavior that I gave in to please the wife, whose voice sounded sincere and in real need of advice. My "father role" took over and, as a good father, I was going to sacrifice for my child. This was the exaggerated, mistaken, superego imperative. At an even more primitive level, the flashing fantasy of some sort of romantic involvement with the wife was preparing the possibility for that by being extra nice to her. This fantasy was triggered by the id, as mentioned earlier, appropriately called the "inner dummy" by Weiner and Hefter (1999). When they canceled, my ego connected again with reality. Had it not been so, I would have had to accept the two inconvenient (and questionable) conditions they had proposed.

Remember that, aside from the obvious differences, the same points mentioned about transference apply also to countertransference. Everything that the patient goes through the analyst goes through as well. I hope this helps to clarify what transference is in its psychodynamic complexity. There is always some element of regression in transference. On my part, again referring to the case just mentioned, as a child I was taught to be a gentleman on every occasion, and to leave others feeling better than before they met me. In my behavior with this couple (or rather, with the woman), there was also a manifestation of the repetition compulsion or urge to reenact that early command implanted in my psyche. If I am not aware and careful, I cannot act in any other manner. In any transference, at least one of the inner drives will appear—either pleasure, or love and attachment, and/or the complicated one of destruction (both the fear of it and the magnetic pull toward it) in so many forms. In my case, the flashing romantic fantasy about the woman (whom I had not yet met), embodied a mixture of psychic tendencies: the attraction of sex, the security of attachment, and the self-destructive possibilities on the personal and professional levels. There was also the fear of it, coming both from anxiety about rejection and mockery, as well as from the possibility of engaging in unfaithful, unprofessional, and unethical conduct. What do we do with this type of awareness? After acknowledging and identifying the transference elements, there is actually nothing "to do." (When a person acts on transferential reactions, it is said that she "acts out," as opposed to "working through," as Chapters 13 and 14 discuss.) Thus transference keeps us humble, helps us to know ourselves better, and reminds us of the constant need to be in touch with our unconscious in order to lead a satisfying and good life. This is why, first and foremost, I consider psychoanalysis to be the Zen of the Western world.

*　*　*

To sum up, in the clinical counseling or psychotherapy session don't look for transference but do expect it. When you find it in yourself, don't do anything at the time, but after the session analyze it. By the next time you see the same client, you must know what it means and what in the client elicited the transference in you. When you suspect transference in the patient, again, don't act right away. Think about it after the patient is gone; try to find the connection between the client's alleged transferential behavior and what you know of her generally, and in particular, of her past. At the next session, observe her behavior carefully in order to assure yourself that what you perceived as transference is truly there. If that's the case, you may now bring up (best in the form of a question) the connection you perceived, and you must help her to realize the difference between the current situation with you and what happened to her in the past. If she accepts this, smooth sailing. If she does not, leave it alone until you notice the transference again. Then bring it up once more. If she still rejects it, explain rejection in simple terms, as an attempt to avoid uncomfortable, stressful awareness of realities in ourselves. If she accepts this, therapy continues smoothly; if she does not, as before, do not try to convince her. Leave it alone, knowing that if your perception is correct something similar is going to appear again in the near future. When it does, you connect what is happening then to what happened before, when she resisted it. By this time, the patient may be ready for your brief explanation about resistance and the repetition compulsion.

Someone may ask about the ethics of acting as if nothing is happening and thus deceiving the client. My response is that honesty does not always mean full transparency. It is also common sense to realize that adults cannot reveal indiscriminately everything that comes to their minds. Bad timing and rushed interpretations can be very unethical.

Conclusion

Rather than consider transference as something to be avoided in ourselves and ignored in the therapeutic counseling sessions, or as something to correct in our clients, both they and we grow in self-knowledge by accepting transference as a natural occurrence, inevitable and enriching, often unpleasant, complicated, and liberating. From everything we have discussed in this chapter, it is obvious that transference is inevitable. But it is also enriching, because by paying attention to it many mysterious things in our psyche move to the level of consciousness. It is complicated, as we learned, but it is also liberating because we can trace back the transferential connections, instead of being annoyed or guilty because of them. It liberates us because when we can make conscious the unconscious reactions that surprised us before, it suddenly gives us more power, control, and better choices over how we respond to our drives and inner dynamics. Read what follows. Notice what makes you uncomfortable. Look into it and notice what you learn from your self-analysis.

One of my old colleagues at Long Island University in New York, who had no training in psychoanalysis, told me once, many years ago, something that is very psychoanalytic. He said that his erotic attraction to many of the beautiful female students was even more intense than when he was much younger. He explained that he realized he was distorting reality. Older men may deliberately seek young sexual partners to feel good. But that was not his case: he realized that he perceived himself as young and attractive to them while in reality they looked up to him as an asexual wise old professor. This "making the unconscious conscious" helped him to freely accept his senior academic role and to look at those beautiful young women as if they were his granddaughters. Recognizing those transferential truths saved him from guilt and embarrassment about his uncomfortable feelings but enriched his experience of aging and helped him to be at peace with himself.

Check now your reactions while you read the last few lines. What annoyed you? Were you judgmental of my friend? What was it in you that made you react the way you did? This checkup may put you in touch with real but hidden dynamics in you.

My friend died a few months after our conversation. Among the many fond memories I have of him, this chat stands out as a good indication of his insights, wisdom, and goodness. His neurotic need to appear young made him perceive very young women as possible romantic partners. But then his healthy ego accepted the reality of the situation and forced him to view them as "adopted granddaughters." My intention in sharing this anecdote is to show that the psychoanalytical concept of transference is experienced by all humans, and that it is understood, though without calling it by its technical name, by those who are not afraid of introspection, like my friend.

To become familiar with transferential realities, look into yourself when you experience a strong reaction of attraction or dislike to a person that you barely know. Get in touch with the fantasies you have about yourself in connection with the other person and ask yourself what would you say and do, and how the other person would respond. Most people dismiss situations like these and distract themselves with other things. My contention is that you can grow in self-knowledge and understanding if you pay attention to your own transferential reactions. Again, the Western Zen of psychoanalysis! Moreover, familiarity with ordinary transference will make you a better counselor and therapist when these reactions happen with a patient or in the patient's own life.

Chapter 7

SUPEREGO: THE "I THAT STANDS ABOVE"

Many today speak of the higher self, the luminous energy field, the soul, and similar concepts. All these constructs can be included under Freud's notion of the superego. Originally, before Freud developed the dual-drive Eros and Thanatos theory, the superego was considered to be limited to one's conscience, that internalized voice of parental and cultural authority, acting as an inner judge. However, Robert Waelder (1932), a physicist who turned toward psychoanalysis and became one of Freud's inner circle, knew about the principle of complementarity of quantum physics, out of which he developed the principle of multiple function (pp. 68–83) to explain the superego. He tells us that the superego "is the element by which man . . . goes beyond himself taking himself as an object [of observation]"; a spiritual or nonphysical "agency" above instinct and culture. It is historically interesting to note that Freud never objected to this reading of his theories by Waelder, even though the German-writing disciple published most of his work in the decade before the master's death. According to Waelder, as elucidated recently by Frattaroli (2001), especially in his chapter on Freud's theory of the soul, the evolution of Freud's thought from libido to Eros points in the direction of spirit. What Freud had considered earlier to be a sublimation of libido later became a strong dynamic in its own right. Eros is the energy of life, present in humans and manifested in the best of human nature, like culture, art, science, compassion, heroism, forgiveness, and caring, as well as in the entire universe, from the magnificent majesty of galaxies hundreds of thousands of light years away to the millions of infinitesimally small subatomic components in our own bodies. Like all the energy in the universe, Eros is in matter yet transcends matter. This is the élan vital, the ultimate energy that forces us to wonder about the possibility of a superior, superhuman intelligence responsible for the existence of the universe and the ruling of it. Because the perspective of this force seems so different from ours, it transcends our human understanding.

Eros and Thanatos

In understanding these ideas, before we consider their practical use in psychotherapy, we cannot forget that Freud found that his theory of libido (the urge to avoid anxiety by satisfying one's desires, be they pleasurable or aggressive) had to be reconsidered after the horrors of World War I. The war gave rise in his thinking to the conceptualizations of the repetition compulsion and of Thanatos (the death instinct). To give a simple example, this means that what we today call PTSD (posttraumatic stress disorder), the unavoidable tendency to repeat in one's mind the horrendous experiences of the nightmares of war or any other extreme trauma like that of September 11, could not be explained by the libido theory. Rather, the need to repeat old reactions in new stress situations can be seen as an unconscious and twisted way of returning to the familiar, even though it is very painful and upsetting. This repetition is a misdirected and regressive unconscious drive that tries to restore inner order, to find stability, to undo the damage done, and to avoid the changes brought by the impact of the trauma, as if by going over it again and again it will become less powerful and less painful. It is a neurotic escape from the current anxiety by trying to find refuge in earlier, known though ineffective, ways of coping. Ultimately it is an effort to end it all—to move away from life to Thanatos via the death instinct.

The superego is the means by which we become aware of both Eros and Thanatos as being part of us. The two become a practical way of explaining two basic drives of meaning and motivation in all humans, which, ideally, must find a balance with each other in our experience of living. Examples include security vs. adventure; constancy and stability vs. immediacy and impulse; synthesis vs. analysis; empowerment vs. helplessness; integration vs. disintegration; and the spirit vs. the flesh. But only when Eros triumphs do we find good mental health, as when we have been able to expand our consciousness of these two realities in life and have resolved the tension of Eros and Thanatos in favor of the former—in yet another instance of the unconscious becoming conscious. What does this mean? That we have gained control of the biological forces of the id operating through the automatic reflexes of the repetition compulsion, thus allowing us to feel more autonomous and free to choose and act from our true self, which in turn means to allow room for Eros in us to take over. It is this facilitation of Eros in us, manifested by responsible free choices, that is the hoped-for outcome of psychoanalytical therapy.

Now we can return, with practical understanding, to the nonmaterial (or spiritual) aspect of the superego and of psychoanalysis. I emphasize that "spiritual" here means everything that is not material. By the way, the difference I find helpful to use in distinguishing between soul and spirit is that *soul* refers to the nonmaterial reality in each human being, while *spirit*, or rather Spirit, is the invisible energy throughout the entire universe, in and with which soul participates. Thus, the animistic idea of soul in animals and even trees, rocks, mountains, lakes, wind, and so on, is a rather poetic extension of the awareness of Spirit or energy in all things. The unique type of energy in every object, simple and complicated, big and small, is considered by many mythologies to be its soul.

The practical side of the nonmaterial

The practical part of this aspect of the superego is that psychoanalysis is not just "therapy," a method to correct or cure something that is malfunctioning or wrong in the patient (the symptom), but is also and equally a means of helping the patient to get in touch with her soul—that is, all the feelings, desires, values and attitudes, expectations, hopes and perceptions of one's surroundings that are themselves made up of things, events, and especially people. By using this approach we make it possible for the patient to "have heart," to stop being a robot, to cease acting as if she were preprogrammed for the rest of her life. We may make the client aware of Eros and Thanatos, the two contrary tendencies within her (as if they were different parts of her) so that she is able to identify, distinguish, and use the two parts for her human fulfillment. By allowing her ego to side with Eros, she agrees with the superego and rejects the excessive demands of the id. Examples are as numerous as the people who employ introspection, and they all come down to learning to be caring, positive, tolerant, joyful, hopeful, creative, confident, and productive. This orientation also puts the client in contact with the "good energy" as Shamanism and other similar religions call it. The good energy of the "I that stands above," with which the client connects when she comes to accept Eros, brings her to a spiritual level of operating. Acting with heart probably refers to this. The analyst encourages her to practice doing this, first when the client is face to face with him and then on her own until the following session. This suggestion is made in order to help her experience the difference between mere acting and acting with heart, with soul, so that she convinces herself of the advantages of being under the influence of Eros.

This approach is positive and healing in several ways. First, it gives the patient the power of free choice, liberating him from the compulsion to reenact, and activating his own responsibility, independent of external constraints. Second, it makes him realize that his self is not a simple entity but that the I is a complex inner identity with more than one constant part. Third, it enlarges his honesty and truthfulness by making him conscious of his intentions, emotions, and actions. Fourth, it starts him on a fresh way of reacting to situations and making decisions about them, taking new risks by moving away from the self-concerned center—libido changes into Eros. And fifth, a consequence of the latter, it expands his perspective of reality, allowing him to reach beyond the domain of the senses and the physical, and thus upgrading him and his life to the spiritual plane. As part of this expanded perception, he sees himself as being essentially connected to the universe, both physically and, in terms of its awesome mystery, at the spiritual level. L. Watson (1979), a researcher of unusual events, summarizes these advantages by stating that "the importance of experiencing oneself, of being aware [being conscious of what was unconscious] is that it allows a far more effective way of adapting to new and varied situations" (p. 135).

As you see, there is a large overlap among the five points mentioned. The power of free choice comes from the awareness of the different parts of one's personality. For instance, one part wants to explode, the other demands self-control; one moves the person to act out of impulse, the other considers the consequences of his actions; one puts on airs of importance and omnipotence, the other reminds him of his real limitations and weaknesses; and so on. Free choice is the consequence of recognizing that he does not need to act just in one fashion, that he can always decide which way to go. In the therapy session, you go with the client over different scenarios or possibilities for handling a difficult situation. In this way he will begin to classify both id- and ego-based solutions, enabling him to recognize the advantages of each part as they influence his perceptions, preferences, and values—and especially his decisions. He cannot any longer hold on to the belief in an immutable center in his own being, despite the false sense of security that may give. Throughout history, dishonest teachers, politicians, and religious leaders have shown the dangers of that view. Yet this lack of security, paradoxically, at the same time brings enrichment, because every situation is new and is accepted with a fresh attitude of adventure and discovery. Reality becomes for the client something larger than what his senses can reach, either by themselves or with the aid of sophisticated technology, and thus he has to reach for the immaterial, the spiritual.

Clinical vignette

One case example may clarify the above comments. The client, Malaq, was a 57-year-old physicist, very aware of his superior intelligence and habitually arrogant in all his dealings with others. His wife was leaving him in order to move in with a woman who had been her best friend. He had not suspected anything before she announced her decision. Malaq, who some days worked as long as fifteen hours in his laboratory, described his reaction as a bomb that had destroyed his private life. He refused to take psychotropic drugs for the depression and stress he was feeling because, he said, he knew their chemical composition better than those who prescribe them, and he was afraid of their "toxicity." He started therapy with me for the first time three months after the devastating event. But he did not want to talk about his marriage or his wife. He was concerned and angry because for the first time in his life he had been experiencing what he called "writer's paralysis," or the inability to concentrate on the reports and articles he had to write on his research. He complained about "blanks" in his thinking process. When in the second session I suggested that these "symptoms" had started right after his wife's decision to leave the marriage, he answered abruptly and angrily, "Symptoms of what? I thought you knew that symptoms are manifestations of sickness." I refused to get into his attempted argument and simply said firmly: "You're hurting as hell for what your wife did to you and you're hiding your hurt and you're refusing to face it." He didn't respond and kept looking at me, the anger gone. Then I continued that I suspected he knew there was a relation between the symptoms and his wife, that I hoped he could use his scientific mind to explore this and that I was here to help him do it. At this point, therapy (the process of healing) started. He admitted that he had never been a loving husband and that he did treat his wife with indifference and lack of love, taking her for granted and almost resenting her very existence as interfering with his first love, work. Even at home, after the long hours at the lab, he would read scientific literature and work on his home computer. Malaq discovered his emotional duality between home and work, realizing that for him, his wife had become a useful tool at home that made his job easier. His deep grief about his wife leaving him had to do with the inconvenience of having lost a very competent "servant, valet, secretary, and Jack of all trades."

This insight led him to surprising progress in an unexpected manner. He explained that his work had become an addiction; that because of it he had neglected his children and his wife. He stressed that he was not feeling guilty for them ("They are okay") but sorry for himself. Notice his choice of words in describing himself: "So much weight on science, as if it were the end of everything else. And I missed out not only on my family but on music and art. I used to enjoy them, but then I didn't give myself time to do it. Science was calling!" After a thoughtful pause, he added: "In over thirty years of science I know that there is more to matter than what we reach with our instruments. But I stuck to matter and punished myself." I was so impressed with this statement that I wrote it down verbatim. Malaq is one of many people who is now able to get in touch with the spiritual (in one way or another) as a result of an insight obtained in the process of psychoanalysis.

Deeper understanding of reality

Concretely now, we can view "the spiritual" as a dimension of strength in our lives. Because we think, we are not limited to the reach of our bodily senses. Thinking, our constant nonmaterial activity, allows us to reach what I call the Infinite Thought, at least in a very imperfect way. In an unconsciously psychoanalytical way, Nelson Mandela (Finlayson 1998), in his inaugural speech of 1994, stated that our innermost fear (does he mean "unconscious fear"?) is that of being too powerful (independent and isolated, self-centered and detached from the rest of mankind?) because then we disregard God (is this included in my concept of the "I that stands above"?). Stressing the spiritual, he refers to humans as children of God born to make manifest the glory of God. He sees that glory within us— does Mandela mean the spiritual, as explained above in this chapter, which sets us apart from all other living beings in the planet?

For many the concept of "God" is a symbol of absolute power, fulfillment, and completion. Hence, we hear expressions like, "With God I can do anything," or "In God is my strength," which, besides the religious meaning that some find in them, I understand as a proclamation of the spiritual reality of humans. It is as if one were saying, in accepting one's spirituality, one can do everything, or my spirituality is my strength. Therefore "God" connotes strength beyond the reach of the senses, something spiritual. This strength then comes from consciousness—what has become conscious after it was unconscious—or, in simple language, strength comes with the reality beyond the reach of the senses that is recognized as an integral part of the total human picture.

However, the word "God" is rejected by many, who see it as involved in what are considered outdated or meaningless rites and ceremonies. It is worth noting that when atheists explain their mental position, what they definitely reject is the way organized religion presents spiritual reality, not necessarily the validity of the spiritual. In this respect, it is also interesting to note that Abraham Lincoln, who was not affiliated with any church or religion, although often quoting from the Bible, never mentioned God on his own but talked of "the Creator," a term that assumes supreme intelligence, control, and purpose. Awareness of the spiritual, full-superego consciousness is what I am interested in. In the attempt to capture this unknown, people call it, besides God, the Higher Power, the Great Spirit, the Fullness of Being, the Cause of all Causes, the Great Mystery, and many other names: "You who are known by a thousand names and you who are the unnamable one," as an Inca prayer reads (Villoldo 2000, p. 135). Many scientists and philosophers who reject religion acknowledge this extrasensory reality in the universe, even though what they call it differs and can become confusing. Thus Timmerman (2001) sums it up in this short formula: What language is to thought, religions are to the awareness of the supernatural. Or, as a Methodist minister who went through the horrors of the Twin Towers destruction in New York City told me, "Religion is for those afraid of hell, and spirituality is for those who have gone through hell."

Application to psychoanalytic work

Going back to clinical practice, we can apply in our work some of what has been theorized by quantum physics at the present stage of scientific development. To review, matter is not really the solid objects (atoms) that we are familiar with, as Newtonian physics held. The subatomic particles discovered by quantum physics explain matter as having a dual character of waves and particles. Bohr's (1927) *complementary principle* states that both are complementary descriptions of the same reality. Therefore, both are needed to give a complete picture of matter and its nature. As a consequence, the more we insist only on particles or on waves, the more the other aspect becomes uncertain and the more we distort reality. In the same vein, Heisenberg's (1958) *uncertainty principle* emphasizes the interconnection between all things in nature. Quantum physicists describe nature in terms of connections, including that between subject and observer, making it clear that at the limits of perception, whatever is observed is altered by the mere act of observing it (Capra 1982, Zukav 2000).

Paralleling these findings, Waelder's (1932) *principle of multiple functions* begins from a point that gave Freud trouble (to the extent that he even abandoned his first theory of anxiety)—namely, that anxiety must be explained by two different theories, that is, as overwhelming the id, and as a danger signal created by the ego. Waelder extended the dualism to human life in general, describing the ego as being driven and being directed in relation to the id and also in connection with the superego, as well as connected with the death instinct in the repetition compulsion and to the external world in general. The ego is always passive and active, overwhelmed and driven. We cannot emphasize one of these two functions at the expense of the other without distorting the picture of what the ego is all about.

In the psychoanalytic connection, where there is also an exchange between an "object" and an "observer," countertransferential experiences will help you understand where to place the emphasis of your attention and what you have to change in order to balance your approach. Your id wants to react the way you feel and your ego wants to remain within superego confines. As a clinician you must consider the patient with as much acceptance and respect as possible. To ignore her human dignity is to ignore her soul, and therefore to manifest a lack of connection. Rogers (1961) taught that in order for a patient to change and improve, she must sense that you regard or "receive" her genuinely, without negative judgments nor with the desire to change her according to your lofty preferences, values, and norms. Her personhood, all she is, makes up her spirituality, and for her to benefit from her connection with you, she must sense that you honor her soul. How? By recognizing her uniqueness as an individual. As we saw above, her being, personhood, and spirituality transcend your perception of her, which is unavoidably contaminated by your own personhood. If you ignore or neglect the spiritual aspect of the patient, it will be impossible to help her. You must respect the "I that stands above" for her to reach it herself. This is why, to make it possible for her to shed her masks, as in the Jungian concept, you must approach her without your masks. We can't forget that the goal of all psychotherapy is to help the client be her true, complete, self, or, as quantum physics teaches about material things, to be what she is with all her waves and particles.

In practice, when you experience countertransference, you have two main options. First, the passive reaction: you may refuse to continue seeing a client because you don't like him or feel uncomfortable with him. Another option, the active reaction, is to purify yourself. By this I mean that by overcoming your negative reaction to this patient (the ego function) you may have the opportunity

to grow and enrich yourself personality-wise. Self-reflection and consultation with a trusted colleague or mentor are the means to purify
yourself, to become aware of your inner reactions and feelings. I see
this aspect of the therapeutic work as spiritual in that the clinician
has to care for the patient and be concerned about her. This is real
love, an essential component of the therapeutic relationship, as
Mitchell (2000) explains at length elaborating on what he calls
"relationality." When cognitive-behaviorists claim that the method
is more important than the relationship with the client, I see in the
claim further evidence of their missed goal; to help people in psychological need you must consider the people first. For us, the
patient–therapist relationship is the most important variable in the
process of human change, as Breuer and Freud pointed out as early
as in *Studies on Hysteria* (1895). I mentioned in Chapter 6 that the
positive side of any type of countertransference is that the clinician
must develop toward the client the same type of genuine positive
feelings, respect, attention, and consideration that clients have toward the clinician, or at least that the practitioner expects clients to
have toward him.

Another aspect of the spiritual dimension in clinical work is the
recognition by the clinician, as well as by the client himself, that
progress in the work is a clear manifestation of his soul. Progress, as
we mentioned before, is evident basically in his becoming more and
more what he truly is. Now he can be himself. Before that seemed
impossible. And in humans this "self" always includes the "I that
stands above." This higher self, included in Goleman's (1995) concept of *emotional intelligence*, encompasses many of the old-fashioned
virtues of acceptance and tolerance of differences in others, empathy, genuineness, sensitivity to others, caring for them, treating them
fairly if not kindly, working responsibly at a high ethical level, and
so on. The emergence of these behaviors in the patient is a common

and typical outcome of psychoanalysis. People experience a positive transformation and identify-in-action with their I-that-stands-above. In terms of what this chapter has been discussing, people become more spiritual.

Finally, psychoanalysis is a special process that helps, first, to make the individual aware of his interdependency, and then to activate it, first with others (because we are always part of systems, like family, coworkers, compatriots), then in the world at large (all the goods that I enjoy thanks to the labor of other humans, even in far distant places), and finally on the entire universe, beginning with our planet (my influence on nature and its effects on me). Mostly these three areas of awareness overlap and grow together.

It is rather obvious that in order to obtain these benefits the clinician must live accordingly. Only when this is the case can she encourage her clients to recognize and activate the qualities of interdependence. Her questions, such as "You know others who have it worse than you?" will not sound empty if she truly lives with the awareness and humility of her privileged position in life. The truth is that everybody is privileged if he compares himself to someone who is less well off than he is. And this awareness, by the way, is an important aspect of living in the present—a very psychoanalytical ideal—having left behind the past that was not constructive and enriching. Wasn't psychoanalysis intended to be the method to learn from our past? If we can do so, we will learn from the past and leave behind what does not work for us now, to restate a basic developmental idea in all schools of psychoanalysis. Regarding the future, mental health requires planning for it but, simultaneously, being ready for any surprises; as John Lennon said, "Life is what happens while we plan for it." The more the person can act in the present, the freer she is, the more she has matured. That means that the person is also free not to act according to her past if that does not fit her now. The old repetition compulsion is overcome. Psychoanalysis destroys the myth of "destiny," and stresses one's responsibility to act constructively and with adult self-love; here, lack of compulsion and the presence of free choice are manifestations of the spiritual in us.

An afterthought to his chapter comes from the reflections of Bettelheim (1982) when he discusses, among others, the mistaken English translation of Freud's word *Seele* to designate mind or psyche. The German noun used by Freud, a consistently careful writer who used words selectively and carefully, means *soul* in English. Bettelheim states unambiguously, "Freud [in 1938] emphasized that his life's work had been devoted to understanding as fully as possible the world of man's soul" (p. 75). Bettelheim's thesis, which I share, is that Freud considered the non-material or spiritual aspect of being human and that we cannot fully understand what his message is regarding the nature of humans unless we incorporate that spiritual part in our thinking.

Chapter 8
HYPNOSIS IN PSYCHOANALYSIS

Freud conceived the idea of psychoanalysis after learning about hypnosis. Can we consider hypnosis "the mother" of psychoanalysis? Not exactly. However, hypnosis is a method that activates the unconscious for the benefit of the individual, and Freud developed psychoanalysis to work with the unconscious. Because one comes from the other we can state, in a general sense, that psychoanalysis was born from hypnosis. Most nonprofessional people don't know how closely hypnosis is related to psychoanalysis, and neither do most lay hypnotists realize it, though they frequently refer to the unconscious, calling it by different names. Most practitioners use hypnosis for symptom removal or for medical problems (symptoms too!), forgetting that the most effective use of hypnosis is for exploring the unconscious.

A look at history (Freud 1925, Gravitz and Gerton 1981) shows that Freud as a youngster had been at a "magnetism" demonstration by a Herr Hansen, a well-known hypnotist of the time, and that he became very impressed by what he saw. Much later and already a physician, in the last years of the nineteenth century, he was exposed to hypnosis as practiced by the leading French psychiatrists—

Charcot and Janet in Paris, and Bernheim and Liebeault in Nancy. Back home in Vienna, Freud began using hypnosis, or the *cathartic method*, as he called it then, especially to help his patients recover repressed memories and to control pain.

But this did not last long. He mentioned scientific reasons for his hypnosis discontinuance, mainly that hypnosis distorted the nature of the relation between the patient and the therapist, but there were also very personal reasons (Kline 1958). He was beginning a new treatment method, *free association*, that he claimed as his own discovery and possession, and did not want hypnosis to subsume free association or to be confused with it. An element of frustration also seems to be involved, because, as Puner (1947) notes, believing that "deep trance" was necessary for effective hypnosis, Freud found that many patients did not attain it and thus made him fail. Perhaps the most important subjective reasons were, first, one or two events (Gravitz and Gerton 1981) where a woman patient, "as she woke up on one occasion threw her arms around my neck" (Freud 1925, p. 48). The second reason seems to have been the condemnation of clinical hypnosis by professionals Freud respected, especially his former teacher at the University of Vienna, Dr. Theodor Meynert.

But the evidence is that Freud, like some of his early disciples, considered hypnosis a valuable tool to use in working with unconscious material. The just-mentioned article by Gravitz and Gerton is important in this respect, giving us evidence that Freud utilized the services of Franz Polgar, a stage hypnotist to whom he referred some patients in order to facilitate his psychoanalytical work.

Diverse uses of hypnosis

In those days hypnosis was very authoritative, the hypnotist taking control of the situation and telling the patient what to do. Now we call that style traditional hypnosis. However, at least in the last fifty years or so, we have a new way of using hypnosis, mainly thanks to the work of Milton Erickson (Rossi 1980). I called it the *new hypnosis* (Araoz 1985) to describe a method that is patient-centered, permissive, naturalistic, and much more interactive than the traditional style, without losing any of the psychodynamic value. Today, generally speaking, clinical hypnosis can be used in four main ways; either (1) behaviorally, for the removal or improvement of psychogenic symptoms, following the medical model; or (2) for strictly medical conditions, including pain control, anesthesia, activation of the immune system, lowering of blood pressure, giving birth, and so on; or (3) as a method to work with and find the meaning of unconscious dynamics, anxiety, motivations, fears, "shoulds," and so on, that affect the quality of life of the individual. This latter use is also called *hypnoanalysis* (Wolberg 1945), stressing the value of hypnosis to bring to consciousness what has been repressed and still remains in the unconscious, negatively affecting the individual. Currently, with the recognition of intersubjectivity in analysis, we can describe hypnosis in object-relations terms, as a reverie that becomes a transitional experience to facilitate the healing of early deficits. This intersubjective experience is healing because it is used as a symbol of the patient's own inner experiences (fantasies) that make up his subjective world, thus leading him to develop subjectivity. Finally, the last modality of therapeutic hypnosis is (4) for personal growth as well as self-enhancement and enrichment, from better sports performance or more acute memory or keener concentration to inner peace, contentment, and mindfulness.

From what he saw, both as a young person and later as a professional, Freud developed psychoanalysis as a practical application of many of the phenomena common to the hypnotic trance. He channeled and tailored the basic hypnotic phenomena for clinical mental-health work. In hypnosis he found an effective way to reach the unconscious, out of which came free association (hypnosis in slow motion?) for the improvement and resolution of neurosis. By the way, true free association is a typical example of new hypnosis because in this way the patient enters an alternate state of consciousness, another way of describing a trance.

Fenichel (1945), in his masterwork on the theory of neuroses, explains hypnoanalysis quite clearly (though as it was then still used, in the traditional, authoritative manner), and seems to justify it by suggesting that many chronic neurotic symptoms may be the result of what I (1981) have called negative self-hypnosis (NSH). The patient convinces himself that he cannot accomplish something and reinforces that thought with his repeated imagery, self-talk, and general attitude; he is unable to stop reenacting the neurotic patterns that make him anxious and unhappy. Pointing to NSH may serve a therapeutic function, when it can make him aware of how he is sabotaging his own well-being and realize that he is using a hypnotic method against himself that the clinician can help him change for his benefit. The most effective way of making him aware of his NSH is by suggesting that he change the imagery and self-suggestions into realistically positive and optimistic ones. Once he has done this, you help him recognize the good feelings he experienced while focusing on more positive thoughts.

The place of hypnosis in analysis

So, how can you use hypnosis in analysis or psychoanalytic therapy? First of all, keep in mind that I am talking about *new hypnosis* (Araoz 1985), as different from the traditional approach of Fenichel or Wolberg, mentioned in the previous paragraphs and used in Freud's time, and that many clinicians still use today. Basically, new hypnosis considers that true hypnosis involves any nonlogical or sequential and outside-reality-oriented way of using one's brain. Moreover, any spontaneous reverie or fantasy that emerges in the course of analysis and to which the clinician responds genuinely is hypnotic. Bion (1962) presents reverie as a capacity of the analyst to resonate with the patient. This, of course, is an experiential reaction to the client (what he has just reported), which establishes a special empathy and connection between both. This is reminiscent of the analytic couple described in Gitelson's (1952) important article that is a precursor of current analytical thinking on intersubjectivity as discussed by Solorow, Brandchaft, and Atwood (1995) and "relationality" (Mitchell 2000). The clinician using new hypnosis helps the patient switch from "objective" to experiential ways of thinking; in thinking as if it were real, one may reach and recognize internalizations and representations, as well as Kernberg's (1980) units of object relations, which organize the chaotic ego. In brief, hypnosis works with the psychological structures that always use inner images that modify (and distort) actual others.

Second, the clinician perceives hypnosis as a different (and more convenient) method for the patient to obtain more effectively what he wants to attain in psychoanalytical work without hypnosis. In other words, hypnoanalysis means that the clinician is fully involved in psychoanalytic therapy and improves it with this technique. I see the improvement as cutting down on intellectualization, rationalization, and other resistances, as well as allowing the analyst to join the patient in a nonintrusive, natural way. This joining happens when the client reports a fantasy, or a waking dream, and the analyst accepts it; by so doing, the clinician enters into the same psychic production. Through this process, the therapist empathizes with the client and experientially knows what the problem is all about. Because she is the therapist, some new ideas about its resolution start to form. Thanks to hypnosis, she has a better experiential understanding of the possible unconscious elements in the clinical picture; the patient's fantasy is related to concrete aspects of his personality. In this sense, hypnosis deals with primitive, preoedipal, unconscious material more directly and purely than mere ordinary language and talking.

Typically, after having understood the nature of the patient's problem, and without even mentioning hypnosis to him, you encourage the patient "to relax" or "to go inside of yourself" or "to get in touch with your inner self," or any other suggestion of this nature. I often find myself using expressions like "your innermost self," "your inner mind," "your very soul," or "the center of your unique self." What is important is the message you want to convey, not the exact sentences you use. And the message that is conveyed is a dawning of awareness of the patient's secret, intimate self or personality part. In order to help in this process, you may suggest that the client become keenly aware of her breathing, and you take the time to do so and avoid any pressure to rush. Also helpful are the old, traditional recommendations to close one's eyes, to feel physically comfortable, to imagine that the body is completely relaxed as it happens during healthy sleep, and to visualize all worries and resistances moving away from her (or she leaving them all behind). This is a way of preparing the client to recognize distractions and of teaching her how to deal with them. All this you say in a very calm voice, as you try to be relaxed yourself. Any image, memory, or connection the patient reports may have important meaning to her. Nothing is nonsense. Because of this, if the person visualizes something that her resistances and worries are encouraging her to disregard, you instead invite her to notice their appearance, form, and size. That is to say, you show her by your interest that everything that comes up in her mind can be meaningful and should be treated seriously.

Then you may instruct the patient to focus, as gently as possible, on the problem or issue that she is working on or wants to work on. You may continue as follows in a slow and relaxed voice (and, I stress emphatically, that this is merely a sample of what you may say). Note that the double slash [//] indicates points where one may pause briefly in order to facilitate the patient's introspection.

"You want to feel the problem // as something that is now part of your life. // But you don't want this in your life. // // You may find a comparison for your problem; // sense the problem // metaphorically as . . . // Let your unconscious bring up one or more images that represent your problem." // (If the person does not seem to understand this, give examples: "Some people talk about an earthquake, or a strong wind, or a bonfire.") "Keep breathing slowly // and relaxing // to give yourself time // to come up with an image of your problem. // There is no rush. // You can trust // your unconscious. // Let it bring up a metaphor that represents your problem; // the image, let it come // if not now, // later or in your dreams // tonight // or perhaps tomorrow night."

This type of suggestion may be briefer or longer, depending on the patient's response. In any case, one must be careful not to talk too much—and never too loud or too fast. If the metaphor appears, you remind the patient that it will give him a better grasp of the problem and its solution. Notice that this is the first time you mention "solution." The full acceptance of one's problem is required in order to look seriously for a solution. Another very important point to make at this juncture is to emphasize that he can leave it up to the unconscious to work toward the solution, as long as he takes the metaphor seriously and goes over it again and again, not in a rational, logical way, but in an experiential one.

All this will probably fill an entire session. At that point it might be good to stop (or rather interrupt), reminding the patient to repeat this practice again and again, especially just before going to sleep. If, however, the metaphor did not appear in this first hypnotherapy session, you focus the patient on trusting the unconscious and look-ing forward with curiosity to that symbolic representation of the problem and its solution: Will it happen unexpectedly, in a flash? Will it come up in his dreams? In any case, you also recommend that he practice this by himself as often as it is reasonably possible. And, please, never say, "I want you to . . ." which is an easy way to elicit resistances that were not active before. It's also a condescending and arrogant order. Simply tell the patient what to do. He should not do it for you or because of you but for his own benefit. Intruding in a nonpsychotic person's mind is very seldom beneficial.

Following up in use of hypnosis

At the following session, you inquire if the patient did practice the mental exercise he did with you. From my experience, the success of hypnoanalysis depends greatly on the mind-work the patient does between sessions. If he has not practiced, handle it with the tech-nique of personality parts that goes right to the unconscious con-flict of resistance. One of his personality parts wants help to resolve the problem; the other part rejects a method proven to be effective. Assist the patient in identifying these two parts by visualizing him-self first as one part and then the other. The two parts may engage in conversation about the issue at hand. This will help him own them fully, and by contrasting their different desires and goals, he can decide which part will run his life. Hypnotically, the patient can refer to these two parts in a cartoon-like fashion, visualizing himself as a living paradox, listening to the statements of each part and choos-ing the one that will have the real power of decision in his life.

Clinical applications

The following cases may clarify two hypnotic techniques. Felix, a middle-aged divorced man who, after several years of philandering, fell in love with Marie-Sue, "the perfect woman for me," still felt himself missing the excitement of his many earlier one-night stands. After asking for his explanation of the conflict, he said something about "two parts in me." I suggested that he try to give a name to each one of those two parts. In order to come up with the right names for each part I suggested that he try to relax in order to let his "inner mind" give him the answer. He identified one of his personality parts as Peter Pan and the other as the happy professional. In that first session he went from "I still want that freedom" to "I know Marie-Sue is good for me." I asked him what had happened and Felix mentioned that in the hypnotic experience he had seen himself as ten years older in each situation: kicking himself as Peter Pan for having let Marie-Sue go and, in opposition, as the happy professional, feeling very good for having found happiness, stability, and emotional security with her.

When a given patient has practiced his mind exercise on his own after the hypnotic experience during the therapy session, you will first find out if he has obtained any important insights. If this is the case, you invite him to look at it hypnotically, as if the insight had already changed his life (what I call "mental rehearsal") so that he can start to assimilate the changes and feel good about what he wants to have or experience in his life. Or, if he is not ready to do that, he may recognize through this hypnotic technique the obstacles he is facing and what he can do to remove or bypass them. After the type of work described with Felix, the analysis is usually directed at the dynamics that made him be in that state of uncomfortable doubt and insecurity, or in other words, what was behind the symptom.

This was the case of Steffie, aged 27 and single, whose presenting problem was that she found herself being too easy, complacent, and accommodating to others in general. I suggested that she try to imagine how she would act if she were not being too easy on others, since otherwise she ended up by hurting herself. Steffie selected a situation with a coworker who frequently took advantage of her by asking her to do things that were this other person's responsibility. Relaxed and with her eyes closed, she visualized the scene in great detail and very vividly for about seven or eight minutes. When she stopped the mental rehearsal and returned to the ordinary way of thinking, she was pleased with the insight she had obtained in the hypnotic practice. She saw that she would feel much better considering her own feelings first and responding to other people's requests accordingly. She repeated and practiced the same mental exercise on her own after the session, as I had recommended. In the second hypnotherapy session she changed the scene and visualized herself "acting right," in her words, with close friends and relatives who had always counted on her, no matter how inconvenient their requests and expectations were. In that session, she repeated the same mind exercise several times with different people in her life, always ending with a new feeling of empowerment, self-respect, and pride. She was reminded again to practice at home until the following session. Meanwhile, and what is especially important from the psychodynamic point of view, is that she realized that her being so "pleasant" came from her mother's "teachings." The mother had always stressed that she, as a girl, had to be pleasant and "nice" to everybody, that she should never consider her own feelings but always do "what's right." Hypnotically, she saw herself as 9 years old with her mother micromanaging everything Steffie was doing. I suggested that, in her fantasy, she could go to her room after the scene with her mother. There she could be in touch with all her feelings. She expressed helplessness and frustration because "I am a good girl but Mom is never pleased with me." At that point I reminded her that she can further use her imagination and visualize herself as she is now (an adult) stepping into that picture of little Stephie, so that big Steffie can make her feel good about who she is. This took several angles and changes until, hypnotically, she was able to make peace with her mother, who had died two years earlier, and to reaffirm Steffie's love for her, even though she disagreed with the mother's teachings. Steffie spent subsequent sessions strengthening her resolve to be "a full adult," considering first what was good for her and accepting the fact of disagreeing with her mother about a woman's proper role, as often happens with two adults. This important second-order change generalized, or "spread out," as she said, to many other aspects of her life, such as dating and relationships with men in general, as she took better care of her appearance and health, and gave herself time to enjoy concerts and outdoor activities as well as pursuing a different career in which she could develop her mind. (She was an office manager when she started therapy but she began the necessary graduate education and years later became a business college professor.) With the help of hypnoanalysis, Steffie stopped repeating a behavior that she recognized as childish and subservient, and the rest of her analysis helped her to utilize the inner resources of her unconscious to grow as a human being, to be happier as a person, and to feel better about herself. Of course, this was not brief therapy; all this work took her over four years to complete. The new college career gave her a more realistic sense of service to others, as well as a new healthy sense of self-pride and respect.

As Steffie's case shows, the psychoanalytic work continues with and without hypnosis by utilizing the initial insight, often along with fresh, subsequent insights that appear in the course of therapy. Frequently, you need to prod the patient gently with questions like, "What else is hidden in your metaphor?" or "Keep thinking of other aspects of the (main image or object in the metaphor)." Whatever the client responds is used, not to talk about it but to experience it internally, as if it were real, for which I use the Spanish word *vivencia*, a vivid inner experience (Araoz 2004).

Short-term psychoanalytic work?

With hypnosis, then, there is a realistic possibility of compressing the process of psychotherapy. As you noticed, the patient is given the chance and responsibility of doing much of the introspective work outside of the regular therapy sessions by repeating the techniques of hypnoanalysis on his own. Therefore, this type of therapy is not a shortcut and does not dangerously diminish the psychodynamic work but it intensifies it. All experienced clinicians have had patients who attend sessions from one to four times a week but do not give any serious thought to therapy in between sessions. However, in current hypnotherapy, the injunctions to review the gains made during the regular sessions, and to repeat the mind exercises that were practiced, are part of the therapeutic process. As you noticed, this type of hypnosis does not involve protocols or neat formulas. It surges up from what the patient is experiencing, so that the work becomes very free and creative. No two sessions are the same.

Generally speaking, troubling symptoms are often strengthened by the process of negative self-hypnosis (NSH), a form of resistance in which the patient repeats messages to himself that are self-defeating, discouraging, or limiting—in one word, negative—the death instinct at work. Nonhypnotic modern therapies propose behavioral tasks for the patient to do between sessions but do not place great importance on the responsibility of the patient to mentally and emotionally work on his improvement deliberately and perseveringly. Hypnoanalysis is concerned with NSH, which is another form of Freud's repetition compulsion, a force that sucks the person into the pathological, negative, and limiting aspects of his life. Felix was in danger of NSH when he concentrated on the excitement and fun that his sexual escapades used to give him, and had to refocus on his conviction of being happy with the ideal woman he was in love with. Interestingly enough, his unconscious brought up the idea of his feeling that he was past his prime age. Steffie, also, could have allowed NSH to bring her back to obey her mother's memory by doing what she was taught by the mother. But her unconscious emphasized that she was now an adult, so that she now needed to look at her mother from that perspective. If we are unaware of NSH, the process of cure is impeded and slowed down. My feeling is that resistance can often be understood in terms of NSH, especially when the patient continues to repeat mentally, consciously or most often unconsciously, the neurotic patterns that foster anxiety and inner psychological pain.

As I have stated earlier, what can be done psychoanalytically can be done better hypnoanalytically (Brown and Fromm 1986). This means, first, that the one who uses this technique must be well trained both in psychodynamics and in new hypnosis so that she clearly knows what she is doing and does it with confidence. Second, and very importantly, it means that hypnosis by itself cannot do what psychoanalysis does. In other words, someone who is a good hypnotist, as many stage entertainers are, but who does not have the qualifications to practice psychoanalysis, would be guilty of serious ethical misconduct by attempting to use hypnoanalysis and moreover could do serious psychological harm to his subjects.

* * *

The reasons for using hypnosis in psychoanalysis are not merely historical, as explained above, but in fact based on theory. If most of a person's psychic life is unconscious, as our references to Freud indicate, and if access to unconscious meaning is important, then the new hypnosis gives us a natural and effective method for the patient to enter the unconscious, thus making conscious that which was unconscious, and allowing the individual to deal with what was out of his control. Much of the strength of any psychopathology in a person's life comes from the fact that reason cannot easily reach and deal with psychopathology. Hypnosis is a convenient tool to do just that. On the other hand, as was already mentioned, we can see that much of psychopathology remains alive thanks to NSH. For that reason, paradoxically, we can assume that the patient is already practicing hypnosis (against himself, to be sure) and will find it "natural" to use a variation of the same basic technique, this time in his favor and for his well-being.

Freud and later psychoanalysts employed hypnosis without having formulated clearly the theory underlying their clinical practice. Thanks to the works referred to in this chapter, we have an advantage they did not have, and with adequate hypnosis training can make our psychoanalytic work more effective, more active, and even more enjoyable.

Chapter 9
PSYCHOANALYSIS WITH COUPLES
AND FOR SEXUAL PROBLEMS

During my psychoanalytic training, working with couples was just starting to be considered. Those who fought for it were followers of the analysts who developed object relations theory, such as Melanie Klein (1932), Fairbairn (1954), Winnicott (1965), and others. Fortunately, the trend became stronger and established a new specialization in the world of psychoanalysis. The historic beginning of what was then called "family psychotherapy," with people like Norman Ackerman (1968), was rooted in psychoanalysis. A few years later Helen Kaplan (1974) was criticized by many traditional psychoanalysts for what they perceived as not paying enough attention to psychodynamics in her "new sex therapy." Despite those early objections, many psychoanalytical institutes now have complete programs specializing in couple and family therapy, and a large number of psychoanalysts practice family therapy.

The application of basic psychoanalytic concepts, especially that of the unconscious, following the teachings of Bowen (1978), has become one of the important orientations in current couple and family therapy practice. In general, it is necessary to understand what transferential elements may contaminate the real relationships within the marriage and the family. Couples often relate to the distorted mental representations they have of each other, rather than to the real person. This is transference and projective identification, originating from distortions of perception and expectations, and it is especially evident in sexual difficulties of people who are in committed relationships—married or not.

The layers of human sexuality

The majority of couples who seek therapy for human sexuality problems have other relational problems of which they are not fully aware, or that they do not mention because they believe, in our age of managed care, that a behavioral solution of the sexual problem will improve the entire relational picture. The solution to relational problems does help their sexual relationship, but that may not necessarily happen the other way around. This view fits quite well with Freud's (1905a) theories on human sexuality and his much later Eros principle. In other words, the symptom is not the whole story. The most common type of human sexuality problem is in the area of functioning (Araoz 1998), although problems of sexual preferences, significance, and orientation follow in that sequence.

There are at least six layers of human sexuality, manifested developmentally from primitive and basic to mature and related to Eros. The first layer, at the core of sexuality in humans, is that of one's *gender identity*. Then follows the spontaneous move toward a choice of sexual partners, designated as *orientation*. The third layer, influenced by one's culture, is that of arousal, called *sensory preferences*—involving the smells, sounds, touch, and so on, that stimulate one's sexual drive. The fourth layer, that of *functioning*, from sexual desire to orgasm, which in ordinary language is referred to as "performance," is what most people consider all there is to know about human sexuality. *Social mores* come next, meaning the behavioral attitudes expected or tolerated from each one of us by the mere fact of being male or female. And when finally the *meaning* of sexuality changes from pure personal satisfaction and relief to spiritual fulfillment, we find the superego layer of significance and meaning, as explained elsewhere (Araoz 2005). Psychoanalytical thinking is beneficial in working with all these layers because in stable relations psychogenic sexuality problems (those not caused by medical conditions) are inevitably connected with relational problems. On the other hand, when there are no problems for the couple at any of the six layers, the relationship between the two partners is generally and universally (in all areas of it) satisfying.

Theory and practice

In a psychoanalytic approach with couples, object relations theory (see Scharff [1996] for a comprehensive view of object relations), and especially attachment theory (see a good presentation of diverse views in Johnson and Whiffen [2003]), give us important insights and tools. Because it is based on many years of application and studies that have given us research data, I now recommend the object relations approach with emphasis on attachment theory to my graduate students and those who choose me as their supervisor. I explain that many of the difficulties couples experience are related to the early developmental experiences with their parents, especially the mother, as Melanie Klein (1932) discovered in her psychoanalytic work with children. CBT techniques alone do not solve the relational difficulties that come from way back in each spouse's life experience.

There are three working premises in the psychoanalytic approach: (1) that attachment, or seeking and keeping close emotional contact with people who are part of our social existence, is a component of our human existence throughout our entire life; (2) that we inevitably depend on each other, so that secure interdependence enhances one's identity, self-esteem, and general functioning; and (3) that sexual difficulties are symbolic manifestations of the entire relationship and give much information on it. Because of the closeness, healthy or neurotic, that marriage provides spouses, it is a hotbed of transference (Araoz 1974) and many neurotic manifestations. The most frequently encountered problems within the couple system seem to be perceptual distortions, exaggerated idealizations, and unreasonable expectations. Underlying control issues and neurotic projections are also part of the full picture. In theory, then, we can assume that couples (and generally nuclear family members) often deal with what I call "phantoms," or distorted images of the other in the close relationship. There is no solution for relational problems, including sexual ones, until the partners recognize their mental distortions and accept each other with the imperfections and limitations that make them unique.

As a consequence of these premises, the goal in systemic psychoanalytic work is to help people recognize their own individual expectations, in most cases built from cultural beliefs and perceptions that originated in childhood. The therapeutic goal is achieved when patients have changed in several different areas. They have learned to question their negative reactions to each other, connecting them with distortions coming from each other's past. They have acquired the habit of looking into themselves every time they engage in self-talk centered on mental complaints or criticisms about their spouse. They are comfortable correcting the established new reaction pattern, and in translating insight into behavior. This new habit of questioning their reactions to each other leads to the following changes: (a) they set realistic expectations of each other; (b) they increase their willingness to accommodate to each other and please each other by being more optimistic and positive; (c) they find new practical ways of perceiving their life situation in the marriage or close relationship so that each individual becomes an active contributor to the well-being and happiness of the other partner; and finally (d) they become sensitive to unconscious dynamics that compare the real spouse-with-all-his-limitations to the unrealistically ideal spouse with all the fictional and wished-for virtues. In sum, there is a switch in perception, attitude, and behavior that takes place thanks to the psychodynamic type of therapy.

To achieve these goals, many methods and techniques developed in the last thirty years or so, under the label of *systemic* theory, have been tested and proven beneficial. Among them are hypnotic techniques to reach the unconscious, employed because the required changes become smoother as well as more authentic and lasting through the use of hypnosis and self-hypnosis (Araoz 1998). One of these techniques is mental rehearsal, mentioned in Chapter 8, which can become an essential part of therapy. As you may recall, it consists of vividly imagining oneself in a typical situation of distress but mentally acting or reacting more effectively than usual. What I find interesting and significant is that in most cases people spontaneously start to free-associate and to make meaningful psychological connections on the basis of the mental rehearsal practice. It can literally create a new reality for the client because, as we know, what we experience as real in our mind tends to become our reality. Hypnosis is the method for doing this.

Clinical case study

The following is a detailed description of work with a couple that illustrates this therapeutic approach. A shorter version of this case was published elsewhere (Araoz 2005). The couple came for hypnosis, expecting a magical cure. As I always tell patients, I replied that

I use hypnosis once I understand what the problem is but I do not start with hypnosis. Lincoln, 42, was a federal investigator for the Immigration and Naturalization Service, and Luna, 38, was a documents translator at the United Nations. Both had finished college and had been married (the first time for both) for ten years. Their children were Bobby, 8, and Lulin, 6. In the first two sessions the wife complained bitterly about the husband's driving, and connected it to his poor sexual interest and functioning. Of course, he denied with anger the sexual connection, while her comments in the car started agitated verbal fights that usually made the driving even more dangerous. After the two initial conjoint sessions, they had individual interviews.

In Luna's first individual visit she kept asking, "What's wrong with me sexually? Why doesn't he want me?" and described in detail her naked self-admiration in the mirror, her love of dancing, of self-pleasuring, of having sexual intercourse, and of enjoying the partner's body, especially his penis, with great sensuality. She cried, expressing her frustration and her fear of sexual rejection, which together placed her in an impossible situation: she wanted sex with Lincoln but was afraid of his reaction because it had been so long (over three years) since they had enjoyed "good sex."

Because of her sense of desperation she was eager to try hypnosis for the first time in her life but also accepted the need to give me a good picture of the situation before using hypnosis in the second session. She agreed to bring to mind the good times she had had with her husband, not denying my comment that she was now too focused on the negative aspects of the situation (the NSH). In a form of age regression, she reexperienced mentally the happiness and inner peace she had felt previously many times in sexual encounters with Lincoln. In trance there was a noticeable change in her when she mumbled that during the time they had been distant sexually she had felt more and more inferior to him, as if she were much younger and he were her father. With strong emotion, she mumbled, "No, you're not my daddy!" Still in hypnosis, she returned to the present and mentally rehearsed an adult encounter (not sexual) with Lincoln in order to clear the air. After hypnosis she talked about this. The memory that had come to her was of her father reprimanding her for her sexual feelings when she was only 13 and he had burst into her room when she was masturbating. The fantasy she had of the conversation with Lincoln gave her a sense of peace and hope and the resolution to go over all this with her husband in our next conjoint session. To counter her NSH, I encouraged her to repeat privately what she had experienced in hypnosis, and to say to herself that she could have all that again. After her hypnotic experience she also explained that the situation with her father had been resolved many years before and the relationship with him had been very good since.

So far, we realize the workings of the unconscious in what happened to Luna during this first hypnotic experience: what was not in her awareness begins to come up spontaneously yet meaningfully. Note also her healthy reaction in her refusing to accept any identification of her father with Lincoln. Consequently, I did not pursue this issue at all. However, for my own understanding of this couple's sexual problem, I had to wonder about the meaning of the memory that came spontaneously from this woman's unconscious; it had been a negative experience where pleasure was punished. Was she, after that incident, more concerned than before with the goodness of her sexuality? This question comes from her admiring herself naked, from the importance she places on "self-pleasuring," and from the general sexuality she described. Note that these are psychoanalytical questions, not judgmental ones. Notice also that at this point in therapy nothing should be done with these possibilities. They are reserved for the future.

When I saw the husband alone I also mentioned the hypnosis they had requested initially. Lincoln, while expressing the frustration of the "bad situation," between himself and his wife, did decide to try mental rehearsal. You may remember from earlier in this book that this happens when a person visualizes in detail how it would be to already be accomplishing what seemed impossible before. Once in hypnosis, and to his surprise, the first image that came to his mind was that of his wife driving and he being a passenger and feeling very good about it. I encouraged him to stay with this mental image for a while because this situation is one he did not allow to happen in reality. In one of the conjoint sessions he had stated, "I can't stand her driving like an old lady." Still visualizing the scene, he abruptly changed his voice and general demeanor, adding, as if he were talking to himself, "This is the damn child in me, you see? She is a very good driver, more cautious than me, that's all." This moved spontaneously to his free associating, leading to an age regression of when he was 15 or 16, as a difficult youngster, always rebelling, disobeying, and doing what he wanted; "Nobody can do anything for me," he mumbled, "and nobody can tell me what to do." He also relived moments with his father, who had a younger daughter and who was separated from his mother. The feelings toward his father were very negative, and he said out loud in hypnosis, "I'd rather be dead than be like my father." In his hypnotic reliving, he heard his father telling him that women are on earth to satisfy the sexual needs of men and because of this they should always be kept under the man's control. His reaction was again one of rejection and hate for a man he did not respect at all.

After the hypnotic experience, he told me that he was 15 when his father stressed on his birthday that he should be independent, self-sufficient, and "a real man." For his father, a real man does what he wants and the hell with what others think, say, or expect. He warned him not to trust his mother or any other woman for that matter. His father had always been a philanderer who abused women psychologically without any remorse.

It must be noted that he had not talked about his childhood or early adolescence in the previous therapy sessions, nor had his wife mentioned anything about his family. He acknowledged that his driving, disregarding his wife, and doing very imprudent things all had the same negative quality of his father's teachings, which he despised. After discussing the hypnotic experience in detail in the following individual session, further mental rehearsal helped him to visualize himself as more considerate with his wife, and more sensitive to her fear in the car with him. He acknowledged that his driving was regularly risky, aggressive, and "adolescent." And he also made the connection of this aspect of their marriage with their sexual functioning, where the control issues were showing up metaphorically. Separating driving from sex, I encouraged him to relive mentally a good sexual experience with his wife, which he had no difficulty doing. For this I used hypnotic self-exploration in order to encourage him to really understand if there was any connection between driving and sex. I invited him "to just check this out." When he objected, I responded that he might discover something important about himself and that his wife might be aware of some truth about him that he might not yet recognize. On the other hand, if he finds out that there is no connection at all, he can deny it without any doubt and with conviction. He agreed, so I asked him to go back to the general relaxation that he had experienced before and, this time metaphorically, to imagine his having an open mind (the image that he had was that of an enormous oyster that was slowly opening up), and then to ask himself if there was any link between driving and sex. "I always thought cars were sexy," he mumbled. "My wife is not sexy anymore," he continued in a sad voice. "I don't react to her . . .

I react to the car." He quickly switched back to the ordinary way of thinking, opened his eyes, and said, "This is nonsense. What the hell am I doing this for?" Considering this a form of resistance, I responded that at times we can't believe the connections that are hidden in our mind, and said, "So, go back to it and find out if it is yes or no." After a few moments of silence, he said, "Yeah, I want to punish her. I'm tired of masturbating—and I hate that word—but it's all her fault and I can punish her in the car." He repeated these ideas a few times with different words. Later, out of hypnosis, he confessed his frustration. Because of religious convictions he could not have sex with anybody other than his wife, yet he was constantly bothered with the thought of sexual activities many times a day when he saw attractive women. This led him to frequent masturbation. Initially he felt guilty but then his wife's lack of interest (according to him, an "old lady," and not just in driving) changed his feeling to anger, on several fronts: he now believed that he enjoyed self-pleasuring to the point of not needing sex with a partner, and he also resented his wife's acting as if everything were okay between them. I advised him to talk to his wife about it and he strongly indicated his preference for doing that in my presence.

What happened with this couple is rather typical, as we found that their issues developed in the subsequent conjoint session. The problem they came up with was not a sexual one, but was closely connected with a sexual aspect of their relationship, and it had then become symbolic of the relationship. So the sequence is: First, a repressed (not-acknowledged) nonsexual problem manifested in their sexual interaction or lack of it. Second, the sexual problem emerges as a symbol of their marital relationship. In the case of Lincoln and Luna, both agreed that the marriage had become dull, colorless, and bland—and, very important indeed, that each was blaming the other because of their unrealistic expectations. The area of secrecy—with non-shared feelings or reactions and blaming the spouse—had become larger with hints of control issues. Third, there was less trust and willingness to talk with each other about important things. The lack of sexual activity and interest followed naturally. Again the blame: Lincoln saw his wife as the cause of his need to masturbate, while Luna also confessed to increased self-pleasuring as a result of Lincoln's lack of interest in her. Because of this she felt deep frustration as she was also very heterosexual and sensual but would never accept sexual involvement with others.

In the joint session I brought up what Lincoln had mentioned about his father, and he confessed that he was using his father as an excuse but that his early attitude of extreme self-sufficiency was still at work. He had become unfair with Luna, expecting her to read his mind and please him sexually, and because she did not, she had become unattractive in his mind, as well as the cause of his unhappiness. What both wanted was a closer relationship with greater trust and companionship. Unconsciously they had used sex as a symbol of the entire relationship. But the most obvious problem, which was much less embarrassing to bring up, was that of the tensions they experienced while driving together. So it became their presenting problem.

This case demonstrates one of the reasons why I call this approach psychoanalytic. The process is centered and dependent on the unconscious dynamics that are at work while the patients are not aware of them. It is psychoanalytic also because of the emphasis on metaphors (for instance, driving together stands for sex, and sex stands for a good, trusting relationship) that are taken seriously in therapy as holding their own meaning for the patient. And, finally, it is psychoanalytic because it is rooted in Freud's ideas, both of sexuality (1905a), in seeking a person (object) to satisfy one's libido, and of Eros (1932).

The following sessions were also conjoint. Lincoln and Luna were able to level with each other and to effectively express their frustrations and hopes. They began to get along much better with each other and they slowly resumed sexual activity. However, after three weeks of improvement, it stopped. In hypnosis, I brought up psychoanalytic questions, such as: "Allow a possible explanation for this to come up. Check your feeling reaction to what's happening. Check if there is a connection between this and something else in your life—especially from the past. If you could use a metaphor to describe what's going on, what comes to mind?" and so on. In response, events that might have caused the "distance" over three years ago and that were still a mystery started to emerge.

About a year after the birth of the couple's second child, Luna had become pregnant again. However, this terminated in a late miscarriage (eighth month). Lincoln, painfully, saw the dead fetus and was tremendously upset by the event. What triggered his excessive negative reaction was a tragic accident that had taken place when he was 9 or 10 years old when his 4-month-old sister died in a house fire. This happened at a time in his life when he enjoyed playing with matches. There was no evidence that the fire was caused by little Lincoln, and in fact, according to the fire department's report, the cause of his sister's death seemed to have been an electrical fire. But he took it for granted that he had killed his baby sister and later repressed the whole memory, never having dealt with it psychodynamically. On the other hand, Luna, not knowing anything about the way Lincoln's sister had died, blamed herself for the miscarriage and for Lincoln's devastating reaction to it.

Once we had these tragic and complicated events to work with, I was able to use several hypnotic techniques to help them resolve the negative impact they had had on the couple. The first was a regressive dissociation. First, in individual sessions, I asked Lincoln to imagine himself vividly as the little child that he was at 9 or 10. Then I suggested that the adult Lincoln step into the picture and begin to talk to little Lincoln the day after the tragedy, and give him sound counsel. Luna used a similar image, by talking to an imaginary good friend who was blaming herself for a late miscarriage, and advising her on how to react to it in a healthy way. Both were able to do this and to identify effectively with the "talked to" character in their hypnotic experience. We repeated this mind exercise several times during two individual sessions for each spouse, and I recommended that each of them repeat the practice alone in the next few days.

At the following joint session, I instructed them together "to reverse personalities" so that in hypnosis she could express—as if she were her husband—the repressed tragedy and the new way he wanted to handle it. He was in the office, out of hypnosis, listening and once in a while clarifying or correcting what she was stating in his name. Progressively, he became mature and realistic in his comments, having separated himself from the little boy who had been blaming himself for the tragedy. The same practice was repeated with him taking the personality and role of his wife, expressing her grief and the way she wanted to change her reaction. She also became increasingly dissociated from self-blame and guilt. This part of their therapy took twelve sessions, five individual and seven conjoint.

After these therapeutic practices, they felt maturely close to each other, understood, and cared for. Their sexual enjoyment increased and they found a form of self-renewal in their sexual encounters, which now were quite frequent. Intimacy and sharing the most personal feelings and thoughts were now the norm. Their marriage had now become a trusting friendship and a celebration of their life together. The hard labor of therapy had produced its fruit. They continued in therapy once a month "just to make sure that we stay at this level and that we have a chance to review our relationship." A year later they celebrated the end of their work with me.

*   *   *

Summary

While we can accept the premise that psychogenic sexual problems in stable relationships are manifestations of other relational issues producing anxiety in both partners, sex therapy alone cannot really help them resolve the entire predicament, because it focuses on the symptom without considering the underlying problem(s). The physical intimacy of sex in committed relationships is fully satisfying when it reflects the spiritual intimacy of two free human beings sharing their lives and love. It has then reached the Eros level.

Hypnoanalysis is helpful because it allows patients to have a fresh, meaningful experience of themselves as integrated in a relationship. This becomes a real *vivencia* (Araoz and Goldin 2004). Hypnosis is centered here on the hidden psychodynamics that affect the partners' sexual enjoyment. Once more, the symptom is just the tip of the iceberg. Because committed sex is such an intimate experience that becomes a vivencia, the hypnotic trance, as a similarly unique, idiosyncratic, personal event, is a very effective means for relational and—consequently—sexual healing.

As a general rule, it is necessary to consider the current difficulty that brings a couple to therapy as a manifestation of unresolved issues of the spouses that originated early in life. The presenting problem disguises the real problem. They don't know what it is and you don't know either. But your job is to help them make the connection between what is bothering them in the present and what they have experienced in the past that is coloring the current events. The clinical way to go about it is to ask (each in turn) if they have ever felt this way before; to go over the current circumstances that elicited negative feelings (fear, hurt, anger, stress, abandonment, and so on), and to connect them with previous events; to find out how they handled the painful situation in the past, and to help them bring to the present moment some of the attitudes, including any mental tricks or thoughts that helped them then. Finally, the partners may each be able to recognize their projections onto each other, and thus become more factual about the things that bother them. In a word, by choosing to go beyond the symptom, they can grow and enrich their lives through a more direct experience of the here and now.

Chapter 10

PSYCHOANALYSIS WITH FAMILIES AND IN GROUPS

This chapter is merely a brief introduction to two areas of psychoanalytic work, both of which are extensive and require specialized
training. My intention is to give you, the clinician, a taste of these
exciting possibilities for clinical work and encourage you to consider
further training in the use of psychoanalysis in family therapy and
in group therapy.

The fundamental psychoanalytic principle at work in both families and groups is, as always, first and foremost, the unconscious.
From this source, and in no particular hierarchical order, you find
powerful dynamics like denial and resistance; transference (displac-
ing early experiences onto current significant persons); idealization
(unrealistic exaggeration of another's personal attributes); projection
(attributing to others uncomfortable traits or feelings of one's own);
and reaction-formation (changing the unacceptable feelings, ideas,
and/or behaviors to acceptable ones). This is by no means a complete list, nor is it intended to exclude the presence of other defense
mechanisms or unconscious ways of dealing with anxiety, common
to family and group therapy. Bion (1961) covers practically every

important point that someone working psychoanalytically with groups should know and keep in mind. A few simple examples of unconscious manifestations in both groups and families may clarify some of the psychodynamics listed above.

Denial and resistance do not need special mention because most people are familiar with them, although denial can take on unexpected forms, as we shall discuss in the last chapter. Transference, on the other hand, often appears in groups as well as in families. For instance, in a men's group Ed complains about Ben: "He's . . . you see? Constantly criticizing me," perhaps perceiving in Ben the critical older brother who made his life difficult in childhood, an experience that has colored all his relationships with equals. In a family, it may also be transferential projection when the mother, who is frustrated with the husband, keeps asking the son (who is very sweet, kind, and patient) to explain something further when it is already crystal clear, causing the son to burst into anger. The mother is seeing her husband in the son and reacting to the husband through the son in a way she cannot do with the husband in this projective identification. Idealization may show up when a group member always defers to another and comes to her defense every time anyone contradicts her. In a family, the father may use idealization when he frequently compliments, praises, and admires everything the daughter is doing, disregarding both small and big mistakes on her part. Projection can be used by a group member when she insists on talking to another, whom she obviously does not like, "You don't like my voice (or my hair, or me!)," or, in a family, when the mother keeps castigating the son for a behavior that is a reflection of her own, like interrupting others. To provide an example of the complex psychodynamics in groups, we can consider Carl, an artist who is in a state of denial regarding his homosexual orientation, and who responds with reaction formation and repression in the group when he affirms that his interest in taking photographs of nude men is nothing but artistic, while insisting that the other group members can only see the prurient side of the pictures.

Being with others elicits these dynamics, and by recognizing them clients can take action to change them, first by going over the "remnants of the past" that trigger these responses, and then by shifting their focus from the "ghosts of the past" to the individual(s) they are dealing with in the present. This effort must be translated into changed perceptions, expectations, and behaviors toward the group's current participants; fortunately, the fellowship of the group is also a great help in doing this.

Family dynamics

One of my coauthored books (Araoz and Negley-Parker 1988) emphasizes the use of hypnosis with families, rather than on the psychoanalytic aspect of the work with them. The truth is that parents, more than children, benefit from the realization that they frequently reenact in their own family the attitudes, expectations, and behaviors they learned from their own parents and, generally, from their early family life. Thus, what begins as family therapy most often develops into a concentration on the parents themselves. Because of this, I like to distinguish two types of family therapy, the first for parental issues (often with educational components), and the second for relational issues, including intimacy.

Family therapy, in common with group therapy, has many unconscious elements. For example, the son may blame everybody else for his misbehavior, and the mother may blame other children for the son's troubles, while both deny that there is anything wrong with what they do, the mother idealizing the son and he reinforcing his mother's distorted view. This dynamic appears frequently in group work, where many in the group unconsciously reenact family situations with other group members. Unreasonable expectations are frequently at work in family therapy. The father may keep complaining that the house is not as tidy as it should be (that is, the way his early family house was kept immaculate by an obsessive-compulsive mother). Transference is always a distortion of perception. Or the mother attributes her spanking and other excessive methods of discipline to good child-rearing, becoming an expert in reaction formation, and so on.

One important difference between group and family therapy is that with a family you have fewer people to provide input and feedback than in a group. The clinician must be extra careful to detect enabling, codependency, and other neurotic defense mechanisms. The father who complains of the selfishness of his daughter is not able to deny her anything. The mother who laments the promiscuity of her 18-year-old also asks him for details of his escapades, claiming she is doing this to make sure he's not in trouble. Chances are that if material like this came out in a group session, one or more of the group members would confront the mother. But in a session with a typical dysfunctional family the clinician cannot count on the healthy reaction of the other family members, and he must be very alert so he can gently confront them.

Even if you have been trained in group and/or family therapy without psychoanalytic emphasis, it is not difficult to benefit from the in-depth method if you always keep in mind that the symptom is not the whole story and that often the symptom is a metaphor for the underlying problem. Questions like, "Do you think this may have a hidden explanation?" or "What might be the meaning of this?" or "Can he be saying something with his constant smirk?" or "What does this remind you of?" can start the family on the road that leads to real insight and self-knowledge. If the reaction to these questions is shallow or seems to evoke a mood of levity, you are there to help them think about your questions seriously. You may share with them your own hypotheses about their current circumstances, or even explain briefly that one can see in recent history many cases where the symptom was not the whole story (see Frank 2004).

A family therapy case

A mother called to request an appointment for her family. When I inquired about the problem she responded with a long story about the children hiding some information from her that only started to make sense after several therapy sessions. In the first family session she explained that the father took care of the boys on many Sundays, when she had to be out of the house due to her work. She had become suspicious of what was going on because the two brothers, Rich, 15, and Lou, 13, were very general in answering her normal questions regarding what they did all day, or what they talked about with their father. She wanted to know and they kept giving her the typical young adolescent response: "Nothing." She sensed that something was making the children uncomfortable. The husband had been no help when she tried to find out the truth from him. Eventually, Lou admitted that the father, Al, told them "secrets" that made them uncomfortable, and the older boy, Rich, angrily agreed, adding something to the effect that his brother was stupid to have said that. But both boys stood firm, without revealing what the secrets were.

I suspected a conflict of loyalty and a potentially very damaging power play for control. I assumed Al was putting the two boys in the middle between him and the mother. I further imagined that he was showing anger toward his wife in a passive-aggressive way and that he was disregarding his sons' feelings, perhaps making them pay for something, through a process of identification with them. Because the children refused to reveal the secrets, I continued the sessions with the couple alone, guessing that it would be safer to protect the children from any possible family surprise that might have been too painful for them to learn.

What came up in the following conjoint sessions was that Al had hated his own father from the time he was very young, first because he had embarrassed Al many times in the company of his father's male friends by forcing the child to show his penis to them, all agreeing with the father about its adult shape and size, admiring it and sometimes even touching it. Later, at age 11 or 12, the father started to take Al to a brothel, which he referred to as "my cousins' house" and made him wait in the company of the "cousins" while he occupied himself with one of them in another room. In the brothel, too, he boasted about his son's penis and forced the child to expose himself to the cries of awe and praise of the young females, some of whom touched it and kissed it; some even took a picture or two of the young boy with the big penis. His greatest humiliation came from the erections that he often had under the circumstance, to the laughter and giggles of his audience. Al admitted that the young women were very nice to him but that he felt extremely uncomfortable about the comments they often made about his anatomy. He also suspected and feared that something "bad" was going on in there when his father, who had said he'd be back right away, took a long time in returning. Now, as an adult, Al knew that he had been sexually violated. In any event, he hated the whole thing, especially that his father swore him to secrecy with threats of severe punishment if he ever told anybody about "his cousins," because Al's mother, the father explained, was not on speaking terms with this part of his family and she disliked them all; she (Al's mother) did not want his father to have anything to do with those cousins.

The psychoanalytic approach requires that the clinician ask herself many questions before coming to any definite conclusion. In this case, without having enough information at this early stage of the family therapy process, I started to ask myself questions such as: Was the current situation an urge to make the wife pay for what those women had done to him as a child? Was he now following the steps of his father, whom he hated, by identifying with him and forcing the father in himself to feel the shame that his father did not feel? Was he using projective identification with his own children, putting them through the same humiliating experience, saying to himself that if his children can take it, it can't have been that hard for him? Al's father forced him to guard uncomfortable secrets; was he now imposing the same on his children? By using the children as atonement, was this Al's way of diminishing his anxious pain and humiliation? Remember that these questions should not be actively pursued at this point in family therapy. However, to propose them to yourself makes you more observant of the process of therapy and more ready to utilize them at a given moment, ordinarily as an observation or a question. For instance, "What's your explanation for putting your children, with the secrecy, through a experience similar to the one you had?" Or, "It sounds to me as if you might have confused your wife with your mother or with those girls, in your inner mind ending up by punishing your wife," or something similar along these lines.

When all this material came up in the conjoint sessions, the mother became upset at several levels. She suspected that the husband was doing the same thing that his father had done; she felt hurt that he had not trusted her with the story of this painful chapter of his childhood and puberty; and she felt guilty that she had not been able to protect the children from this pain. In responding to her anxious questions, Al's big secret slowly emerged. It had nothing to do with brothels and call girls. He had told the boys that he had taken some cocaine (on three occasions in the last year) and that they should never do it because, "You see what happened to me? I'm a doctor and know better but I keep doing it." Al kept emphasizing that this conversation had been an attempt to educate the boys about drug use. We had another family session at which the children were informed of the revelation. The wife and sons were relieved and the father felt better—"Now that everything is out in the open"—Al promised to seek treatment to resolve his childhood problem, to which his cocaine use was linked in his mind. Regarding Al's childhood problem, the children were told that Al's father had been very mean to him. Al recognized that hurting the children in the way he did was also an attempt at alleviating his own pain. Both husband and wife accepted the fact that they had to solve many loose ends in their marriage, and decided to continue in couples therapy. Together we agreed to seeing the couple once a month and Al twice a week. About a month later the wife requested a referral for her own analysis.

In his individual analysis, Al described his mother, a strict follower of religion, and how she was very outspoken against the sin of using drugs as well as very controlling of Al. He expressed his long-standing resentment of the woman who was still dressing him like a girl when he was 6 or 7, perhaps, he now wondered, to somehow cover up his unusually large penis. She had insisted that he must become a doctor "to take care of your mother who loves you so much." She had died just the year before our family sessions. The fact that he had hidden this sin of drugs from his mother made him feel very guilty, and he used the two young boys to make a sort of delayed confession that he believed his mother should have heard. In one of the unexpected ways of his unconscious mother–wife "identification," by confessing to the boys and keeping this secret from his wife, he was making up for not having told his mother. At the same time, because he saw his wife as a representation of his mother, with whom he was angry because of her control over his life, he was also holding onto his secret as a way of punishing his mother, his wife, and himself.

The truth that came out, thanks to the psychodynamic approach, made the family free. Each individual benefited from the introspective work that follows the theories and approaches of object relations, which is centered on infant development that influences internal structure (Fairbairn 1952), in this case perhaps especially through Al's fantasy life as a child because of his anatomical peculiarity, leading to the splitting of reality into good and evil, the latter to be destroyed. This perspective is enlarged by Winnicott (1982) when he emphasizes the partnership of mind and body of both infant and parent (especially mother). This thinking expands the writings of Klein (1946) that led to the practical aspects of attachment theory. Feldman (2002) uses the metaphor of a mental movie to explain the "continuous flow of projective and introjective processes that goes on between human beings and forms 'the meat and potatoes' of human communication and understanding" (p. 16), to the extent that very often we pay more attention to our "internal objects" than to the real people with whom we are dealing.

Dynamics of group therapy

The dynamics that lend themselves to in-depth work with families have similarities to those in group therapy, as Bion (1961) repeatedly implies, and as I have experienced in clinical groups (private practice), in corporate group work (seven years with the American Management Association leading a five-day intensive workshop on effective management), in military groups (ten years at West Point in the Tactical Officers Education Program), and in clergy groups (several years after I resigned from the Jesuit Order).

As a general principle, the clinician can use the group to help an individual member change by encouraging the others to give feedback. But the group leader has to be sensitive to the delicate dynamics at work in every group. As Bion (1961) explains, commenting on the three basic assumptions that can confront a "work group," recognizing transference to the clinician and among group members requires sharp skills and great sensitivity on the part of the "leader." The basic assumptions are: (1) the group meets to be sustained by a leader; (2) the group gives hope and optimism; and (3) the group provides active interaction among members. He summarizes them as "dependence, pairing, and fight or flight." The psychoanalytic group therapist guides the group and also protects it from lack of empathy or negativism, from inappropriate anger, and from wasting time. She is, as Rogers (1961) called it, a facilitator. The group members help each other under the attentive oversight and leadership of the facilitator, who keeps the interaction going, asks the facilitating questions, and points to nonverbal behaviors and other forms of unconscious (and therefore unclear) communication—not interpreting anything prematurely, but always asking first for the reaction of the group members. Thus the group becomes the "social microcosm" of Yalom (1995) in which the members learn tolerance for differences and how to cope with new situations at the reality level, rather than the defensive level; they learn to be constantly engaged in reality testing, and they grow in emotional intelligence, as Goleman (1998) would call it. Where the id was, the ego starts to appear and grow. They also learn to express themselves more effectively using congruent language, so that content, tone, style, and body language all express clearly what they want to communicate.

In one of the corporate self-help groups (the term "therapy" was not used), a man named Sandy was one of the members. He was a top executive in an international men's clothing company, had been in a previous group, and now unconsciously intended to take over as the leader. The group members were from different companies and had not met before, but I had been given background information on each participant. Sandy had recently been demoted for an incident involving alcohol abuse and lascivious behavior at a company party, and was forced to attend AA meetings for an entire year before he could resume his previous position. It had been a case of "Do it or leave the company." Even though he had agreed to take the penalty imposed, he was very angry, resentful, and humiliated, and kept denying any alcoholic problem. However, the others in the group did not have this information.

From the moment the group started, Sandy was antagonistic and bellicose. He called Tex "Baldhead," after they had introduced themselves by their names. I asked for the group's reaction. Tex was the oldest in the group, and gently said he didn't mind. The others reacted negatively; Jill said that she did not like Sandy's facial expression and tone of voice when he said it; Nick stated that he would have punched Sandy because of his smirk, and that Tex had previously given his name to the group—"Who the hell are we to give each other nicknames?" Sandy's retort was sarcasm: "Are you all blind or am I having hallucinations? He is a baldhead, no? What's all the fuss when Tex doesn't mind? Is this going to be a touchy-feely, be-nice-to-everybody bull situation?"

I asked the other seven members to "put in one word" the feeling they perceived in Sandy at the moment he said it. Four said "angry," two said "hurt," and one said "cocky." Sandy turned against me accusing me of inciting the others against him, a good example of projective identification. Again I asked the group to react to his comments. Among the reactions, the group was telling Sandy that he was afraid of feeling, that he was insecure, that he was sadistic, and so on. Of course he showed resistance and denial, digging himself deeper into the negative box in which the others saw him. I kept reminding the group that they were expressing impressions and perceptions without knowing about Sandy's experiences, maybe painful, that had led him to act this way in an effort to protect himself from further anxiety and emotional pain. Perhaps the others were not accurate and fair. Sandy's initial reaction to my comment was,

"A lot of crap." I invited him repeatedly to check if the others were even ten percent right in their opinions. After several denials, he finally agreed to check out one of the labels. He chose "sadistic."

Briefly, one explanation of sadism comes from Melanie Klein's (1932) controversial theory of self-destructiveness, expanding on Freud's death instinct. She finds that many who have not gotten the right attachment to the mother (and the father) in the first two years of life resort to splitting off the deprived, painful part of the self, and project it into the outside world: "I am good and they are bad." This is an overly simplistic split that if not recognized or resolved may continue into adulthood, and for those using it, justifies in their eyes their being sadistic and cruel. The bad self is put outside, projected onto others, so it can be hated there. Because this split originally happens due to frustration and the anxiety it elicits, there is anger and rage. Therefore, this psychic mechanism goes a step further so that the destructiveness that would be directed to the bad self of the inner world is detoured to other (outside) targets where the inner bad self was projected. Sadism is a projection of one's destructive self onto others. Karen Horney (1950) explains it with her "externalization of self-torture" (p. 147).

Going back to Sandy and the group, they explained to him what they perceived and felt about his sarcastic comments. Eventually he started to admit that "perhaps you have a point there," and very slowly he began revealing important aspects of his life. Sandy's nastiness, anger, and sadism were his defenses against lashing out more violently at the world that had been so harsh with him. His mother had died giving birth to him. The woman his father found to take care of the baby, according to what he found out later from relatives and neighbors, was a strict disciplinarian but not a loving person. Among many other things, she started his toilet training at about 18 months, with severe punishment for "accidents," even depriving him of food. He became very sick and had to be hospitalized for more than three weeks, during which time neither this caretaker nor his father visited him—again, according to information he obtained much later. He was under this woman's care till he finished grammar school. Many times he complained to his father, but his father scolded and punished him for being a sissy, although he finally agreed to put his son in a boarding school where everything was fine for the first two years. Then one of the teachers forced him to satisfy his sexual desires, both orally and anally. This went on for a year or so until the authorities found out about the situation. The teacher got away scot-free when rumors of their involvement became public, and accused Sandy of immoral behavior, for which he was punished. His father never questioned the school's verdict and transferred his son, at the age of 14, to a military academy that Sandy hated, where he stayed until high school graduation. Sandy claimed to have been "depressed" ever since.

To shorten this long story of Sandy in group therapy, the other members gave Sandy the help he needed to face his inner demons. Without their gentle confrontations, understanding, caring, and advice based on shared experiences, Sandy would have finagled his way through his recent experience without getting anything of value for himself. He was always in a defensive mode. However, the group's insistence and kind understanding allowed him to come out of his defensiveness. They also motivated this man, who had never been in therapy, to start his psychoanalysis, which he continued for several years.

* * *

As mentioned above, you need specialized training to work psychoanalytically with families or groups. With this brief overview I want you to consider that psychoanalysis is not merely a caricature that many people accept as true, but that in fact it is a valuable perspective that can be applied to many other modalities. The belief that there is strength in numbers applies here in the group, too. Because of this, the clinician must be prepared to handle many unexpected difficult dynamics. However, for the same reason, there are more resources and strengths to work with, as we found in the group just described. In the family presented earlier, the psychodynamics of father and sons were intermingled but the family's inner strengths also combined to effect the healing of the entire system.

Therefore, I hope that this primer-like sample of psychoanalytic thinking in situations with multiple clients might make you curious and interested in learning more about how to use these methods effectively by obtaining postgraduate training in these fields.

My statement also comes from the conviction that the uncaring choking-off of psychotherapy by managed care, and the expansion of the oxymoron of "health insurance" will force newcomers to the field to become experts in family and group therapy. Those with good analytical training in these modalities can offer a great deal of help to patients.

Chapter 11
THE CASE OF TITUS

Please note that in this chapter I'm trying not to concentrate on theory or on mere psychoanalytic speculation. That's why I'm trying to avoid technical terms (and jargon?) so that you, the non-psychoanalyst, may be able to clearly understand what we do when working in this modality. My focus is on helping you, the clinician interested in enriching your practice with psychoanalytic thinking, have an idea about how the treatment proceeds by demonstrating to you, through the case of Titus, the beneficial results of this approach. Note that in what follows I use square brackets [. . . .] to indicate my own thoughts, not what I said to the patient.

First session

In Chapter 4 you met Titus, the wealthy lawyer who was afraid of going crazy because he was not happy even with the vast abundance of material things he had accumulated. This was his presenting problem, and his demeanor, and particularly his speech, both in content and tone, made him appear desperate. You may remember that he made me anxious with his urgent demands for help that evoked in me the thought of his possible suicide. We decided to begin therapy with two sessions a week.

[My thinking also jumped to diagnosis. Quickly I went over the nosological categories. On the one hand, it seemed that obsessional neurosis could fit him because of his preoccupation with having things. But the question of why this was the case remained unanswered. On the other hand, character disorder also was a possibility (although most probably he was not psychotic, like the personality disorders listed in Cluster A of the *DSM-IV-TR*. Here I was thinking of those habitual characteristics or traits of his personality, like his efforts (in his showing off) to be recognized and respected through his possessions and status. Was this a manifestation of oral needs or of oral character? Was his compulsive need to have things explained by his existential anxiety ("I am nothing without these things")? Or, before this, with women—holding on to them (Lacanian "others") and now to things in order to feel alive? Was his previous womanizing, much like the current materialistic obsession, excessive enough to think he might be showing perversion in the Freudian sense? Or, going back to the insecurity hypothesis, was he trying to make sure he had overcome the poor and deprived background he came from? Or could this be a form of phallic narcissistic character? All this was going through my mind, but at this early stage of the analysis I was not able to be sure, nor could I have been. However, speculation of this kind must go on to eventually make sense of the clinical picture in order to decide how to proceed.]

The first session was spent in gathering information, assessing his motivation, giving him guidance on the rules (such as punctuality, fees, and so on), and also what is expected of him and what he can expect of me and of the treatment process. He asked many questions about me, my background, and about psychoanalysis as a form of therapy. I accepted his questions and answered truthfully the ones

THE CASE OF TITUS 149

I could answer. I also suggested that he pay attention to his dreams and to where his mind goes when it wanders. This ended the session. After the first session, I mentioned the case to a colleague whose half-serious reaction was that he should get rid of all the luxuries and extravagant "things" in his life. Perhaps that would have been the cure, at least of his anxiety and urgency, but it certainly was not the prescription for Titus at that time.

[Psychoanalytically, I was interested in finding out what psychic role all these possessions played in his life. Was this a big mask, hiding his real self behind all these material possessions that gave him societal respect? Was this a manifestation of his self-dislike? Was he replacing growth, satisfaction, and happiness with all this glamour, and by having so many things to take care of that he had no time or energy left for "being" himself? Or was all this his "search for glory," as Horney (1950, pp. 17–39) calls it, dominated by neurotic drives? Had he accepted the devil's pact of Faust's story, trying to attain infinite glory by losing his soul?]

Second session
In the second session, I asked Titus to concentrate for a moment and check what came to mind when he thought of his possessions. We spent a couple of minutes focusing on his breathing and general sense of relaxation.

[This had to do with my initial comments to him in response to his questions on my work with hypnosis, in which he showed great interest; he was again hoping for a shortcut, not viewing hypnosis as a means to know himself better. This decision also referred to the above questions that I had been asking myself after the first session, in which I usually get a general feeling of the client.]

He spoke, already in a hypnotic tone, saying that possessions make him feel important (smiling now), accomplished, and successful.

I asked him how being important, accomplished, and successful related to him. Slowly he whispered (the smile gone), "My father," and continued, saying that his father was "an alcoholic loser" who had given much grief to his mother and three siblings and that he remembered, on his ninth birthday, being the oldest of four children (two sisters and a baby brother), promising himself that he would never be like his father. Later, when he was 15, his drunken father was killed crossing a street and Titus became the "man of the family." Actually, he was the main financial source of support for them, doing so by cleaning three different stores, practically sleeping only four to five hours a day.

All this was said very slowly, in a low voice and with deep emotion and tears.

Shortly thereafter, in the ordinary thinking mode, he believed there was something "spooky" in the fact that his little brother turned 9 when the father died, the same age at which he had made that momentous decision never to be like his father. He added, going back in his mind to review his many possessions, that by "accomplished" he meant that he had accomplished his goal of having become the opposite of his father, and that his "things" were there to show it.

[So, why is he still so unhappy? And what can I do to help him, not just to recognize intellectually what he is, but to have a vivid mental experience of it, so that he can fully "own" what he is? I have to help him move from "having" to "being."]

I asked him to check his explanation of what was happening with him and his possessions. After reflecting for a moment, he said slowly that this is what he needed me for.

[Anxiety in me again.]

Obviously agitated, he added that he was lost for an answer and had no clue; how did I dare ask him for his explanation? He emphasized that he was afraid of not being able to stop getting more and more things and that he had no explanation for this conundrum.

[Was he showing a transferential expectation from me or was this a reality-oriented statement? Not being sure at present, I kept the question to myself and asked him to go back to that special relaxation he had enjoyed before.]

Looking for a metaphor, I asked him to find a comparison for his possessions, like when someone says that this is like his security blanket. Titus was very relaxed at that point, breathing rhythmically while he whispered, "My protection, my defense," and continued that as long as he had all these things, he was not like his father. I suggested that he visualize something real that came to mind as "his protection and defense" [I thought, like a shelter or armor].

A long silence ensued, after which he said that he saw himself in a dark forest at his current age but, somehow, he felt the presence of his father nearby. He added that in his fantasy, every time he turned around to see his father, he disappeared and Titus kept missing him. I said something about his father's ghost in his imagination, following him—or him running away from the ghost of his father. Perhaps this image was saying something about his being afraid of becoming like his father. He partly agreed with the concept of avoiding any similarity to his father, but there was no feeling in his statement. Hoping to help him enhance his ego and his emotional distance from his father, I suggested that he visualize his father on one side of his mind screen, paying attention to any detail in this mental picture.

[Note that I made a suggestion, but only because it was an amplification of Titus's own thinking about his father. There is only a short distance from thinking about an important person in one's life to visualizing that person.]

Titus did this quickly and with ease, now expressing contempt for his father, blaming him for not having had a father when he was a teenager, and rejoicing in the fact that he was dead. Then I asked him to see himself on the opposite side of his mental screen, also in great detail. When he captured this image, I directed him to visualize himself growing and his father diminishing, and to also experience the feeling of becoming stronger than his father. All the way to the left side of the mental screen, in contrast with the father who had receded to the opposite end on the right and had shrunk to the size of a pitiful mouse, he pictured himself as a glorious giant, healthy, strong, well-dressed, standing in a position of triumph, with head and arms raised, smiling broadly and repeating with joy, "I made it!" I guided him to linger on this mental picture until the father disappeared completely and Titus took center stage. At this juncture I brought him to the symbolism of his possessions by asking where they were and what place they occupied between him and his father. The answer came slowly, "I have won! I have shown that I'll never be like him." Before he was finished, I reminded him that now he knew what picture to pick when he wants to feel good about himself.

We discussed what he had just experienced. He was pleased with it and believed that this had been a valuable mind exercise. On this basis, I invited him to go back into hypnosis. This he did, and without any direction on my part, he saw himself as before, triumphant; he started a soliloquy in which he reassured himself that he was too young at the time (from 9 to 15) to do anything for his father and that he was proud and deserved praise for what he had done to help his mother and siblings. Noticing a possible sense of guilt that did not show up earlier, I indicated that a part of him still needs reassurance so as not to feel guilty, and that now the triumphant, adult Titus can reassure himself, strongly and firmly, allowing himself to have memories of his success in the midst of the difficult times he went through helping his mother, younger sisters, and brother.

These memories would help him to increase his sense of pride and satisfaction for what he had done for himself and his family, and thus eliminate whatever guilt he had about not helping his father.

Discussing this practice after doing it, he agreed to repeat it on his own in order to "get rid of my father completely."

Third session

In the third session he was happy to have realized that, through the years, in all his business and legal activities he had always been "extra honest" as a reaction to his father, who was a conniver, a liar, and a petty crook. This insight made him understand that he did not need all his possessions in order to be different from his father because his way of practicing law made him completely different. But at the same time he was becoming aware that he was still treating his new woman friend, Milagro, like another possession. He explained that he was proud of her, and boasted about her with friends, but that she was like one of the important things he possessed.

[It was too early for me to bring up his fear of intimacy, as if he would lose himself by trusting her; so, trusting his unconscious, I asked him for his dreams.]

He reported a dream where he saw himself in a rather modest yet elegant apartment, with brilliant natural light and exquisitely decorated. He was arranging an altar where he was placing an image of Our Lady of Los Milagros in the midst of beautiful flowers that had a very delicate scent. He was feeling very good in the dream and loved this apartment. Then he was surprised to find that somehow a picture of his that he liked was among the flowers surrounding the statute of Our Lady of Los Milagros. Titus's own interpretation of the dream, when I asked for it, was that a more simple life would make him happy and that Milagro was special; he added that among all the other beautiful objects he owned, he had an altar for her in his heart. His picture in the altar, he interpreted as meaning that he and Milagro belonged together "as part of something holy." When he said this, he surprised himself and added that he did not yet dare to admit that he loved her and that the altar represented love and that he had to stop treating her like a possession. He had worked hard to get her to pay attention to him; now that he "had" her, he didn't take enough good care of her. He described how he lavished her with gifts and plays and luxurious dinners but he admitted that he did not give her what she wanted, attention, thinking of her with love, and spontaneous tenderness.

[Intellectually, Titus knew what to do but he did not realize what stopped him from doing it. Was the dream an explanation of his inability—because he worshiped her like a Madonna?]

He continued, asking if it was appropriate to bring her to the next session and explained that the reason he had finally decided to start psychoanalysis was because she had persuaded him. She had become a Kleinian psychoanalyst in her country of origin, even though now she specialized in applied psychoanalysis as an editor of a respected journal on psychology in political, social, and cultural events. She was the one who had made his going into therapy a condition for their dating. This condition came up, first, because of what she called his neurotic lifestyle and fast-paced living. He had accepted it and reflected that it would be horrible for her two children if things did not work out after they got familiar with him. Milagro's children, in their late twenties, were already practically independent, and living on their own. We discussed this important aspect of his current life and decided that there was no need to rush to have a conjoint session because Milagro would notice the progress he was making and, due to her psychoanalytical background, did not need that type of appointment. Regarding his passing argument about Milagro's children, for whose sake their relationship had to work, I asked him to look into it for the next session.

Titus was still far from truly committed to self-knowledge. He was in a hurry. I led him to focus on his progress regarding his father and he agreed that he had to slow down with Milagro as well as with his therapy.

Fourth session

In the fourth session, Titus reported another dream. This time he was also in that beautiful apartment overlooking the ocean, but this time with Milagro. He recognized it as an embellishment of Milagro's actual residence. He didn't see the altar of the previous dream but she was in bed like a goddess welcoming him and he approached her. He started making love to her as if he were worshiping her, feeling a great sense of peace and happiness, coupled with a new playful freedom. Now she was a person, not a statue or another possession.

[Is this his resolution of what Jungians would call the Madonna complex?]

The dream confirmed for him that he was ready to make the commitment to be with her permanently, after over a year of dating and nine months of not having seen any other woman. Remembering Freud's rule of abstinence, about not making any big changes precipitously during psychoanalysis, I reminded Titus that this was just his fourth session and that a well-trained analyst like Milagro would not be convinced that any momentous transformation had taken place so soon.

[I was aware of his gentle resistance and of the fact that his transference was still quite weak. His tendency to rush kept coming up repeatedly but he accepted intellectually my slowing him down. In other words, I knew that he was not going to go elsewhere, looking for a quick-fix method. Moreover, the fact that Milagro had set his analysis as a condition for being with her, also gave me a lever to slow him down.]

Fifth session

In the fifth session, Titus talked about his three siblings, all of whom were now successful and financially comfortable thanks to his help through the years.

[Is this a sign that the patient has severed the mixed emotional ties with his father and keeps reinforcing his independence from him by reviewing what his father had not done for his family and Titus did?]

The mother had died seven years before. One sister, married, with two children, had become a lawyer and was a partner in a well-regarded legal firm. The other had been in a lesbian relationship for many years. The two women were artists and owned a prestigious art gallery. His brother, now 48, had been married for 20 years and had also two teenaged children. He was a cardiologist teaching at a medical school and working in a group practice. Titus's relationship with them was very good, all three feeling very comfortable and relaxed in his presence and treating him almost as if he were the father. Titus saw them frequently and talked to them on the phone regularly. His early memories of his siblings made him proud; indeed, he had been like a father to them, taking care of them, affectionate, protective, guiding and disciplining them. I asked him to imagine an old-fashioned pharmacist's scale and to place in one of its plates all these positive things about his family, and on the other, all his possessions, in order to figure out what gave him the greatest pleasure and what he valued most. First, he imagined the scale heavier on the side of the possessions but then he pictured it even. I asked what this mental picture meant to him. He explained that now he felt comfortable with the

THE CASE OF TITUS

balance between these two aspects of his life, relieved that he could be well off without feeling that he owed his siblings anything. He started to say that he wanted to simplify his life but then, as an afterthought, he mentioned Milagro, saying that he should not change anything about his life without considering her.

[I heard this as an indication of his desire to commit to the relationship with Milagro and also as an indication of his not treating her as a possession.]

I remarked that he sounded pretty sure of what he wanted to do, with which he agreed. I invited him to go into hypnosis and, trusting his unconscious once more, to check what would come up in his mind. What appeared in his imagination showed him that he needed more time to decide definitely. He saw himself still holding on to all his "toys," as he called them: the houses, the cars, the club memberships, the wealthy socializing, the expensive restaurants and wines. I suggested that he let Milagro get into the picture. He found it difficult to do it, recognizing that part of him did not want to change. He expressed his fear that marriage might change Milagro and that he wanted her the way she was with him now. Again, his "toys" gave him a sense of security. I reminded him of the security role his possessions had with regard to his father. He saw his "things" now as providing the certainty that marriage will not provide. Since he had referred to a "part of me," I suggested that there must be at least another part also. He tried but could not get in touch with "the other part" and we finished the session with my recommendation to go over all this in private and not to allow himself to take anything as definite yet. Not yet.

Sessions 6 to 19

In the next fourteen sessions (sessions 6 to 19) of working through, Titus experienced the typical anxiety that introspection often produces. During seven weeks, he worked on what he considered his having allowed the toys to control him. He compared himself to an addict, always wanting more. And he realized that this craving was depriving him of happiness. He did not enjoy his possessions, he just possessed them, worrying about them, making sure everything was in order, making them ends in themselves rather than means to his enjoyment and satisfaction.

[Is there some truth to his fear of having addictive traits, perhaps genetically passed on to him by his alcoholic father? It could also, more simply, be that he has obsessional traits. Or is this more resistance against intimacy and emotional closeness with another person? When he was a baby, was his mother distracted from him by the behavior of his father? If so, she probably could not be the Lacanian first Other, and that probably would have deprived Titus of the Winnicottian "good-enough mother."]

During this period he kept dreaming (twelve times during the first three weeks) of being in a strange and scary place surrounded by his toys, but they were alive and kept mocking him. He remembered words like "We own you," and "You are our slave." This repeated dream had become a nightmare and he would wake up in a cold sweat and very afraid. He had even started to delay his going to bed at night for fear of the nightmarish dream. In the sessions, we worked on spontaneous images from his unconscious to neutralize the nightmare; he imagined having a magical power that would scare the toys and make them run away from him. He finally succeeded in stopping the nightmare. In trying to find the explanation of his nocturnal mental torture, he had an important insight. When he had decided not to be like his father, he never hesitated—never doubted that he was going to succeed. But now that he had succeeded, he did not know how to stop succeeding; just when he thought he had made it big, he had a new problem: too much success, too many things

THE CASE OF TITUS 159

showing his success. He worked on his images of success and the way he compared himself with people he considered successful. I guided him to imagine himself with fewer things. This became a useful mental rehearsal, as in the technique described in Chapter 8. After visualizing himself with fewer and fewer possessions, he was ready to do something about it. Proactive, organized, and methodical as he was, he began to simplify his life. He made an action schedule and decided not to invest for an entire year in any unnecessary article, trip, club membership, or the like.

[I began to get anxious, suspecting a flight into health, and tried to slow him down. He reassured me (reassuring himself) that he felt like a sailor in a small, overloaded ship, caught in the middle of a storm and getting rid of dangerous weight. "It's this or capsizing. My life is at stake," he emphasized. We worked on the sinking boat fantasy many times and each time he was more determined to lead "a normal life" so he could be happy with Milagro.]

Before he was finished with this "purification" (another metaphor he found helpful) he sold seven of his twelve cars and kept only one motorcycle. He also sold his expensive cuff-link collection of over 500 pairs. Instead of the large amounts of money he paid for membership in one-of-a-kind clubs, he joined a foreign organization of "Lawyers for Real Justice" and donated the proceeds of all these sales to a reputable civic organization. He also donated hundreds of articles of clothing that he had accumulated. He told me that he had finally found "the other part" of his personality that was responsible, reflexive, and unselfish.

[These weeks of working through represented the real struggle between the id and the ego. Titus experienced the "id resistance" and had sufficient time "to become more conversant with his resistance with which he had now become acquainted, to work through it, to overcome it, by continuing in defiance of it, the analysis work"

(Freud 1914b, p. 155). This work culminated in the succinct formula proposed by Freud (1933, p. 80) and repeated by me many times, and which, in the literal translation from the German, as used by Lacan (1977, pp. 128ff and 299ff) applies correctly to Titus, "Where it was, I must come to be."]

Sessions 20 to 22

In the next three sessions (20 to 22) Milagro joined him to go over different points, including relational issues of individuality, identification, and separation. They also discussed love and personal freedom. He recognized that because of his relationship with his family of origin, he had the misconception of considering the woman he was with dependent and "inferior." But also, because his mother was rather passive, reluctant to make decisions, and procrastinating, his fantasy was to be with a woman who was the complete opposite, though he was afraid of strong women.

[This might be a last-minute resistance. What does he mean by being afraid of strong women? Milagro is no weakling and he has been getting along well with her and enjoying her in every way. It may also be a confused yearning for the mother he did not have in the first years of his life; or perhaps a complete idealization coming from that lack.]

This attitudinal opposition had been the difficulty in his first marriage and he had not become aware of it till now. We agreed that these were issues for his individual therapy. Milagro first mentioned her fear of his "flight into health" that made her insecure about Titus's improvement. On the other hand, she was also seriously apprehensive, thinking that all the good qualities that she saw now in Titus would change and become points of contention after they were living together. However, she acknowledged that this was her own insecurity that she had to deal with in her own therapeutic work.

With several cautions and as an (unconscious) test of their feeling confident and emotionally secure with each other, they set a date to move in together and to live in her house overlooking the ocean— the house of his dreams. Both agreed that the conjoint sessions had been beneficial in many ways.

Sessions 23 to 45

Sessions 23 to 45 were used to work out Titus's "true self," as he liked to call it. He learned to fantasize hypnotically the future of his new self, without all the possessions, and thus to check his feelings. This we did, using mental rehearsal repeatedly and for different possible situations in the future.

[During this period I had a dream about Milagro coming to the office and asking me to help her find Titus, who had disappeared. She was seductive and said something to the effect that she had missed him for several days and therefore she and I should make love to cure her loneliness. In the dream I felt a strong conflict between sexual desire and professional ethics. I quickly helped her into the coat she had taken off and rushed her out the door in search of Titus. I returned to the office (I think) to lock the door and Titus came out of hiding, shushing me and smiling. He said, "You passed the test, I can trust you now." When I went back to meet Milagro, she was gone and I woke up. The dream brought to my awareness the uncertainty and fear I had felt, unconsciously, about the changes Titus was making. My doubts were: Was I doing the right thing guiding him in the new direction? Could I handle his change? Was I imposing my values on him? On the other hand, in the dream Milagro was my resistance; by focusing on her I could distract myself from the hard work of dealing with Titus's problems. Also, I saw in her apparition a confirmation of the unity she and Titus had become; she connived with him to test me. I felt good about their communion.]

Session 46

In session 46, I told Titus part of my dream.

[I realized that in my countertransference I was seeking his confirmation and assurance, but I believed that sharing this dream would benefit Titus.]

He responded, in a friendly and relaxed way, that he had been sure of me for a long time, and added that the dream must have come from my insecurity.

[I realized that he was right. In cases like this, I find it better to give the point some thought, not to pursue it then and there with the client. That I did. I did not dismiss my primitive id attraction to Milagro, which simply made me aware of the need to be as objective as possible with her and what I heard about her through Titus. Second, the dream had brought my insecurity up to consciousness (the patient is often right in these observations triggered by events in the course of therapy), which was a response to the rapid pace at which this case seemed to have progressed. In a few months this man seemed to have gotten many insights and made many changes. I also understood that the dream was telling me that I had not yet found the true Titus, although his appearance after being hidden in the office seemed to contradict my fear. In either case, there was insecurity on my part.]

Sessions 47 and 48

I shared my reflections on the dream with the patient in the following session, session 47. On this occasion, Titus proclaimed his great change from things-oriented (what he called the "phony-self") to true-self, including Milagro-oriented. This led to a discussion about being certain that the changes perceived in therapy were real. He wondered if there were other people who found themselves in similar situations. I brought up group therapy, but because our time was up we left this topic for the next visit.

At the next session, session 48, Titus wanted to talk about group therapy after he had looked it up on the Internet. I responded by stating that learning about group therapy is interesting but that one can really know it only when one experiences a group. He insisted on my referring him to a group, but I focused on his impatience and his need to be sure about the validity of his attitude change. He claimed that he was impatient because he wanted Milagro and him to be together soon. I went back to the personality parts and asked him which part was saying that. He used hypnosis to "listen" to what that part wanted and to discover what the other, more mature, part responded. He realized how much influence his impulsive, non-thinking "part," still had on him, and decided to use this introspective checking method of personality parts between sessions by himself.

Sessions 49 to 55

The next seven sessions (49 to 55) were conducted using hypnotherapy to help with his need to be certain in general, and specifically to check the genuineness of his attitude change. I helped him remember past situations that made him uncertain. He brought up several events in his family of origin related to his father's complete unpredictability. He understood that the early difficulties had created an overreaction against uncertainty. In hypnosis, he kept going over many other situations no human being can be certain about, from the weather to one's health and death. He rehearsed mentally how to react with less anxiety to uncertainty. He even found excitement and joy in looking at some of these circumstances as adventures. He repeated these practices many times during these sessions and was able to integrate the desire to be certain with his impatience to have things done quickly, on which he had focused earlier. Now his buzzword was "integration," on which he worked during this time.

Session 56

Then, in the fifty-sixth session, after discussing it thoroughly, Titus and I agreed on a new schedule to make sure that his personal growth would not be interrupted and that the gains would be lasting. Individual sessions would continue once a week, group therapy with another therapist would begin with once a week sessions and we would have one conjoint session with Milagro once a month. He asked about hypnosis in the group sessions and I replied that we would reserve them for our one-to-one visits.

[The colleague to whom I referred Titus for group therapy, an experienced psychoanalyst, uses traditional hypnosis, very different from the naturalistic method Titus had been exposed to with me.]

This session marked the beginning of a new chapter in his psychoanalysis. Because of this, I suggested that he go into hypnosis and recapitulate the benefits reaped so far. I encouraged him to allow any images to pop up as metaphors of what he had accomplished in the last few months. When he was in hypnosis, happy events appeared to him as sunny, brilliant, clear, and joyful. His smile was genuine and childlike. After a few moments in hypnosis, his unconscious brought up the view from Milagro's living-room window with a mountainous peninsula on the right side, covered with greenery of all different hues. I encouraged him to just enjoy this view, get into it and feel it as something that is part of him and to get into the feelings he is experiencing. He asked a question that sounded too intellectual, to which I responded by stressing the hypnotic experience by saying that later he would be able to analyze and comprehend its meaning. Now he was there, looking at nature from Milagro's living room. This was the time to absorb it, taste it, enjoy it, and experience it. I invited him to get fully into his imaginative concentration, paying attention to small details, close by and far away, of sound, of sensations, of vision, of smell, even of taste—to truly be there. I suggested that he see in this beautiful picture his growth in the last months. All he had to do now is to just see it, taste it, savor it in his mind and enjoy its scent, its shape, its form. After this practice, Titus connected again with the ordinary way of using his mind (what traditional hypnosis calls "waking up") and reported very positive feelings. He said that the beautiful order and precision of the mental representation of the view from Milagro's room was like a reflection of the tranquility and peace he felt in his life now. I advised him to make that his special mental place where he can put himself to become centered in his superego. At this point, I taught him again to practice natural self-hypnosis, this time following the simple BRIMS method of Breathing, Relaxation, Imagery, Messages, and Sign or anchoring, as explained by Sutton (1996).

Sessions 57 to 76
The next twenty sessions (57 to 76) were also part of the working through, following Freud's (1914a) advice, quoted above, about allowing the patient time to work through the resistance. This work included comments on his group therapy experience, which he benefited from, and on the progress he was gradually making in his relationship with Milagro. The few conjoint sessions centered mostly on the couple's unrealistic and fantasy expectations of each other, as well as on increasing their skill in conflict resolution and arriving at satisfactory compromise.

During this time he celebrated the progress made in analysis. He was happy to have "gotten the psychoanalytical habit," as he put it. By this he meant that he often found himself asking questions about his reactions and desires, behaviors, feelings, and fantasies. He added that this new habit had always proven to be beneficial and self-enhancing. Titus wanted to stay in therapy under the same schedule we had followed during the last four or five months. He continued his psychoanalysis both individually and in group. The conjoint sessions with Milagro slowly came to an end toward the last part of the second year. Milagro continued individual sessions with her own analyst. By the time Titus began his third year with me, he announced that Milagro and he were getting married that coming spring. After the marriage I saw them together only two times, and by the end of the fourth year Titus finished his psychoanalysis. He has kept in touch, mailing me greeting cards, and once saw me for a business problem for which he wanted my opinion.

*   *   *

It is impossible to summarize in a few pages the many things that happen in four long years of rather intensive psychotherapy. Nevertheless, the preceding description may give you some idea. The important question for the purpose of this book is this: How can the new clinician, freshly licensed to practice psychotherapy, benefit from psychoanalytical thinking in his clinical work? And the second question is, How can the seasoned clinician, not trained in psychoanalysis, best enrich his practice with these principles? I have kept these points in mind in every chapter and in every clinical case presented.

The answers to these two questions have several levels. In the most general terms, they can be answered by reference to the broad concept of the unconscious. You can always be alert for its manifestations, even if you are applying cognitive-behavioral methods, so popular in the early 2000s. You may also invite information from the unconscious by suggesting to your clients that they pay attention to their dreams and fantasies. You saw in the case of Titus how dreams were meaningful and helpful. For their benefit, as well as for your own curiosity, you may want to work with dreams—yours and those of your patients. After listening to their dream, you can ask them (1) what sense do they make of the dream. You may add, more as a question than as a definite statement, any comments you have on the same dream, for instance, "Do you think that this may have something to do with . . ." (some aspect of the client's life). Then, ask them (2) how they can use the insight or information gotten from the dream to improve their life. Pay attention to what they say and check if it makes sense, given their lifestyle and other circumstances. Frequently, the way they respond to this question invites further analysis, often going back to early experiences. By paying attention to their metaphors and figures of speech, always by means of questions rather than by direct "interpretations," you can help them find unconscious meanings that may be very enriching for understanding themselves. And at the very least you can help them to start thinking, wondering, and questioning.

Another way of answering the same questions about the benefit of the psychoanalytic perspective for the clinician is this: by recognizing that most behaviors have different meanings at different levels, you become more helpful to your clients in a variety of instances. For instance, Joe is very helpful to everyone, not realizing that he acts this way because he does not trust others to do things right; by his doing them he is sure they'll be satisfactory. And later, Joe (who believed he had a wonderful childhood) may become aware of the fact that his mother was an obsessive-compulsive disciplinarian and that his childhood home was run with military exactitude, thus influencing his adult need to have always things right.

The more aware people are of what they do, the greater control they have over their lives and, paradoxically, the more relaxed they are. Yes, new awareness often produces anxiety and anxiety bothers us, so we repress it. But, as we said in Chapters 4 and 5, anxiety can also motivate us to use that awareness for self-transformation. Some ask in what way awareness gives us greater control over our lives.

The response is that by recognizing, for instance, that I am doing something mainly so as not to hurt someone else's feelings, I may be ignoring my own preferences. This awareness allows me to make a better choice next time by putting my own feelings and preferences into the decision equation. Thinking psychoanalytically will mean I will no longer wonder why I usually react one way or another to specific persons, events, or circumstances. You hear often statements like, "I don't know why I'm doing it. It's just the way I am." But with the psychoanalytic attitude you can help clients ask themselves in-depth questions such as, Have I been always like this? What made me start acting like I do? Why do I get anxious if I cannot be this way (or have it my way)? Does this (situation, person, event) elicit reminiscences of some past person or event in my life? Can I imagine myself acting differently? How do I feel when I visualize myself acting differently? And so forth.

* * *

Through studying the case of Titus, you may realize how many possibilities become open to you as a clinician by taking advantage of the psychoanalytic approach. One of these advantages comes from holding on to the belief that human actions are seldom simple and understandable on the surface. What you see is often much less than what is there; the symptom is not the whole story. You can spare your client much anxiety and confusion, pain and wasted energy, by opening her eyes to the possibility that her symptom is connected with other aspects or parts of her personality, conscious or not. It is of real concern to me that other therapeutic approaches refuse to even consider the unconscious, as if it were some sort of superstitious belief without any practical significance.

This brings us back to some basic points I mentioned at the very beginning of this book. First, that psychoanalysis does not accept the medical model of only considering the symptom, alleviating or removing it. Second, that medications (so widely used nowadays for psychiatric conditions) are not the cure but merely part, at best, of the complete treatment program for most of those conditions. And third, that the more awareness the patient obtains about his symptoms, the more power and control he has over them. In other words, people need to look inside themselves and to accept that it is their own responsibility to make changes that will improve their condition. By relying mostly (or even only) on medications, they get into the negative self-hypnosis that convinces them of their helplessness. The psychological model of introspection and self-knowledge, followed by self-acceptance, welcomes the help that medications can give in many instances but it holds on firmly to the benefits of insight and to the reality of the influence of our early life on our current personality. This is not too far from the Romans' advice of "*Nosce te ipsum*," which originates in the Corinth temple inscription "Know thyself." Oedipus, believing the oracle's statement, fled Corinth not to kill those he thought were his parents but in so doing discovered the truth too late, that he did not know what he was doing. Sophocles' main message in *Oedipus Rex* is that not to know oneself will lead us into serious trouble (see Bettelheim 1982, pp. 20–30). The more familiar advice, "To your own self be true," embodies the entire psychoanalytic purpose of full self-acceptance after one has discovered, by using introspection, the truth about oneself.

PART TWO | POINTS AND CLARIFICATIONS FOR THE NON-PSYCHOANALYST

Chapter 12
PHILOSOPHY AND METAPSYCHOLOGY

The first part of this book was essentially practical and intended to help you apply psychoanalytic principles and methods in your work with clients. This second part goes into some of the important concepts and theories to make you comfortable with and knowledgeable about them. I have selected items that are directly related to the application—the praxis—of psychoanalysis.

This chapter presents what you, as an educated practitioner who intends to use psychoanalysis without being a psychoanalyst, must know about two different and basic aspects of psychoanalysis. To understand what psychoanalysis is all about, we must distinguish between its theory and philosophy, on the one hand, and psychoanalysis as a treatment method on the other. By philosophy, I mean its essence and nature. If the reality of the unconscious is at the heart of psychoanalysis, we must concentrate on this first. However, in addition to these two main aspects of psychoanalysis, we also have metapsychology, a term used by Freud to designate his new approach to the understanding and handling of the unconscious, a new field unlike the psychology of his own time, which limited itself to the area of consciousness.

Enlightenment and self-awareness

While I still stand by my earlier statements about psychoanalysis being the Zen of the West, I also recognize that it is necessary to clarify my view. For instance, when Freud talks about bringing to awareness what was hidden before, he was not referring to an integrated program of complete self-awareness, but merely to the clinical work at hand. Thanks to analysis, the patient comes to realize the symbolic meaning of her symptoms; she understands that the hurt she experiences now because of psychological deficiencies in her early relationships can and should be handled more effectively and with less pain. She discovers that her unconsciously fantasized world—that is, the mental images she has about her life, past and current—is harming her, and that she has to revisit the truth of her overactivated fantasies that were unconscious for many years. All these insights have, indeed, the sound of enlightenment. Yet in fact Freud limited the need for consciousness to the symptoms of mental illness because, first, people came to him to get rid of their symptoms, and also because when the symptoms are functioning only as emergency coping devices against the unmanageable inner conflict that produces anxiety, they are not effective, even if they were useful at some time in the past. This limited intent is shown in his statements about changing the id into ego, or replacing one by the other, or letting ego take control over id, meaning that it is the symptom to be cured or the personality trait to be improved that determines and circumscribes the extent of what is to be uncovered.

However, as Fromm (1960) comments, the principle of awareness can be extended to a lifestyle of enlightenment. Here is his definition: "The aim of Zen is enlightenment: the immediate, unreflected

grasp of reality, without affective contamination and intellectualization, the realization of the relation of myself with the universe"
(p. 65). This is, therefore, a pure experience, comparable to the way
the child grasps the immediate world in which he or she lives. By
stating that this experience is "the aim" of Zen, Fromm seems to
stress that it is never fully attained. So too in psychoanalysis, if we
extend and widen the idea of making the unconscious conscious, as
Jung (1956) did, the free association produced by introspection gen-
erates a habit of enlightenment—always uncovering and discovering more details of one's unconscious. The person, then, frequently
not even realizing the similarity of this to Zen discipline, is in the
attitude of enlightenment, where one is gently open to one's inner
self and to the richness of experiencing the world around and one's
relationship with it. Thus, awareness is a practical way to know ourselves. This might be why many former patients, and obviously also
psychoanalysts, get into this introspective habit. As we notice, across
cultures and through the ages, many others who have had no connection with Freud use awareness to enrich their lives, not necessarily to solve problems or cure neurotic behavior. All these people
have found the value of introspection, self-questioning, and open-
mindedness, qualities rooted in the conviction that our past and
developmental experiences have all left unconscious marks in us,
affecting and even distorting our current experiences of self and
universe. Because of this inevitability, we and they are on the look-
out, although relaxed and at peace, for connections between the
present with the past. For instance, instead of just reacting with anger
to the tone of voice of another person, the aware individual tries to
uncover, through introspection, why he reacts so strongly to that
external stimulus. He may find out that the other person holds views
that are against his value system and that he would like to change
her. His angry reaction is not, then, a response to her shrill voice,

but comes up because he feels helpless to change her. And then, of course, further introspection, might reveal that he wants to change her because of his own rigidity and intolerance. At another level, he may become aware that as a child he hated a teacher who had a similarly shrill voice.

I mentioned earlier how popular psychoanalysis was in Buenos Aires when I was a youngster. Many entered analytic therapy. I did at 21, knowing that I had to resolve many issues from my upbringing but also as a matter of status: without having been psychoanalyzed an intellectual person was thought to lack something and it diminished his credibility and seriousness. In fact, many of those who did not go into analysis for one reason or another, so as not to be considered unsophisticated, had meetings, self-directed groups, and weekend retreats where they analyzed their thoughts, feelings, and behaviors. This was a form of enlightenment that helped many to lead productive and satisfied lives.

Overanalyzing

Another example of understanding the philosophy of psychoanalysis is the need for restraint on our part. Not every problem must be psychoanalyzed. Not every behavior our culture considers abnormal or inappropriate is necessarily neurotic. Not every painful life circumstance has a deep-rooted explanation and meaning. Many people come to us for immediately troublesome situations, such as the mother whose 35-year-old daughter has been a drug addict and continues to abuse substances like crack and cocaine. The problem, strictly speaking, is not hers, but it bothers her and she needs support, reassurance, and validation. It is unfair and almost cruel to infer that the daughter turned out this way because the patient was not a good mother, or that for some other reason she contributed to the daughter's condition, or to infer that the mother's need for help at this point is a sign of her weakness, dependency, or guilt. Such ways of using psychoanalytic principles and concepts are an aberration and an insult to the entire analytic movement.

We must be clear about the scope of psychoanalysis. I mentioned at the start of this chapter that there are at least two different meanings involved here. Therefore, when we refer to psychoanalysis as therapy, we reserve it for specific emotional or mental problems—primarily for neurosis in its many manifestations, and for character disorders. In the first category, we have hysterical neurosis, as manifested in psychogenic bodily suffering; obsessional neurosis, affecting one's thinking, logic, and common sense; and finally phobic neurosis, related to environmental circumstances into which the patient projects unconscious dynamics. I like to add to these three relational forms of neurosis "interaction" because it helps the clinician to zero in on interdependent problems, especially in work with couples and families. This neurotic type manifests itself in lack of trust and fear of intimacy, in insecurity and doubts about the relationship, or in selfishness and lack of sensitivity toward the other(s). As an appendix to the neuroses, but separate from them, *sexual perversions* should be listed. The word chosen by Freud sounds much more negative than what it means in context. Paraphilia, because it is not part of the common language, may be more acceptable. Call it what you like, these are behavioral manifestations that must be distinguished from neuroses, since there is no universal norm for sexuality and all "normal" people are sexually deviant, paraphiliac, or perverse, as Kinsey's research published by him and his coworkers in 1948 and 1953 proved, thus confirming the beliefs Freud made public in 1905. Therefore, from a clinical point of view, a perversion is not necessarily neurotic and is beyond treatment unless it becomes an issue between partners. On the other hand, all types of neuroses, as they affect sexuality in different ways, may exhibit diverse types of perversions.

When it comes to character disorders we refer to inner dynamics, mostly cultural and unconscious, with all the personal traits affected by defense mechanisms, values, inner duties, guilt, and fears, including the behavioral manifestation of them. (Nowadays we prefer to use the word *personality* to refer mostly, if not only, to idiosyncratic structures—that is, behavioral patterns and habits. This is, probably, because of the bias in favor of focusing only on behavior.) It must be noted that while we may use terms like "histrionic personality" or any of the other designations given in the three personality clusters of the *DSM*, we refuse to approach them merely at the behavioral level. Consequently, our psychoanalytically oriented work outside these categories may be very important, beneficial, and constructive for patients, but it is not psychoanalysis. As someone who is interested in using psychoanalytic thinking and practices in your clinical mental health work, you will wisely select the recipients of your services according to the broad diagnostic guidelines mentioned above. A clear and uncomplicated presentation, very relevant to the issue of character disorders, is Frattaroli's (2001) Chapter 17, "What Are We Really Hearing When We Listen to Prozac?"

In sum, these two vast areas of neuroses and character disorders are the province of psychoanalysis as therapy. I want to stress that this is the ordinary, regular scope of psychoanalysis. Psychotic conditions are rather the exception, given the fact that today effective medications to reduce the symptoms are universally available. In this book I have repeatedly criticized the practice of medication without psychotherapy, but, like it or not, this is the reality in the age of pharmacology. Nevertheless, I have noted that the psychotics who end up in psychoanalysis are those who themselves had a good experience with this method before they became psychotic, or those who have a relative or close friend who was helped with analysis. Even though most analysts in private practice don't work with active, nonfunctional psychotics, our tradition has wonderful examples of those who did, mostly with hospitalized patients. In this tradition, we find names like Sullivan (see White 1977) and Fromm-Reichmann (1950), among many others.

Dreams

Even though we'll discuss dreams again, it may be useful to add here, in connection with the above, that we have to be careful not to discover pathology in every dream a client reports or that a friend talks about. With a little effort, anyone can always find negative meanings in dreams. In general, it is important not to believe that dream images have a universal or common meaning. You may remember the cookbook approach to dreams published in the past (and taken seriously even by serious readers): teeth mean aggression, one's nakedness means poor self-esteem, and so on. As I mentioned in Chapter 11, it's safer, in terms of avoiding a mistake, to ask the patient for her interpretation and for the possible meaning of her dream. This is especially the case when the individual has been upset by the dream she had. If the person does not have a clue, I change the focus of her mental attention from the dream to the negative feeling she is having and ask her to visualize her feeling, to give that feeling a shape and size, a color, a temperature, and to check if any of these change; then I ask if there is any scent or sound with this feeling, and so on. By paying attention to the feeling that is the result of the dream, not the dream itself, the person usually finds out something meaningful about herself. However, if nothing comes up with those suggestions, ask if she can find some comparison of the way she feels with some natural event, like rain or wind. Once she does, you ask her to elaborate on whatever similarity she finds between her feeling, elicited by the dream, and that occurrence in nature.

As we mentioned above regarding "therapy material," many dreams do not need sophisticated interpretation and are the manifestation of a healthy unconscious or of the dominance of the ego in a person's life.

Applied psychoanalysis

In addition to the two meanings of psychoanalysis discussed so far, there is also the aspect of it being a tool to study human nature, as manifested in history and in important individuals who have changed the course of world events. One of the authors I find charismatic in this respect is Erich Fromm. In *Escape from Freedom* (1941), among his many important studies, he uses psychoanalysis to understand the leaning toward authoritarianism that has produced monstrous changes such as the German Reich or Communist China, and that is still continuing its march on our planet. *The Anatomy of Human Destructiveness* (1973) is Fromm's expansion of his early ideas on politics. He is just one example, among many psychoanalysts, including Freud himself, of those who have used psychoanalytic thinking both to make sense of difficult events and to center them in the actions of humans. Therefore, using the principles of human conduct and interaction, it is impossible to simply say that "That's the way things are." We don't accept from patients as valid a statement like, "That's me, I guess it's my personality" as an excuse against introspection. We would consider it an indication of resistance and by no means as the final statement on the issue at hand. Applied psychoanalysis, therefore, looks at what lies behind and under the facts in historical, social, and cultural phenomena, similar to the way analysis does in therapy. Among many essays of this kind, many instances of this method may be found in the study of unconscious elements in religion by Freud, in his "Totem and Taboo" (1913), "The Future of an Illusion" (1927), and in his essays in "Moses and Monotheism" (1939). But what does all this mean to a mental health clinician who is not a psychoanalyst?

I believe the main lesson to be drawn from the philosophy of psychoanalysis is that we can be (and as clinicians, must be) more sensitive to the unconscious reality in our lives and around us. If you want to take advantage of the richness of psychoanalysis in your clinical work, you can develop an attitude of introspection with yourself and of sober inquisitiveness with everything around you. For example, we know that a habitually late patient is telling us something with that conduct, but we cannot interpret it correctly unless we inquire from the client what the lateness may be saying regarding his relationship to and with the analyst. Without the concept of the unconscious reality in our lives that we are discussing, one therapist might get mad and show it, a second might say nothing, and a third might just ask the client to talk about it and accept the first explanation that the patient offers. You, using psychoanalytic thinking, will make the habitual lateness the main topic of the session to uncover the unconscious truth of this behavior. In so doing you help the patient understand himself better, while you are becoming aware of the meaning (the message) of that symbolic conduct. And what's the value of this insight? You make the client–therapist encounter more authentic by honestly bringing up what (rightly!) bothers you, and in so doing you get to know the patient better as a human being and thus get yourself more ready to deal with him as a real person. To ignore the possible "other things" that are part of the total psychological picture limits your interaction and makes the counseling/therapy superficial—or, rather, does not allow it to exist at a deeper level of understanding and caring (see Mitchell 2000). All this being said, I want to stress that to speculate without full information is misleading and unfair. Moreover, it is an insult to psychoanalysis and confirms the erroneous ideas that many people have of it.

Metapsychology

To explain the new theory that was beyond the realm of psychology in Freud's time, he used this term, meaning "beyond psychology." Consequently, all that metapsychology was trying to do was to explain what was unexplainable by psychology (the discipline that studied, as stated at the opening of this chapter, conscious behavior). But the difficulty here was that the evidence upon which an entire system was built came from one-to-one observations that were easy to challenge by anyone other than the observer himself. A scientific system requires a careful theory of mind that includes unconscious phenomena. But this then came into conflict with the problem of multiple causation; are the so-called unconscious phenomena caused perhaps by unknowns not accounted for? The list of problems is long. Waelder (1962), whom we met in Chapter 7, the physicist turned psychoanalyst in the last decade of Freud's life, goes over all the important points of scientific validity. There are many points of view from which to explicate unconscious phenomena, from structural to adaptive, and on through several others, depending on which psychoanalytic school you choose, but the important and central issue is to comprehend how unconscious psychic reality originates in the individual. To address this question, psychic reality in general, and psychic identity more specifically, must be defined. Simply put, the former refers to all the nonconscious things that are such an important part of human existence. The latter, however, does not lend itself to a simple explanation. To help us understand these complicated concepts, I like to take advantage of the work of Jacques Lacan (1977) who since the mid-1960s has had a powerful influence on psychoanalysis in Europe and only recently is becoming known in the English-speaking world (Dor 1999, Nasio 1998, Verhaeghe 2004). For Lacan, psychic identity, synonymous with subject identity, designates the uniqueness of the individual who is never an individual without his or her relationship to what Lacan calls the Other (Verhaeghe 2004), so that "the subject's identity develops in relation to the Other and this has immediate effects on the way he or she relates to all others" (p. 136). Note, first, that for the individual there is no psychic reality without psychic identity. Second, note also that the Lacanian Other is a general term to indicate all significant others, not just those of the early years, though ordinarily beginning with the mother and the rest of the parental "objects." The same word also includes language, the common means by which Others influence the individual and she connects with them— both are interdependent through language. Thus the two concepts of psychic reality and identity are dynamic, living, and constantly changing, in a perpetual process of exchange between the self and Other(s) as well as the external world in general. So now we return to the question: How does the individual become a subject and, thanks to his psychic or subject identity, a part of psychic reality? It all starts with the relation that is formed between the person or subject and the Other. Note that this is not an interactive relationship but describes the way the split or divided self relates at two different levels and from two different structures, internally and externally (fantasy and reality). There is an inner relation to the other-in-oneself, which is the active drive, and simultaneously an external relation to a part of the Other who is also split or divided. This relation happens through language (including body language) and speech. There is nothing mysterious here if we recall what transference is all about, and understand that the corrective experience of transference is an important process of developmental growth for the patient. In normal (healthy) circumstances, the formation of object identity grows into fulfillment, from the very beginning, through this repeated process of language relation between the subject and the Other. Thus, subject formation never ends, because one's identity keeps being affected by every meaningful life experience. Among these are developmental stages, like graduations, marriage, one's children, career landmarks or changes, losses and disappointments, and many more. In optimal circumstances, these events refine and enrich our identity. However, when the original Other lacks the ability to respond adequately to the subject, a defective and pathological relation is formed, which means that the object identity ends up damaged or deficient and in need of serious restoration. However, a very important observation is that this process of identity acquisition is not linear, with one new event only adding to the previous list of experiences, but circular, so that old experiences give meaning to new events and vice versa.

The benefit of clarifying these concepts and, generally, of being interested in them by reading and studying as much as we can about them, is that it enlarges our specialty to know these ideas and formulations and how to apply them. As a psychotherapist who wants to enrich her work with psychoanalytic principles, you need to understand these basic concepts, particularly those closely related to subject formation or to how the individual becomes a subject. To summarize without getting into the details of this process, subject formation takes place when the subject is able to separate from the Other. Separation here means autonomy, effective decision-making and functioning, mental security, and emotional self-sufficiency with joyful acceptance of reality, even when it is tough. This is the sense of empowerment that ultimately remains the goal of analysis.

Recapitulation
Our brief attention to the philosophic and metapsychological explanations of the unconscious may seem a deviation from the practical, "how to do it" approach of earlier chapters. Nevertheless, if you quickly scan the chapter and reflect, it gives you material to explain and justify what you, a non-psychoanalytic therapist, are doing with

these various psychoanalytic concepts, methods, and techniques. First, you read about the two very different aspects or conceptions of psychoanalysis, as pure theory and as a philosophy that can become a new way of being in the world for a person who chooses it. This latter use of psychoanalysis is a method of self-transformation, growth, and enrichment that requires self-discipline and, ideally, a long training period (self-analysis) resembling the arduous regimen expected of a Zen or Taoist disciple, with enlightenment as the goal.

The second meaning of psychoanalysis is what this book is all about, and my idea is to present and explain psychoanalytical concepts and application for those clinicians who are not analysts. I mentioned earlier that in my many years of teaching in a graduate program of mental health counseling, I often found and continue to find many students (young adults for the most part) who are not satisfied with staying at the surface, concentrating on the symptom, as if nothing else could be done to help the client. My contention is that you can enrich your mental health work with psychoanalytic concepts applied to your therapeutic efforts.

However, and accompanying that view, you also read some ethical considerations about avoiding overanalyzing and not losing one's common sense. The practical consequences of this warning are that psychotherapists of any kind must have a balanced life involving recreational activities, hobbies, or personal interests (other than professional), enough quality time with one's family, and enough regular dealings with people other than patients and colleagues. The one whose only interest is his profession may well need to recognize that as a deficit and lack, not as a virtue. In this connection, we moved then to dreams, a special area where overanalyzing seems to be quite common.

Next, in order to highlight the extended value of psychoanalytic thinking, we touched lightly on applied psychoanalysis, that branch of thought that uses and adapts these principles and ideas to history, and to social and cultural realities in general, as well as to religion in particular.

Finally we dared to enter the area of metapsychology or of those mysteries of the unconscious that were outside the field of psychology in Freud's time. The purpose was simply to make you aware of the true and real meaning of the term. Here we focused on one's psychic identity, since one's knowledge of that is essential in order to help any human being who approaches us with problems, anxiety, questions, or confusion and doubt. And because in the order of priorities, the first is to assess the client's (psychic) self identity.

I hope that when you look at this chapter in this light you'll agree that we have dealt with very practical issues in a very brief manner. Now is the time for you to think concretely about using these ideas for the benefit of your clients. But first, find a psychoanalyst or an analytic therapist whom you respect and whom you can use as a consultant. Then decide with whom and in what type of case you could begin to consider the unconscious in a therapeutic way. Begin with an "easy" case and use it as research, to be fully aware of what you do and what seems to work.

Chapter 13

THE WORKING ALLIANCE, INTERPRETATION, AND RESISTANCE

This chapter highlights a few points on technique. It also studies what the psychoanalyst does in this form of therapy. As we have said before, many, including non-psychoanalyst mental health professionals, still believe the caricature that depicts the analyst as passively listening and barely responding, with any responses being dogmatic interpretations of what the patient has said or omitted, and let the patient who disagrees with the interpretations beware. While durable, that image is a complete distortion of what the analyst does in today's practice. Here we will take a close look at concrete, detailed psychoanalytical work. Contrary to that mistaken cliché, we pay attention to what analysts, at least since Greenson (1967), have called the *working alliance*, and more recently *intersubjectivity* (Stolorow et al. 1995), both closely related to Sullivan's (1953) interpersonal analysis and to what others, for example Rogers (1951), have referred to as *unconditional positive regard*. That is, we consider that the person of the therapist is actively and genuinely involved in the work of therapy, and thus becomes the most important variable in "the cure."

Once the function of the therapist is clear, we can move on to begin to comprehend what he or she does, meaning the technique used, which goes by the general term of *interpretation*. Finally, because of its connection with interpretation, we will investigate the dynamics of the patient's resistance.

The working alliance

In truth this is a transferential phenomenon, and as Greenson (1967) defines it, it is "the relatively nonneurotic, rational rapport which the patient has with his analyst. It is this reasonable and purposeful part of the feelings the patient has for the analyst which makes for the working alliance" (p. 192). Later on the same page he clarifies this definition by stating that it is formed by the common efforts of the reasonable part of the patient and the analyzing ego of the analyst. Here, Greenson comes across as emphasizing the attitude of the client; his or her readiness to work and become healthier. However, the fact that he chose the word "alliance" to refer to this phenomenon makes me believe that he was very aware of the important part the analyst has to play in this alliance. More recently, and returning to the position that Racker (1968) established with his emphasis on countertransference, many have stressed uncompromisingly the need for the therapist to be genuine, careful and caring, sensitive and respectful with the patient. This is the core of intersubjectivity, as Mitchell (2000) explains in his description of relationality.

This also is essentially what makes analysis work, as Freud (1921) remarked when he said that "the vehicle of success in psychoanalysis" (p. 105) is the sympathetic understanding of the therapist. Therefore, we must know how to produce this alliance and how to avoid interfering with it. The most important consideration on the part of the therapist is mature honesty; with himself first, acknowledging his feelings, and with the patient. Most importantly, this quality cannot be faked, since, if someone hypocritically attempts to fake honesty, sooner or later he will betray himself and show his true personality and nature.

Consequently, the mental health worker is required to lead a life of empathy and to be everything that we expect the "cured" patient to be. She must be at peace with herself and the world, enjoying the daily happenings of life with tolerance, patience, and humor, and have all the other attributes belonging to someone with excellent mental health. Inevitably, the only way to attain the goal of establishing a working alliance is to have gone through one's personal analysis, as we have stated before, or through another similar program of unadulterated self-knowledge and transformation. My bias is for psychoanalysis, since anything less may not allow us to act with fairness and equity toward our analytic patients.

Interpretation

When we are asked to interpret something, we are expected to explain (or to translate), to clarify something that is obscure, to throw light on something, and to uncover a meaning that was not evident before. Freud's (1900) first book is a prolonged treatise on interpretation, and is not limited to dreams. Repeatedly he reminds the reader that to interpret means to find a hidden meaning. Because of this common understanding, the first surprise for many not familiar with psychoanalysis is that an interpretation is much more than just interpretation. Ordinarily, it is a verbal expression of what the psychoanalyst understands and feels about the client, his life in general, and his problem(s) in particular; often this expression is nonverbal, or a combination of both. What the analyst understands about the patient comes from what the patient has said, that is, memories and fantasies, fears and wishes, projections and visions of the future as well as his dreams, and how the patient reacts to them. But the patient has mentioned many of these things in passing, with no intention of explaining or uncovering secrets of his life. Nevertheless, all these psychic phenomena and more give the professional a profile, an idea, of the client. Interpretations, therefore, most frequently relate to the unconscious. They also include things known to the patient but in an incomplete way, often distorted and inaccurate. Because this type of therapy is meant to increase the patient's understanding of his unconscious dynamics and motivations, every interaction between the patient and the clinician is in pursuit of that goal, and every communication or intervention, that is, every interpretation of the therapist, ideally at least, is expanding the client's self-knowledge and effectively increasing his control over his life and destiny. As we said before, empowering the client is the ultimate goal. Each mental health worker develops a unique and ego-syntonic manner of interpretation— brief and to the point or verbose, self-disclosing or storytelling—all with reference to the knowledge the therapist already has of the client or encapsulated and isolated. But regardless of the therapist's great expertise in interpretation, one is never exempt from the need for tact, kindness, and sensitivity, as well as the openness to correct oneself or modify one's perception and impressions, from which interpretations come.

Interpretation being so crucial, it is necessary to take the time and effort required to learn how to do it well. Fenichel (1945), with the clarity so characteristic of him, comes to our aid by presenting the ideas of Freud in an organized manner. He assumes that the analyst will have no great difficulty determining a neurotic conflict because of its intense emotional content. On this premise and because "we should always be able to explain what we are doing, why we interpret and what we expect each time from our activity" (p. 52), he develops three guidelines for interpretation—economic, dynamic, and structural—all of which, by the way, can become ineffective if deprived of the free attention and intuition of the therapist, the two prerequisites to any form of interpretation. The "economic" guideline refers to timing; interpret when the patient is ready to accept what you say. When is that? Usually we decide when to interpret from what the patient says, consciously and unconsciously (slips of tongue, using a mistaken word, etc.), from his body language, and from our own countertransference. The "dynamic" guideline for interpretation refers to unconscious resistance shown by the client, which if ignored will counteract any further progress. Finally, the "structural" guideline directs itself to working at the ego level. In practice, what Fenichel teaches us is that to make an effective interpretation (remember, this means any therapeutic intervention to clarify what's going on in the session and to uncover its meaning for the patient) we must concentrate on what carries more emotion for the client, we must address resistance first and foremost, and we must avoid guessing about the unconscious and stay with the ego material, using the data and facts that we have collected to help the patient with his problem. In a very helpful way, Fenichel is repeating what Freud (1914b) had stated earlier when he suggested that one should start at the "analytic surface," a felicitous term that emphasizes the therapeutic (analytic) content, not any other material that might be obvious (the weather, some slight illness, or anything similar).

In addition to Fenichel's guidelines, others (Levy 1984, Etchegoyen 1999) have contributed to the understanding and use of what is considered the central therapeutic activity of the analyst. The list of interpretation categories is open to the creative initiative of researchers and practitioners. Thus, Etchegoyen (1999, pp. 426–436) summarizes all interpretations under four headings, historical and current and under the latter, transference and extratransference. Very briefly and from our practical point of view, historical interpretation is a way of reconstructing the past in order to give back to the client an idea of the position she had in the traumatic past. Current or present interpretation, as the designation implies, has to do with real difficulties the client may have in her environment and with her overreaction to or ineffective way of handling them. Etchegoyen places the other two categories under the "current" interpretation. Transference interpretation deals with the distortions in the therapeutic relationship due to displacement into the analyst of feelings, attitudes, and behaviors originally experienced with significant persons of the past. Extratransference interpretation, on the other hand, relates to a response when the patient does not accept the interpretation as coming from the therapist, but as coming from the person the transference makes the patient suppose is the therapist. In Etchegoyen's words, "The risk . . . consists in the patient receiving them [the interpretations] with a transference perspective" (p. 431). But as the author reminds us, the risk of misunderstanding in one of such interpretations can be corrected with a subsequent one.

Etchegoyen proposes that, ideally, the complete interpretation would show the present transferential conflict, its connection with what happens in real life, and the infantile conflict from which the distortions in both places originate, thus including the three convergent levels of operation and three instances of the unconscious and its fantasies altering the individual reality.

Regardless of these important concepts and distinctions, experience has taught many seasoned mental-health providers that educated common sense is indispensable for effective interpretation in therapy. But because common sense is a very broad term, here is a review of some of its manifestations. The following are listed at random, not in order of importance: know what to say and when to say it; use productive material from the accumulated information you have about the client; discriminate between fantasy and reality and don't act until you have clarified this difference; when in doubt, don't spout—you most probably will have a second chance to say what you had in mind, or you may change your mind; when in doubt, don't act, that is, don't take unnecessary risks; as a general rule, keep your personal views apart from the client's problem, knowing that self-disclosure should be the exception; always be relevant; and to improve your style and effectiveness, be acutely observant and control your urge to talk; then self-analyze the origin of your urge, your fantasies, and your countertransference. Obviously, you may add other guidelines of your own.

Resistance

This is an inevitable reaction to self-examination that surprises the novice because of its contradictory nature. Even the most sophisticated patient, with clear knowledge of what psychoanalytic therapy is all about, especially the insight and psychodynamics parts, will find himself using defensive efforts to shun the very essence of this type of therapy, that is, self-knowledge. According to Freud's (1926) account, when he first encountered this response, and before he realized that resistance was unconscious, he believed that a firm, cognitive approach would do away with this obstacle to therapeutic progress. Yet the "obstacle" came as an automatic defense against contact with repressed material, namely, the memory of traumatic events that were responsible for the neurotic symptoms. It was only when he discovered the unconscious nature of resistance that he gave it the important place it has in analysis today, where it is essential to interpret it. In order to uncover resistance so it can be interpreted, he developed the technique of free association. This method helps the client (who is not aware of the defensive maneuvers she is using to avoid getting into emotionally loaded subjects) to get in touch naturally, and without intrusion, with her unconscious information. Free association—the new method Freud considered the fundamental rule in psychoanalysis (and about which he was quite possessive, because it was his invention) consists of verbalizing, without any censoring, whatever comes to mind, regardless of whether it makes sense or not, whether it is logical or not, or whether it is proper, good, and decent or not. Parenthetically, I must add that by using free association to overcome resistance Freud was indicating his trust in the unconscious; the unconscious knows what the patient consciously does not know and, through free association, it brings up some of that knowledge to consciousness for the benefit of the patient.

Wilhelm Reich (1933) considered resistance to the fundamental rule a manifestation of a negative character trait, not merely a symptom, and Etchegoyen (1999) explains it clearly: "Different from a symptom, a character trait is syntonic [something that does not bother the person and has practically become a trait of the personality] by reason of its being strongly rationalized, and it serves to link floating anxiety with what Reich calls charactero-muscular armour, the expression of narcissistic defense" (p. 391).

What does this mean in practice? That the practitioner must be alert to what others (Alexander 1927, Glover 1926) have called asymptomatic or characterological neurosis, because if the latter is encountered the practitioner must move to second-level analysis or, in the case of a non-psychoanalyst using psychoanalysis, refer the patient to a specialist in psychoanalysis. Dealing with character disorders is difficult because the client does not perceive his conduct as neurotic, pathological, or inappropriate; he is so defended that what everybody else condemns he praises and what everybody else abhors he loves. I remember a young couple with a baby 6 months of age. The wife put pressure on the husband to come for marital therapy because he still went out with "the boys" every Friday after work. The point of contention was that often he did not come back home till three or four in the morning, even after she had called him before midnight and he had assured her he was on his way home.

Moreover, by the time he got home, most of the time he was drunk and/or high on drugs. However, he blamed her for calling him on the phone when she knew he was relaxing and having a good time; he complained that she was too controlling, too needy, too immature. He also brought in the troops: all his married friends did the same, none of the wives were so nagging, and so on. In a word, she was wrong. His was an angry "put up or shut up" attitude. When asked why he lied to her, he actually stated that she made him do it so he could get her off his back. To which I responded, "And you're here to get her off your back also." When he agreed, I suggested that we do something to get her off his back. First I found out who else in his life had been on his back. Of course he mentioned his mother. Being the oldest of three boys and a girl, he was blamed for many things the others did, not him. Once we got to the point where he was responding to me (that was by the fourth session) I asked what he could do to get his wife off his back. The man was basically healthy and sensitive, strongly attached to the baby and genuinely protective of the wife in public. Working from those strengths, he started to lower his resistance to change by going through several compromises (once a month he would not go drinking with his friends; he would come home after five hours at the bar; he would act as if he were a helping husband with the baby and get up early to feed him, etc.). After having a few relapses, he finally recognized that he could not be single and married at the same time. At this point he started his own analysis twice a week.

I summarize this case briefly to remind you that resistance is real and often "thick" but also to stress that using rational methods is usually ineffective. You waste your time arguing with someone so resistant because of his unconscious defenses. As you noticed, therapy could not start until his defenses had been lowered. I chose this case because this man's motivation to change was absent at the start. His only motivation was "to get his wife off his back." Only when he accepted the long-term gain of being happy with his wife and enjoying their child did he get ready to change and to pick up on his arrested development. As a matter of fact, after a month or so of twice-a-week visits, he asked to have a third session every week.

Resistance may also be politely hidden, the patient seemingly agreeing with everything the mental health professional proposes and does. But I don't believe there is any insight-oriented, psychodynamic therapy or counseling without resistance. However, in some cases resistance is a sign of health, not pathology. Here, I am referring to instances when the professional is too harsh, or prematurely intrusive, or insincere, or too businesslike, among other possibilities. This is because defensiveness, up to a point, is healthy. The circumstances of psychotherapy allow for the revelation of personal information, but one must also keep in mind the working alliance, as discussed earlier in this chapter. Before the patient feels comfortable, a process that later becomes routine may first appear as disrespectful, invasive, and threatening. At that point, the client's defenses are appropriate, self-respectful, and mature. In the next chapter, we will discuss acting out. That client behavior is also common when the therapist is at fault with her own conduct. Greenson (1967) puts it succinctly when he asks why the patient is resisting. He answers that "the immediate motive for defense and resistance is to avoid pain, i.e., painful effects . . . [of] some painful emotion like anxiety, guilt, shame or depression, or some combination of them" (p. 107). Because of this, every time we experience defensive resistance, we may introspect and become aware of what we have done or not done to elicit this reaction. This is putting psychoanalytic thinking in the service of the effectiveness of our work. I remember several instances where the professional would quickly blame the patient when it was evident that the former had handled the situation inadequately. In a mental hospital where I did some work, any complaints from patients were quickly ignored with the explanation that it was expected that mental patients would complain. The people in power never took time to investigate what the complaints were about. I have heard private practitioners talk in the same arrogant, superior, holier-than-thou attitude, as if saying that mental illness deprives a person of all judgment and objectivity. Resistance is often the label used by inadequate mental-health workers to hide their mistakes or to justify them. Our honest introspection will correct this aberration.

But despite some of the above-mentioned comments, resistance is real and we must know how to handle it. My bias, again, is that if you have had the experience from the other side of the situation (as a patient), you will recognize with compassion and kindness what resistance is all about. But if you have not had that advantage, stay firm with the conviction that resistance is a clear indication of the client's ambivalence, questions, and doubts about the changes that intellectually he knows he must make in his life. The moment you start getting angry at the patient because of his resistance, you must take an honest look at yourself and become aware of your expectations, of how much your "ego" is involved in your role as "therapist," and ask yourself if there might possibly be something in your conduct that the other person is picking up as your dissatisfaction, your rejection, or your disappointment with him. If you expect resistance, it will be easier to handle it.

Summary

The three aspects of psychoanalysis I put together in this chapter are indeed related. You may imagine interpretation in the center, with the working alliance on the right of it, and resistance on the left. This mental image indicates that the bridge between the resistant patient and the successful therapist is the way the latter relates to the former. As you notice, then, interpretation belongs to the analyst, resistance to the patient, and the working alliance to both of them; without the cooperation of both nothing happens in psychoanalysis. Brandchaft (1992), in speaking about Ralph Greenson, writes of "the analytic situation as one of an interaction between patient and analyst in which each participant plays a constitutive role in the outcome" (p. 324).

Volumes have been written about the praxis of psychoanalysis, in which the working alliance, interpretation, and resistance are pivotal. In spite of the diverse language used and opinions presented, there is agreement among all the schools that the practice of psychoanalysis hinges on these three activities. Interpretation and resistance depend on the working alliance to such an extent that a person who is unable to form the alliance cannot benefit from psychoanalysis. As Greenson (1978) wrote, "The working alliance deserves to be recognized as a full and equal partner in the patient–therapist relationship" (p. 200). The importance of the alliance is that with it the dichotomy between the analyst (as right, healthy, in touch) and the patient (as wrong, sick, out of touch) is minimized. "Reality" for the patient may very well be different than what the professional perceives, and if the analyst is not open to that possibility, again, nothing constructive will happen. This is because the reality relevant to treatment is subjective reality, or the impact things have on the person, and it pertains as much to the clinician as to the client. Without the subjective reality, we only have concretization, or subjective experience transformed into objective realities, as we often encounter when someone asserts that something is absolutely true based merely on his single experience of it. Schwaber (1983) expressed this accurately when he wrote: "Attributions of objective reality . . . are concretizations of objective truth" (p. 103). The intersubjective approach that we have presented is a practical method to use to prevent concretization.

Chapter 14
WORKING THROUGH AND ACTING OUT

The previous chapter included related topics, and so does this one, and these, like the ones discussed earlier, are not "clean or pure" concepts either. "Working through" relates to insight and "acting out" to regression, and both are connected with repetition. None of the connections between and among these concepts are made in an exclusive way, since there is also regression in working through and insight in acting out, once it is analyzed. Therefore, we are standing before a vast and varied panoramic display of concepts, out of which we will extract a few practical points for the non-psychoanalytic clinician who has decided to enrich his practice.

Working through
Freud (1914b), in his essay "Remembering, Repeating, and Working Through," defines working through in terms of analyzing the resistances that often appear even in accepting things intellectually (as if that were enough), barring the emotional, gut-feeling of owning a truth. The analysis produces insight that lets the patient make contact with the hidden emotional meaning. Or, from another

perspective, working through is the effort to bring to consciousness the repressed inner conflicts ("complexes" as Freud called them) with their many ramifications into early experiences. Brenner (1987) claims that by this expression Freud simply meant the effort needed to overcome the resistance by which the patient deprives herself of insight. This is the connection between insight (having the immediate experience of the original emotional truth underlying the problem) and working through (the process by which this happens). The entire point of working through is to help the client become emotionally aware. Thus the work of psychoanalysis is mostly working through. The summation made by Etchegoyen (1999) says it clearly: "working-through (as Freud describes it in his 1914[b] article) leads from intellectual, verbal or descriptive insight to ostensive insight, which we can now say is also always emotional" (p. 677). By "ostensive insight" he means "when the person suddenly feels he is in direct contact with a particular psychological situation" (p. 673). This type of experience I call by the Spanish noun *vivencia* (Araoz 2004), which means insight, gut-feeling, and more; it is a vivid fantasy with great detail of something that I have experienced in the past or of something that I imagine I can realistically experience in the future. The type of emotional insight we are dealing with here is a *vivencia*, but realize that not every *vivencia* is insight.

Working through is doing good analysis and, because of the normal resistances, it does not happen in a few sessions. Just as normal development takes time, the conversion of insight into active change is also slow. Good analysis, just referred to, means that the person is helped to recognize the influence of previous conflicts on her current problems or dissatisfactions. To do this, it is necessary for the client to accept the connection between her current unhappiness or her psychic pain and events of the past. Furthermore, the client has to undo her neurotic defenses, her resistance. Only then can she truly begin to change.

Working through is also where we get into the misunderstood idea of *regression*, which for many has negative connotations. However, in many daily life situations, we accept regressive behavior; people cling to each other in tears and sobs when they are in great pain or jump for joy and yell incomprehensibly when they are very happy. In therapy too, when an adult gets in touch with long-repressed feelings, she cannot remain emotionally an adult; she regresses. The total experience is a *vivencia*, and this is what Kris (1936, 1938, 1950, passim) called "regression in the service of the ego." The client has to experience herself as a child in order to put a hurtful situation in the adult perspective; "Then I felt that way," she may say, "now I can accept that pain as belonging to my past and release the pain from my adult life." Whether we like it or not, we may have to go through this *Durcharbeit*, as Freud called what we translate as working through.

A problem may arise if the clinician inadvertently fosters regression by making the patient more and more dependent on him. This can happen in subtle ways, as when the client is put in an uncomfortable position and cannot make a decision without checking it first with the therapist, or when the client is overwhelmed by ordinary events and is asking advice on trivial matters, and this behavior is not brought up to be analyzed. Regression of that kind is not in the service of the ego but infantilizes the client.

The call to genuineness
As with other topics presented in Part Two of this book, much more technical material could be discussed. However, for my purpose of acquainting you, the non-psychoanalyst, with analytic concepts and

applications that you can use in your mental health practice, I believe the concepts of working through and insight might be summarized as follows. To begin with, today we respect intersubjectivity as a most effective form of analysis. The focus and center are still with the client, but you become a participant-observer and guide. The entire process is a mutual, conjoint adventure. You allow yourself to react emotionally to what you hear and observe and to share with the client your feelings about it. You don't give or produce insight in the patient by advising or telling her what to do; you merely facilitate it by gently concentrating on the point you believe the client should be aware of. The interplay between the subjectivity of the client and that of the therapist, as both become observer and observed in the interaction, facilitates and enriches the outcome—namely, insight leading to change and improvement. Intersubjectivity requires the Rogerian unconditional positive regard, mentioned earlier, including respect, tolerance, patience, compassion, and empathy.

The premise is that much of what the client does in this process is real and healthy, very different from the opposite tendency of finding pathology even in the most insignificant actions. Therefore, if the client does not accept the therapist's comments or insights, the therapist tries to understand patiently and empathically the client's point of view and meaning. In a sense, this is an effort to perceive reality through the lens of the patient, a difficult task that some people have described as an impossible occupation. I regard this avocation as more than just a profession because of its demands on time, effort, knowledge, experience, lifestyle, and self. Briefly, a vocation is something one does out of personal love and commitment, an occupation one believes one was born to fulfill. The demands on the therapist's time, effort, knowledge, and experience have been discussed throughout the book. Lifestyle and self, on the other hand, need clarification. If we expect the positive type of intersubjectivity described above, the therapist must have the "3G's"—he must be good, genuine, and generous. Without these qualities, his attempts at intersubjectivity will be fake and the therapist will live a lie.

All this sounds very preachy, but if you read about subjectivity, for instance in Stolorow et al. (1995) or Mitchell (2000), you'll find passion and a fervor for true authenticity.

Acting out

I like to concentrate on this aspect of the client's conduct in analysis because it is closely related to working through, and acting out often interferes with that. The previous concepts cover what happens in the process of self-transformation through psychoanalysis—basically, change through insight into action. Here we must look at what interferes with that health-oriented movement. From a different viewpoint, we are going to delve deeper into the familiar concept of resistance, because acting out is a negative reaction to the therapeutic effort, a distraction from insight that confirms the person in the mistaken notions that keep him neurotic. In this manner, acting out is closely related to the repetition compulsion, the unconscious urge that makes us revert to the past without realizing how much it drags us back.

The expression "acting out" has become so common in our language as a way of indicating an action with unconscious, usually hostile meaning, that it seems almost futile to linger on a definition of the term. It always has a neurotic connotation and it is most often used in a critical, condemning way. But to cut through all the theoretical nuances, it is fair to state that acting out is a behavioral expression of an unconscious conflict rather than an effort to understand it (insight) and take constructive action; it is an example of infantile (ego) functioning in lieu of mature (ego) functioning. It is an escape from facing the truth about something amiss in the individual. Here, it is relevant to point out that *lack*, in Lacanian language, or rather the remnants in adult life of that experience in early life, refers to the feared impossibility of ever having a full answer to the tension of the drive (the primitive needs of the child for attention, food, warmth, love, etc.) from the Other. This is, in part, the defensive aspect of acting out, as if the patient were saying, "I know that the analyst will not react (as I need him to) to my attempt at verbalizing what I don't know that afflicts me, so I have to be quiet." Yet because the unknown conflict is there it nevertheless comes out in the patient's behavior. This convoluted dynamic is what Freud (1905b) mentions for the first time in the famous postscript to his clinical report on his patient, Dora: "she *acted out* [emphasis in original] an essential part of her recollections and phantasies instead of reproducing it [*sic*] in the treatment" (p. 119).

In general, then, when you, as the therapist, deem what the client is doing or about to do to be acting out, you must help her to stop it because acting out always interferes with psychotherapy. That is why Fenichel (1945) insists on making the acting out egodystonic—so that the patient will find it undesirable and thus easier to stop. This is tricky, though, due to the fact that, for it to be effective, the patient has to perceive your interpretation as being genuine, constructive, and caring, not a command or prohibition. As a practical clinical comment, I find it helpful first to explain to the client my observations about what I consider her acting out, and then to inquire if other situations in the patient's life are or were handled in similar ways. This opens the door to the idea of repetition (the urge to reenact) as a form of solving "something" that is there but cannot be identified. In true acting out, the patient has unconsciously developed a modus operandi that appears in different settings but has the same underlying script as a way of trying to remember and understand the "something" that is bothering her. This approach often works, but if not it prepares the ground, as it were, because the next time that I observe similar acting out I can confront the patient again, referencing the earlier situation when I brought it up. And, by the way, if there is a modus operandi, it will show up again soon.

Returning to acting out, in old texts you may be puzzled to find a less familiar word, *parapraxis*, which is an involuntary mistake in our speech, our perceptions, or our understanding, among other mental activities. However, parapraxes are not instances of acting out. These are the daily errors that, yes, most frequently manifest the unconscious, but they are not characterological, that is, they are not necessarily related to important inner conflicts or unresolved primitive problems. What constitutes acting out, on the other hand, appears in Freud's clarifying footnote quoted above in reference to Dora. But to be precise we must note that Freud says she acted out only "an essential part," a portion, of her emotion-laden memories, instead of bringing all of them up in the analysis, which implies that acting out is never a solution but instead a neurotic pseudo-solution: instead of remembering in treatment what was repressed, she acts it out. In Freud's (1914b) words, "He reproduces it not as a memory but as an action; he *repeats* it without, of course, knowing that he is repeating it" (p. 150, original italics). Acting out becomes a metaphor of the repressed conflict; it is a metaphorical remembrance, which makes acting out a special form of resistance, and one not to be taken merely as simple resistance, or as transference for that matter. To repeat, acting out is different because, unlike resistance in general, it involves concrete repressed material and it is not necessarily or directly related to the therapist, as in transference. Simplifying the differences, we can say that neither all resistance nor all transference is acting out.

Therefore, acting out is a behavior that appears not merely in the therapy sessions but in life in general, just as transference does (see Chapter 6, for instance). Thus a man who is constantly boasting of his accomplishments and does not let you forget them could be considered an "acting-out character," as we used to call them in the past. What is he acting out? The need for analysis is obvious, because just by observing his behavior we cannot be sure. Nevertheless, his acting out could be a way of demanding the attention and validation he did not get as a child, as in the case of Titus in Chapter 11, or he could be competing in his mind with another person important in his life, either because that person represents someone from his past or because the real person is someone with whom he has a history of competition and rivalry. This simple illustration brings up another facet of this behavior, which is its language, its message. What is the subject unconsciously saying with his acting out? In the above mini vignette, he may be saying "I am capable, I am successful, I have accomplished a lot," and especially, "notice me, be impressed with me, feel honored to know me."

Another interesting point regarding acting out is its relation to what Freud (1905a) called perversion, which, among other things, can mean a special type of transference. In Freud's (1905a) studies on sexuality, perversion has the same structure as a symptom, but is different because the perversion is pleasurable and thus ego-syntonic; thus all perversions are symptoms but not vice versa. Then, almost twenty years later, Freud found aggressive impulses in perversions in addition to the obvious libidinal ones, thus depicting a reaction that can be either a defense against going crazy or one of the causes of psychosis. If it is true that the little boy fantasizes a penis where there is none in a woman, thus denying the difference of the sexes as a protection against the fear of castration, perversion follows that early traumatic experience. The fetish allows repression of the fear of castration and may act as a substitute for the (supposedly) non-existing penis. Lacanians like Nasio (1998) fix their attention on the

WORKING THROUGH AND ACTING OUT

very defense mechanism of denial in order to understand fetishism. In other words, by using a fetish, the individual can go through the fantasy of castration and then deny it and imagine what does not exist, the penis as a part of the female body. If adult sexuality has an intro-jective basis, as opposed to the projective basis of perverse sexuality (Meltzer 1973), we can agree with the connection between acting out and perversion. Thus not all acting out is perversion, but most perversion is acting out. As Dor (1999) asserts, "defiance and trans-gression are the only two possible outcomes for perverse desire" (p. 43), and both are frequently manifested as acting out; that is, they are recognized not by what patients verbally say about them but by their unconsciously motivated actions, which are always related to anxiety about sexual differences and to the mother's desire for the father, not for the child, as he had fantasized.

Now the same question we have asked many times before ap-pears again: What is the practical use for you of all this? I believe the most important point here is that, as a therapist, you must be ready for your client's acting out, and for the erotization of this. Otherwise, you will be taken by surprise and that may ruin any pos-sibility of constructive therapy thereafter.

The following was a supervision case of a beginning therapist, a young-looking woman in her fifties, who was working with a 39-year-old married male patient who had presented obsessive thoughts about his health interfering with his work and other activities but who firmly refused any medication, insisting that this was a mind problem. In the sessions, he kept staring at her crotch area and, a couple of times, she thought, with a slight smile. When she brought this up, he apologized and explained that he was not aware of it and might have been just thinking about the topic discussed in the ses-sion. But this was repeated several times in the following sessions, to the point that the therapist became very upset, not knowing what to do about it. She had questioned him concretely, saying that he was staring at that area of her body and she wanted to know what he was thinking when he did so. He kept denying anything amiss but continued to do the same thing. She invited him to lie down on the couch but he politely refused. When she brought this up in supervision, I found out that she had been embarrassed to mention it before, even though she had been bothered by it for over a month. She had not talked about this in her own therapy because "it was a topic for supervision," but she also was afraid of telling me about it. We discussed this over three supervision sessions. What happened was that the patient had finally confessed that he knew it was bizarre but he kept fantasizing that she had a phallus. He knew better, but his fantasies included the possibility that she was a male transvestite. He had become sexually aroused thinking about this outside of the therapy session. He was afraid that he was "becoming a homosexual" or, worse, that he was completely mad.

Before proceeding with the case, please put the book aside and take a brief moment to ask yourself what you would do in this instance if you had to deal with this client. Would you tell him that you wanted this stopped? Would you suggest some connection of his behavior with his childhood? Would you firmly ask him to cut it out?

Well, the first thing is not to take this personally. You would spend a few minutes educating the client, before proceeding with therapy. He has to know that this type of behavior is rather expected on his part, an indication of preoedipal issues, and that the resolution of these issues will help him in his progress to full maturity. You would put all this in your own words but you have to explain this eroticized acting out in terms of some lack in his normal sexual development. You would encourage him to talk in detail about his fantasies as if they were a dream. This usually makes it easier for the patient because a dream is something that just happens to me; I can't help it. Then, you would explain that what he experienced is a form of regression, telling him that at an earlier age he had these fantasies, curiosities, and doubts that, unfortunately, were not resolved at the time. Now is the moment to start resolving, and working through, what has not yet been worked out and understood. You would remind him that the way to do this now is to let himself talk about the fantasies that are related to his curiosity of the past. This is working through. Probably the patient will mention his questions about sexual differences that he had as a little child and that were repressed for all these years. Notice that this curiosity is not intellectual (he knows about all this as an adult), but also not rational, as it was experienced (and repressed) in the past. When he starts to verbalize all this, you pay attention to his feelings, encourage him to do the same, and to accept the regressive emotions that come up. Again, this is working through.

From all of the above, you understand how important it is to have a clear grasp on the concepts described in this chapter, working through and acting out, with all the ramifications into transference, regression, perversion, and related concepts. If you intend to use psychoanalytic methods, you must consider the concepts set out in this and the previous chapter very carefully. These concepts cannot be foreign to you.

To sum up

This chapter and Chapter 13 cover the analytic process. What they include and discuss are basic elements of what a psychoanalyst does in his clinical work, and the difficulties to which he must accommodate in order to persevere in the clinical process. I believe that these two chapters, more perhaps than the rest of the book, may persuade you of a view I have mentioned several times: that to be a psychoanalyst it is necessary to have gone through the experience of analysis as a patient. But I also insist on the whole premise of the book: you can do a lot of good for the clients you see by working with the unconscious. Just to be aware of the unconscious and of its workings can motivate people to seriously work through their problems.

The working alliance cannot exist unless you make the decision to work on your issues. The equivalent of the working alliance for the one who wants to benefit from psychoanalysis on her own is a strong motivation and commitment. After all, we have the example of Freud himself and the record of his self-analysis in *The Interpretation of Dreams* (1900). Not that many can be as thorough and honest in their introspection, but theoretically they can benefit from the exercise. Ticho (1967) studies self-analysis, following M. K. Kramer (1959), who described the process after the person has gone through regular sessions. She has this comment: "It is an interesting phenomenon that the science of psychoanalysis, which owes so much to the self-analysis of its creator, largely disregards self-analysis in its literature" (p. 308). Unfortunately, people can also harm themselves with this practice. In attempting self-analysis, one faces one's own resistance, together with the surprisingly strong feelings of frustration, anger, shame, and guilt, just to mention a few. The labor is arduous, painful, and long. Often the resistance takes on many forms, at one time that of regression, at another the mode of acting out. Again, one can monitor this on one's own, but it is hard and it tends to become a full-time job, often straining one's relationship with those who are close. In this process, the resistance, as in ordinary analysis with the help of a trained therapist, goes against one's preferred interpretations of one's actions, thoughts, fantasies, and so on.

I describe this because of my own experience. When living in California after my own analysis in Buenos Aires, I tried self-analysis.

I planned it carefully and dedicated to the task one entire hour a day, seven days a week, for three months. I benefited from it, no doubt, but it became so difficult that I gave up on the ninety-fifth day of my effort. Then I moved to New York and found myself a good analyst to help me; I stayed with him for almost eight years. One of my friends put it succinctly in this question: "Unless you are specially gifted, why would you try to learn a musical instrument by yourself, without the help of a teacher?" Even though I regularly use analytical introspection, I have given up on self-analysis and I do not recommend it. It may be useful for research but not necessarily so for personal growth and enrichment.

Chapter 15
PSYCHOANALYSIS AND THE GOOD LIFE

In a materialistic culture like ours, a person is considered to live the good life when he or she has an abundance of possessions and high social rank, and many privileges. By contrast, philosophers in practically every age and culture, from the earliest Buddhists to the Greeks and Romans, from biblical times to ours, point to a higher level of satisfaction as a condition of living the good life. As I see it, a good life is recognized by what the person is, not by what he or she has. To understand this better, we can look at what psychoanalysts consider the successful result of treatment (see Fromm 1976).

Definitions

The good life is not just a matter of having all drives satisfied (although this seems to be the goal of our current culture), but goes "beyond the pleasure principle," as Chapter 7 hints when dealing on the "nonmaterial" side of being human. Freud (1923a) himself, describing the outcome of analysis, namely the new personality characteristics required to live the good life, emphasizes "secure[ing] the best possible psychological conditions for the functions of the ego

. . . bring[ing] about the most far-reaching unification and strengthening of his ego . . . to make him [the analyzed person] as efficient
and as capable of enjoyment as is possible" (pp. 250–251). This brings
to mind one of Lacan's central concepts, *jouissance*, which he likes to
leave untranslated because of its French nuance of joy and lust, which
also goes "beyond the pleasure principle."

We have another solid source to help us understand who is
ready and capable to live the good life. This is the report (Panel
1969) in an article by Firestein, on some limited research conducted
with senior analysts of one of the most reputable training institutes
in the U.S. regarding what a successful analysis had accomplished.
The responses fell into three categories: object relations, ego
and superego health, and "the pattern of symptoms." A quotation
from the article, confusedly entitled "Problems of Termination,"
follows:

Under the rubric of object relationships [*sic*] the analyst views
1. the level of psychosexual maturation;
2. the degree of impeding transference distortion; and
3. the capacity to experience pleasure without guilt or other
inhibiting factors.

Additional views of ego and superego are provided by
4. the degree of energy depletion by overly energetic defenses;
5. the ability to work productively and
6. to tolerate gratification delay;
7. sharpened capacity to distinguish fantasy from reality;
8. strengthened capacity to tolerate some measure of anxiety and
to reduce other unpleasant affects to signal quantities; and
9. the stability of sublimations.

Although
10. the pattern of symptoms is least heavily relied upon, despite
the patient's greater interest in this aspect of himself, one

> naturally pays some attention to significant reduction of this factor. [p. 225]

Three years later, in the same journal, Dewald (1972) buttressed the previous list with a series of clinical examples.

From all this, we deduce that the good life is possible if a person can be her true self, having removed the obstacles to her potentialities, creativity, and uniqueness. What a challenge to education—from pre-kindergarten to college! However, as we realize, there is no emphasis here on the individual in relationship to the world and the universe at large. This is an important point, and as psychoanalysis has been in a process of change and improvement since its beginnings, we find that early on one of the first luminaries in Freud's inner circle, Carl G. Jung, filled this gap.

An old friend to the rescue

Jung was searching for the connections that the individual actually had or would benefit from having with others, with nature, and with the entire universe. As I said in Chapter 3, Freud had been close to Carl Jung and had thought of him as his successor. Regarding their closeness, one of many quotes from his letters (McGuire 1974) dated March 1909 to Jung says it all: "I have no need to tell you how much such meetings with you mean to me both professionally and personally" (p. 135). Jung, on his part, saw in Freud not merely a friend but a master and mentor, a father figure. Thanks to Carotenuto (1982), an authority on Jung, we have the correspondence, including over thirty letters between the two famous men with some referring to Sabina Spielrein, together with her diary of that period (1909–1914). These provide a detailed narrative of this fascinating story. By the way, all these evidentiary documents were found only in 1955. Spielrein, a medical student in Zurich, was a quite disturbed patient of Jung's about whom he consulted with Freud. Carotenuto gives us the story of the woman who had an important influence on the early years of psychoanalysis and who, we now know, was caught in the middle of the break between the two friends. Their story is closely interwoven with the very lively presence of this patient. The transferential dynamics between Jung and Spielrein made the younger, inexperienced analyst request the help of the master. Spielrein also wrote to Freud when her transference to Jung became too difficult to handle. And all this was taking place close to the time when the break between the two men started to happen. Even after the break, in 1913–1914, she was in written communication with Freud. Interestingly enough, though initially diagnosed as psychotic, she became well and finished her studies and obtained her medical diploma, after which she trained in psychoanalysis, and returned to her native Russia. She had married in 1912, had two daughters, and later practiced psychoanalysis in Russia until 1942 when she and her young daughters were killed by Nazi soldiers because they were Jewish.

This long detour from our discussion of psychoanalysis and the good life is intended to introduce Carl Jung as someone who expanded Freud's ideas, although, strangely, he seems to be considered an outsider to psychoanalysis by many in the field. (The punishment of excommunication for his apostasy?) As I have mentioned, Jung was a committed believer in the unconscious and found in it what he called archetypes, as part of our personalities. These are repeated themes (religious, artistic, and cultural) that appear again and again through time in many civilizations, and make up a collective unconscious that resonates in us as humans. Think of such well-known stories as those of Siegfried and the dragon, part of the *Niebelung*, or *The Lord of the Rings*, among the many other myths so well researched and explained by Joseph Campbell (1968), who makes many references to both Freud and Jung. Through this expanded view of the unconscious, Jung leads us to our connection with the whole universe. What Freud refers to as the healthy ego, Jung calls self-actualization; it is the ongoing act of living up to our full potential, in both cases considered possible because of the attention paid to the unconscious. In comparing these two concepts, healthy ego and self-fulfillment, one recognizes that the difference between them is mostly semantic, though the emphasis is different, with Jung stressing what humans have in common and Freud what makes the individual unique.

Psychoanalytic elements in the New Age?

Much of what we understand as "New Age" thought uses Jungian and Freudian psychoanalytic themes. (By the way, remember that Jungians prefer the expression *analytical psychology*, instead of psychoanalysis). Take, for instance, imagination; Jung called active imagination what I consider "new hypnosis," as discussed in Chapter 8, and what Freud called general fantasy. The greater the use of active imagination, the easier it is for the person to change positively. Another difference: in classical Freudian theory the id acts on the pleasure principle and the ego on the reality principle. For Jung the id or fantasy principle, which stresses the creative imagination, is the source from which art as well as the discovery of new truths (science) come. In Jungian analysis, imagination is constantly encouraged and utilized to make psychic connections and to visualize the new self in the future. In fact, for the individual, imagination is more real than reality itself, a concept that is a familiar one for Freud also. Because of this belief Jungians, perhaps more insistently than Freudians, emphasize the analysis of fantasies, mental images, and visualizations, as well as reveries and dreams.

As I explained in Chapter 8, the use of reverie and any type of mental imagery aids the psychoanalytic work and facilitates insight. If we consider dreams important, we may consider our work with the new hypnosis on the same level as working with "daydreams," or as it is called in French, *rêve éveillé*, with the emphasis on dreaming, even though one is awake. Thus we can intensify and multiply our dreaming, tapping the unconscious for our benefit.

If we turn our attention to New Age thought, we find that among its good points are its stress on a positive psychology. They also inject, through repetition and visualization, productive and constructive messages into the unconscious. Just as people tend to become hate-mongers in an environment of hate, so too they tend to become positive in an optimistic milieu. Realistic positive thinking allows one to create one's own beneficial environment. As an example, instead of saying "I can't" and believing it, one can change his self-talk to "I haven't learned yet" and believe that he is not up against a stone wall. Brainwashing, is a systematic method of seeding negative, hateful, thoughts into the unconscious of a prisoner or victim; and it works often all too well. To encourage people, even analytic clients, to repeat to themselves positive messages while imagining a situation that was considered difficult or impossible before (a process I have tested with patients), brings about positive results. One thing I found out is that those who do this offer less resistance and report more constructive dreams, becoming more seriously involved in their psychotherapy. Is this a way of making the process of working through move along more smoothly? From my experience, the answer is affirmative. This is a psychoanalytic technique because it is trying to influence the unconscious; it also might work for your clients as it has worked for mine. It has a strong Jungian flavor and it deserves to be tried and tested.

Another aspect of New Age thought that comes from Jungian analysis, perhaps without those who propose it knowing that it has a psychoanalytic origin, is a greater social consciousness and awareness. I say greater in comparison with most people in comfortable cultural environments. The circle of object relations is enlarged and enriched. This happens through an understanding that the self has more in common with other human beings than what is different. The person is encouraged to recognize as many physical, social, and psychological elements in common with all other human beings and not to take for granted any of those characteristics. Appreciating and not taking for granted is an important concept in New Age practice.

Practical psychoanalysis

One aspect of psychoanalytic thinking is the general idea of helping ourselves and our patients with techniques that affect the unconscious, whether they come from Jung or not. A few examples may suffice to activate our imagination.

1. Always take advantage of mental rehearsal (Chapter 8) when you have to do something difficult so that you imagine yourself doing it well. You may face the real task with new confidence.

2. Catch yourself when you start using negative self-hypnosis or any other form of negativism like being overly critical, ignoring positive aspects of an unpleasant situation or person, or , engaging in self-pity. You will lower your stress and feel happier.

3. With some frequency, do something for another person that you could avoid doing. This can help you get out of being neurotically self-centered.

4. Purposely try something new, of some difficulty, that you do not particularly like. This may awaken your spirit of adventure.

5. Keep a diary; it may bring much unconscious information about yourself to consciousness.

6. Compose a list of power thoughts (thoughts that are true about you and your life, that give you a sense of energy,

power, and well-being). Pep talks work for a short while in many team sports. Power thoughts perhaps help patients to get out of a negativistic mood for a little while.

I hope you get the idea, which is to learn to profit from deliberately using your unconscious for your own benefit, and that you may also teach your patients to do the same. I often wonder why some psychoanalysts disregard these techniques as simplistic, superficial nonsense. If we pride ourselves on being open-minded, we can try them as an experiment—to be discarded if they do not work but to be kept if they do. They can become an aid and facilitate the influence of the unconscious in our lives. Yes, it would be absurd to even suggest that these techniques are a panacea, or that with them you don't need therapy and especially analysis. I do consider them as ancillary to analysis, nothing else. But this word signifies that these meta-analytic techniques serve us (*ancilla* in Latin means female servant). All the above-mentioned psychological exercises can be helpful and useful for ego strengthening. Look at it this way: one of the classical reasons given for seeking analysis is that the "emotionally ill" person is unable, because of his weak ego, to bring back to consciousness what had been repressed. His unconscious inner drives produce fear and apprehension and his superego is either too strict and demanding or too weak and passive. Therefore, the patient's ego has to become stronger or has to be empowered so that he can face his own unconscious with the id drives and the repressed parts of the self and past experiences. It is true that this simplistic classical formulation is much richer in current psychoanalysis. However, the central hypothesis of a weakened ego still holds. This is what explains the success of hypnotic work in analysis (Wolberg 1945): it serves to strengthen the ego. And, again, this is why the techniques mentioned above can become a substantial means of buttressing the patient's ego, especially when you suggest them to your client as a means of continuing the analytic work between sessions. When this is done, the self is finally freed to fulfill the basic psychological needs in an adaptive form. This affects positively all areas of human functioning in expanding circles, starting with the mature satisfaction of personal needs and positive relations with others—family, friends, coworkers, and service people, as well as connection with society at large: community, nation, world; and finally in relation with nature, from the immediate moment to the vast universe. Thus, I feel that any reasonable tactic that contributes to these ends deserves to be considered, because most analysts will agree that the strengthening of the patient's ego is related to the progress made in analysis; the stronger the ego, the more progress. Therefore, any reasonable maneuvers converging to this end and aiding the purpose of psychoanalysis are welcomed.

I believe in our responsibility to make psychoanalysis practical by teaching people in general and patients in particular that all these things mentioned here fit well into analytic thinking.

Chapter 16
REALITY, PSYCHODYNAMICS, AND SEX

Those who don't know much about psychoanalysis are quick to criticize things that they don't understand. This chapter tries to clarify some areas of basic confusion, such as the special interest in sexuality that we do not find in other therapies. Part of the problem is that a literal understanding of many of Freud's terms fails to grasp the validity of the concepts behind the words, with sexual functions being a central example of this literalism, in which toilet training, for instance, is seen as being symbolic of the first inklings of self-control, and not considered primarily as a physical activity. In the same way, reality and ego functions are often taken literally, as if Freud were teaching us that ego should absolutely dominate human actions and life, when his belief and intention was to have a balance between ego and id, as Lacan's (1977) discourse on *jouissance* seems to indicate. Freud's cryptic statement on replacing the id with the ego applies when the id is dominating and controlling the personality. But it needs to be complemented with the opposite statement in cases when the ego becomes a rigid structure because of a severe superego. These two areas of misunderstanding are explained by the inner forces at work—the psychodynamics.

Reality

In psychoanalysis we are often dealing with two realities, the material and the psychic. From our point of view, psychic reality is the main focus of concern because it exists due to the fantasies, imagination, beliefs, and other subjective experiences of the individual; in the things beyond the seen, as I said at the beginning of the book. We can state that in order to study and work with subjectivity we need to stay in the psychic reality, as Freud (1905b) discovered in the vastly discussed and studied case of Dora, which became a turning point in his thought. Newirth (2003) puts it with masterful precision:

> This dialectical conceptualization of material and psychic reality maintained a tension between the scientific and the moral or romantic viewpoints, freeing psychoanalysis from the constraints of a simple learning theory, and focusing attention on the complex relationship between and inner psychic organization and the individual's actions and experiences in the external world. [p. 50]

Dialectical conceptualization seems to refer to Hegel's "dialectical inversion" of thesis, antithesis, and synthesis. A very simple example would be a patient who, with a depressed voice and expression, says that the weather is nice after a whole week of rain ("thesis"). You respond that his voice does not sound cheerful ("antithesis"), expanding his awareness. He responds, "You're right, I have a good reason to be more cheerful" ("synthesis"), and in doing so the patient accepts the dialectical inversion, which becomes a new thesis: in this case, that he can, must, will, show his cheerfulness and cut out his depressive tone of voice. Thus in analysis we have the thesis, or what the patient says or does; the antithesis, or the analyst's interpretation; and the synthesis, or the patient's response that becomes the new thesis, and so on in the dialectic interrelationship. The application (in psychoanalysis) of this Hegelian dialectic to material and psychic reality, simply put, means that we always try, first, to find the psychic reality in any manifestation of the patient's material reality; and, second, that we propose it to the patient, who, when integrating it, obtains a new truth about herself. This method reveals a tremendous respect for and acceptance of the patient's unconscious dynamics and mental productions, from opinions and simple reactions to wishes, fantasies, and all sorts of feelings. This helps the client move from fixed and unchangeable perceptions, reactions, and decisions to symbolic and metaphorical ones, thus enriching the patient and elevating her to a new and refreshing level of functioning (mentally, emotionally, and spiritually—that is, psychically). But the same process helps and enriches the analyst too, when greater cognitive and emotional flexibility is obtained by a process of reflection similar to the much-recommended mindfulness attitude that enjoys everything in every moment.

By insisting on the psychic reality, we try to genuinely connect with the patient's experiences and to enter into his world without intrusion, entitlement, or arrogance. One important part of this other's world is the entire area of sexuality. This includes the six levels, mentioned in Chapter 9, all meaningful for every human being. To review, the six sexual levels (Araoz 2005) are sexual identification (one's innermost gender); sexual orientation (one's attraction to other people); sexual, erotic preferences (things, from sounds and smells to activities and sensory stimulation that help the individual to become aroused); functioning (the five stages of sexual response, from desire to climax and completion, passing through arousal, foreplay, plateau, and climax); cultural and social gender expectations (the ex-tent of one's activities, as established by one's culture merely because one is male or female, such as crying, dressing, etc.); and finally, significance (the meaning of sexual activity, from simple physical relief to that of a spiritual union, as in the Eastern Tantric tradition). The following section concentrates on the dynamics of sexuality as they relate to psychoanalytical thinking and practice.

Sexuality

Many who know very little about psychoanalysis believe that sex is at the center of it. Of course, they mean sexual activities, as most people do when they hear the word sex, or what more technically we call sexual functioning. The fact is that sexuality is, indeed, cen-tral in the experience of being human. Because of the important place of sexuality in psychoanalytic thinking, it is necessary to clarify this point. You'll realize that this perspective provides a sense of libera-tion in a topic that our culture either represses or mishandles.

The most obvious sexual organ is the penis. The vulva is not as externally obvious and not as mysterious. The mystery associated with the penis lies in its ability to change, almost with a life and en-ergy of its own, as in the erection. The problem starts with the sexual differences that humans ordinarily notice as babies and toddlers and misinterpret. This confusion, however, remains unconscious to us until later, after it has been repressed. Here, what needs to be clari-fied are the meanings of terms like castration fear and castration complex, penis envy, Oedipus complex, and other such popular psy-choanalytic terms. From the start, we have to understand and not forget that these terms refer to the realm of psychic reality that we discussed earlier. The little boy becomes familiar with his penis very early, making this organ significant and important for him. But, as he perceives, his mother, his little female friends and his sisters and cousins, if any, lack this precious commodity. Still unconsciously, he is confused and wonders what happened, while the little girl fantasizes that she must have had a penis but lost it owing to the machinations of others and becomes envious. And here is where the fantasy of castration comes up. We know that the term is unfortunate on many counts; first, it is inexact, since the fantasy refers more exactly to the penis and not to the testicles (castration meaning the surgical—no matter how primitive—removal of the testes); the term is also too bloody, invasive, and frightening. But nevertheless, the word *castration* is used as a symbol referring to a complex and difficult experience of our life that shapes our self-image and our gender. What castration really refers to is the absence of a valuable organ that supposedly was there or might be taken away. The boy would verbalize this by stating, "I have it, but it can be taken away," and the girl would say, "I had it and it was taken way." Those studying different cultures have reported quite frequently on infant behavior (Edwardes and Masters 1963) consisting, among others, of little girls focusing on the male baby's penis with which they play, often pulling and pinching it to the point of hurting the baby.

The sexual difference contributing to our gender identification is therefore more than a chromosomal reality, although it may be rooted in that. For us, it is important to understand sexual difference as a cultural, psychological, and characterological phenomenon. We all go through this traumatic and fantasy event of discovering the sexual differences, of fearing in confusion their significance, and of reacting with awe to the father who, for the boy, might take away his penis and for the girl may insist on having it taken away from her. To emphasize the active role of fantasy in all this, the name given to the mental representation of this conundrum centered in the penis is the *phallus*. This Latin word with Greek roots was used in antiquity to designate the generative forces of nature, and symbols of the phallus were used in celebrations of spring, the harvest, and the birth of children (we still have the custom of fathers offering cigars to friends after the birth of children). Freud (1923b) stated that "for both sexes, only one genital, namely the male one, comes into account. What is present, therefore, is not primacy of the genitals, but a primacy of the phallus" (p. 142). He was not aware of current biological data, obviously, but the symbolic meaning of the phallus is clear. Therefore, when one sees "phallic" mentioned in early psychoanalytic literature, the reference is to the penis in the male and the clitoris in the female, perhaps derived from the embryonic reality in early gestation. However, the metaphoric use of "phallic" also has to do with personality traits that were considered typically male, such as power, aggression, and such. In the literature we find terms like phallic character or personality, phallic mother and phallic woman, phallic narcissism, phallic phase, and so on. I invite you to briefly review this symbolic language.

Ernest Jones (1933), a man Freud trusted, discussed the phallic stage; later, Edgcumbe and Burgner (1975) called it "the phallic narcissistic phase," both preoedipal, and mainly indicates an over-concern with the penis. Here also we find phallic pride and narcissism, said to compensate for the castration fear. If this focus on the penis continues into adulthood, we have the phallic character, which indicates a defense against the anxiety of the oedipal stage and was supposedly found also in women, though less than in men. In this case, the person unconsciously perceives his body as a phallus and equates body functions like urinating or spitting with sexual functions (ejaculation), according to Lewin (1933). Remember that all this is unconscious symbolic fantasy on the part of the patient. I wonder how much the analysts of that era shared in this fantasy and how much nowadays erection medications contribute to the phallic character. The terms *phallic mother* and the *phallic woman*

(Bak 1968) were initially applied to the childhood fantasy (in the phallic phase) that the mother had a penis. This unconscious fantasy is later applied to women who seem to be overly assertive, aggressive, and threatening.

The point of briefly reviewing all these strange and at times esoteric expressions is to remind ourselves that sex does occupy a vital position in the experience of being human and that Freud did not run away from this, nor did his disciples and followers. It is not true to state that psychoanalysis is overly involved with sex, or at least no more than other "schools of thought" that are overly concerned with repressing anything sexual, as for example during Victorian times, which coincided with Freud's early work. But *la chose sexuelle* is never isolated and relates to a host of other psychic dynamics, which brings us to the understanding of psychodynamics.

Psychodynamics

Everything that begins in the mind, such as feelings, memories, and reactions to external stimuli, even though they may be elicited by the body, as when I burn my tongue and feel annoyed, or when I hear a strange sound and react with apprehension, is in the realm of the *psychodynamic*. When I say that it "begins in the mind," I am approaching a construct that is difficult to explain, since there is no mind until there is mind. In other words, we talk about mind when we become aware of a thought or feeling. This is because the mind is not an organ or a site in the brain, but the manifestation of an internal capacity to feel, think, plan, foresee, recall, and more. Freud made it easier to understand with the construct of the three personality parts, so that we can attribute some psychodynamics to the id, others to the ego, and still others to the superego. Thus, the sexual psychodynamics of the id are mostly desire and coveting, involving impulsive action and pleasure, or urge satisfaction. The ego sexual psychodynamics are caring for the other, courtesy, accommodation to the partner's wishes, trust, and mutuality. Finally, the superego in human sexuality produces psychodynamics related to respect, spirituality, generosity, and love. In any one particular sexual encounter, you may find a confusing multitude of psychodynamics intermingling, crossing, supporting, or contradicting each other.

Consequently the concept of psychodynamics is essential in order to grasp what both sexuality and reality mean in analytic thinking. The practical application of this is reflected in the attitude of the psychoanalyst who makes an effort to understand the psychic reality of the patient's attitude, accepting it nonjudgmentally. Moreover, the analyst's perception of any sexual material in the process of therapy always transcends the mere literal meaning and embraces the symbolism of things sexual, trying to reach the emotional meaning of it. In these two reactions the psychoanalyst is in tune with the psychodynamics of the client which are at the core of the cure in the psychoanalytic process.

CONCLUSION AND ENDING THOUGHTS

As the list of Suggested Readings implies, psychoanalysis is such an immense area of knowledge that no single book will make anyone an expert in it. I hope that *The Symptom Is Not the Whole Story* provides you with a good introduction to this rich and difficult topic, so popular and so misunderstood. No matter how much a book covers, there is always much more to say about the clinical application of psychoanalytic concepts. For instance, I have said practically nothing about two important aspects in the use of psychoanalysis—the large areas of diagnosis and supervision.

Supervision

Briefly, supervision is an essential component of psychoanalytic psychotherapy for all beginners. Even senior practitioners like me need consultation. The supervisor must be a legitimate analyst, someone experienced and well-versed in psychoanalysis in order to help the therapist work with what is below the surface, besides concentrating on the symptom and the presenting problem. Therefore, supervision must take place regularly, at least once a week for novices who are carrying a load of fifteen to twenty therapy sessions. Later, the supervision meetings can be reduced to two a month, and with more practice even to once monthly. For more advanced clinicians, supervision often takes the form of collegial consultation and it happens naturally and less regularly. Many seasoned clinicians often consult a colleague that they respect when they have a specific difficulty or question, as Jung did with Freud. Personally, I also religiously attend a small group of colleagues that meets once a month (the sum total of our experience is over 250 years of practice), and I participate in clinical workshops (lasting from half a day to two days) at a minimum rate of four a year. The continuing education hours that many states require in order to keep one's professional license gives us the incentive to take advantage of these offerings and allows us a choice of clinical topics we are interested in. Unfortunately, few offerings include psychoanalysis.

One important point about supervision is that it is only meaningful for both the supervisor and the therapist when the therapist being supervised has had psychoanalytic therapy. Without it, supervision is a waste of time, just as it would be if the supervisor did not have any training in psychotherapy. As I have stated before, a psychotherapist (insight-oriented) who has not had personal therapy is truly not trained to practice what she is trying to do. By now we know that training in psychoanalytic therapy is not merely an intellectual pursuit; it also has to be experiential. This is why, before I accept a therapist for supervision, I make sure that he has had the valuable experience of his own introspective and analytic psychotherapy. A knowledge of the concepts discussed in this book is necessary before one can begin to apply psychoanalytic concepts in therapy. After having learned what this book presents, the beginning psychoanalytic therapist must find someone she respects and trusts from whom to accept supervision, almost as an extension of her psychotherapy. This is because true supervision does not center on technique, plans of action, and immediate results; rather it considers seriously the therapist's reactions, feelings, and clinical behavior. For more on supervision, a good source is Frawley-O'Dea and Sarnat (2001). Supervision is also an extension of one's training in therapy; books, articles, and conferences are recommended to the supervisee, to be discussed at a future session, as part of supervision.

Diagnosis

In psychoanalytic psychotherapy, diagnosis has a meaning that is different from that of the *Diagnostic and Statistical Manual* (2000), with which all U.S. mental health workers are obliged to be familiar. The *DSM* concentrates on the symptoms and considers the "disorder" cured when the symptoms disappear. Psychoanalytic diagnosis always goes beyond the symptomatology. It considers the development of the patient's personality and its effects on his behavior, perception, beliefs, reactions, his explanation of his world, and all his interactions. McWilliams (1994) treats this issue masterfully. Most people agree that without diagnosis, treatment does not make sense because treatment should be directed to a goal. But the analytical goal is the personality itself, whereas the DSM goal is the behavior. For us, diagnosis does not need to be a label or a categorization that places the client in a pigeonhole. In psychoanalysis it is important to have a much broader view, including cultural, ethnic, religious, occupational, and especially relational variables, as well as what is or is not age appropriate.

How can I, then, recommend techniques of treatment in the book, when I do not specify the diagnosis for which they might apply? Before answering this question I must remind you that what the *DSM* represents as diagnosis has very little to do with the traditional diagnostic formulation of types of mental and emotional suffering we find in psychoanalysis. The *DSM* categorizes with labels, as scientists do when labeling characteristics of animal or plant species, the symptoms of psychological human pain. There is no developmental perspective, nor is there an awareness of the relation between the self and the Other, as explained the section on metapsychology in Chapter 12.

With this in mind, my response to the question posed earlier about proposing techniques without a clear diagnosis is twofold. First, in psychoanalytic work there is no rush to come up with a diagnosis; you develop the diagnosis in time as you consider all those variables mentioned above. And second, because the techniques I have proposed are general ones (I call them "master key techniques") that encourage introspection and test the possibility of change, a formal diagnosis is less necessary. Consequently, in the way a master key opens many doors, these techniques can be safely applied to many different conditions.

*   *   *

As with all books, the number of pages, complexity of the subject matter, and the intended readership have all imposed limitations on this one. The story I am telling had to confine itself, and I trust the above comments explain the volume's limitations. I wrote this book as an introductory text for non-psychoanalytic therapists interested in psychoanalysis, and so decided it should not encompass all practical aspects of this extensive field, and thus it did not include discussions on research, ethics, areas of special difficulty, and psychoanalytic thinking in everyday life, among others.

I will consider myself lucky and satisfied if readers find the book helpful in their work with clients, and especially if their clinical efforts are enriched with this, for them, new approach of psychoanalysis.

SUGGESTED READINGS

My advice is that you keep this list in mind in order to proceed systematically. You will notice that, in line with the general orientation of this volume, I have selected books that are eminently practical and useful for clinical practice. They all are strong in the theory they follow but they are not theoretical formulations as such.

I also suggest that you read the following books in this sequence. One will help you to learn more from the next volume. Consider this progression of knowledge as part of your preparation to become an effective psychoanalytic psychotherapist. I must confess that my conscious intention is that you may want to become fully trained as a psychoanalyst. That is, that you may want to invest four years of your life to become a psychoanalyst. You can consider the following list as a basic preparation for fully certified training in psychoanalysis.

Here is the list:

MCWILLIAMS, N. (2004). *Psychoanalytic Psychotherapy: A Practitioners Guide*. New York: Guilford. Although the book is useful for advanced practitioners, it is written in such an uncomplicated style and manner that beginners will find it very helpful. Dr. Nancy McWilliams covers every possible aspect of psychoanalytic practice, from different forms of resistance to countertransference. Her outlook, as a psychologist and as a woman, is very enriching. Common sense combined with solid theory may well summarize her contribution to the field. My book prepares the reader for the vast open field Nancy McWilliams presents.

FRATTAROLI, E. (2001). *Healing the Soul in the Age of the Brain*. New York: Penguin. This is a joyful and refreshing approach to psychoanalytic therapy by a uniquely well-trained and experienced psychiatrist/psychoanalyst. Focusing on Freud's classical approach to psychoanalysis, Dr. Frattaroli presents a strong case against the current rage to cure with pills. His honesty and openness about himself as a psychotherapist offers a good example of modern-day psychoanalytical practice. This is must reading for all current clinicians, especially beginners.

BREUER, J., AND FREUD, S. (1895). *Studies in Hysteria*. New York: Basic Books, 2000. This is a classic that has seen many editions, like this one from Basic Books, which has a glorious foreword by Irvin Yalom, MD. This book is one of the ways we can come closest to Freud as he is doing psychotherapy. I have read the *Studies* more than six times, finding in every reading new insights and inspiration. Perhaps it is extreme for me to say so, but I believe that nobody should dare to enter the intimate work of psychotherapy without having read this gem.

GREENSON, R. R. (1967). *The Technique and Practice of Psychoanalysis*. New York: International Universities Press. This is called "Volume First." Edited by his admirers, Volume Second came out several years after Ralph's death. I consider this volume one of the best for clinical practice. Filled with practical observations and encouraging the reader to look into him- or herself as the clinical work progresses, Greenson's book is like a "manual" that one has to keep ready to hand all the time if one wants to proceed correctly. It should be read after *Studies in Hysteria*.

SULLIVAN, H. S. (1953). *The Interpersonal Theory of Psychiatry*. New York: Norton. Harry Stack Sullivan, MD, is the first 100 percent American psychoanalyst, meaning that he did not train in Europe. Greenson and Sullivan complement each other with regard to the way to do psychotherapy. His advice to beginners and seasoned psychoanalysts is as valuable today as it was sixty years ago. The interest in the patient that is so evident in his approach is refreshing, inspiring, and constantly applicable in our clinical work.

REIK, T. (1948). *Listening with the Third Ear: The Inner Experience of a Psychoanalyst*. New York: Farrar, Straus. I had a hard time deciding whether Theodore Reik should come before or after Greenson and Sullivan. The reason I place his book in the list at this point is because of his refreshing, commonsensical attitude toward psychological healing. Reik's erudition and cultural sensitivity make him a role-model for all of us: we cannot ignore what is happening around us in the world. His focus on what he personally experiences is very useful, especially for the beginner psychoanalytic therapist, and helps clinicians learn how to hold on to their own identity.

HORNEY, K. (1950). *Neurosis and Human Growth*. New York: Norton. Karen Horney was a medical psychoanalyst (psychiatrist) who had a brilliant and open mind, a caring heart, and an empathic sensitivity with her patients. She makes psychoanalysis relevant. She teaches us how to be helpful to our patients. You'll find in her pages many very practical points for clinical work. Her application of psychoanalysis to modern life can still become a model for clinicians today. This is the crowning work of a lifetime of dedication to the basic psychoanalytic principles.

FROMM, E. (1973). *The Anatomy of Human Destructiveness*. New York: Henry Holt. Erich Fromm is unique in his clear and very comprehensive psychoanalytic explanation of many aspects of human nature. All his many books are full of wisdom, erudition, and common sense. This book is especially important because he concentrates on the problem of evil and studies it from different angles and levels. Many patients are self-destructive, and Fromm not only gives us unique insights into their condition, but also proposes effective and doable psychoanalytic ways of dealing with them.

SIEGEL, A. M. (1996). *Heinz Kohut and the Psychology of the Self*. Philadelphia: Brunner-Routledge. Because self psychology, with its roots in object relations, has presented such an important development in psychoanalysis, it is imperative that you know about it. This is an in-depth study of Kohut's theories and clinical applications and, as such, it deserves careful attention by the clinician who is interested in psychoanalysis. Not to know about self psychology today is to be handicapped as a practitioner of psychoanalytic psychotherapy. Allen Siegel's book is unique in that he "translates" many of the difficult theoretical formulations into clear methods and procedures for practice. You'll find here many wonderful examples of psychoanalytic work.

SAUL, L. (1972). *Psychodynamically Based Psychotherapy*. New York: Science House. The uniqueness of this classic book by Leon Saul is that the second half is devoted to clinical material, namely verbatim records of two analytic cases, one covering twenty-one sessions and the other 189 hours. Especially for someone who has not been in analysis as such, this reading gives a good taste of what this is all about.

MOLINO, A., ed. (1998). *The Couch and the Tree: Dialogues in Psychoanalysis and Buddhism*. New York: North Point Press. I add Anthony Molino's book to my list of suggested readings because it gives you a refreshing understanding of the value of psychoanalysis when compared to other (Oriental) ways of looking at human nature. My concept of psychoanalysis being the Zen of the West is superbly justified in this volume: the more we know ourselves, the better we can help other human beings in their quest for meaning and happiness, productivity and social usefulness.

EPILOGUE

I first met Daniel Araoz in the 1970s when I was on the board of the New York City Personnel and Guidance Association. Decades later, when attending the annual awards ceremony of the Long Island Association for Marriage and Family Therapy, I met him again and we became reacquainted. Because I consider him a friend, mentor, and colleague, I am happy to add my comments on this new book of his, which I found most appropriate for working professionals and even advanced graduate students in the area of human services. I believe it to be specifically useful in mental health counseling as well as in marriage and family therapy, two professions now licensed in most states. I also consider it a valuable paradigm, complementing the techniques and strategies of the varied mental health disciplines. In particular, because of its insistence on the reality of the unconscious, the book becomes a basic resource in psychoanalytic approaches when working with individuals, couples, families, and groups. What it offers is a solid foundation in psychodynamic theory combined with a multifaceted discussion of clinical techniques, making it a very useful tool to meet our clients' many needs: physical, intellectual, emotional, social, and spiritual. Given that there are so many needs to deal with in human services, a straight line is very seldom the shortest distance between two points in our field. Mental health practice is such a rigorous and challenging process, requiring a lifetime of application, that Freud himself alluded to it as one of the impossible professions. This is the case, in part, because there are not only numerous obstacles but ethical considerations are also involved in achieving the goal of meeting clients' needs, especially since many difficulties are societal in nature.

For instance, in our age of rapid pace and stress, where approximately fifty percent of first marriages (and a higher percentage of second marriages) end in divorce, the cost in emotional and psychic terms is enormous. A related fact is the large number of children born outside of a regular family environment and raised under disadvantaged socioeconomic circumstances. These contemporary realities, among a multitude of others, have a profound impact on our society, increasing the normal level of stress and anxiety in the general population. We might be in a period of sophisticated moral relativism, where value systems and behavior are dictated by greed and hedonism, as the big corporate scandals of the recent past have shown us. The impact of the mass media on the young seems to have a deleterious effect on them, as reliable statistics on drug use, teenage pregnancy and suicide indicate.

Daniel Araoz's understanding of the superego in its literal meaning as "the I that stands above" points to the need to recognize the spiritual component of human nature, even when a sense of feelgood hedonism prevails, as it currently does throughout Western civilization. This important point has immediate practical application, because without a sense of spiritual (as opposed to material) direction and morality society becomes immersed in nihilism and relativism. Moreover, the mental health profession does not exist in a vacuum; it must respond and address these cultural issues.

Empirical data, coming from my long clinical experience, indicate that a foundation in and study of psychodynamic theory is effective in serving individuals, couples, and groups. In addition, I have found that the use of dreams has been beneficial in meeting clients' needs. Consequently, psychodynamic therapy means positive changes within the context of the therapeutic alliance. Araoz, bridging the gap between academic study and clinical practice, adds to this evidence. He makes it clear that mental health practitioners need an understanding of unconscious dynamics, without which the therapeutic process becomes superficial and less human, with limited, short-term results. As a matter of fact, psychodynamic theory stands at the foundation, prior to any subsequent theoretical explanation of counseling and psychotherapy. Our clients deserve the best we can give them in the alleviation of psychic pain and the restoration of healthy couple and family relations. In short, the symptom is not the whole story, as the title proclaims.

The sections dealing with stress and anxiety (the bane of contemporary life) are especially lucid and constructive. The case of Titus is a fine learning example that uses modern hypnoanalysis and dream work to help the client toward a successful outcome. This case, like all the many clinical vignettes, as well as the theoretical constructs throughout the sixteen chapters, will benefit advanced students of marriage and family therapy, mental health counseling, social work, psychology, and general mental health services, not to mention seasoned non-psychoanalytic clinicians.

Finally, Araoz, the psychoanalyst, insists that all mental health professionals ought to pursue their own psychoanalytic therapy, as postgraduate training institutes require their students to do, because he recognizes that the slow and in-depth exercise of introspective self-knowledge will increase their sensitivity and rapport with patients—and consequently their success as psychotherapists of any school. In the meantime, Araoz, the senior university professor, has made an excellent contribution that will resonate with students and professionals alike because it fills a void in the interface between academic theory and clinical practice.

Roy Inter-Nicola, MS, PD,
NCC*, CCMHC*, AAMFT*

---

*National Certified Counselor, Certified Clinical Mental Health Counselor, American Association for Marriage and Family Therapy.

REFERENCES

ACKERMAN, N. (1968). The emergence of family psychotherapy: a personal account. In J. A. Paterson, ed., *Counseling: Perspectives and Prospects*, pp. 54–72. New York: Associated Press.

ALEXANDER, F. (1927). The neurotic character. *International Journal of Psycho-Analysis* 11:292–311, 1930.

ALPER, G. (1994). *The Puppeteers: Studies of Obsessive Control*. New York: Fromm International Publishing Corporation.

——— (1996). *The Dark Side of the Analytic Moon: A Memoir of a Life in a Training Institute*. San Francisco: International Scholars Publications.

——— (1998). *Portrait of the Artist as a Young Patient: Psychodynamic Studies of the Creative Personality*. San Francisco: International Scholars Publications.

——— (2003). *Self-Defense in a Narcissistic World*. Lanham, MD: Hamilton Books.

——— (2005). *The Paranoia of Everyday Life: Fleeing the Terrorist Within*. Amherst, NY: Prometheus Books.

ARAOZ, D. L. (1974). Marital transference. *Journal of Family Counseling* 2:55–63.

——— (1981). Negative self-hypnosis. *Journal of Contemporary Psychotherapy* 12:45–52.

——— (1985). *The New Hypnosis*. New York: Brunner/Mazel.

——— (1998). *The New Hypnosis in Sex Therapy*, 2nd ed. Northvale, NJ: Jason Aronson.

———— (2005). Hypnosis in human sexuality problems. *American Journal of Clinical Hypnosis* 47:229–242.

ARAOZ, D. L., AND GOLDIN, E. (2004). The importance of "vivencia" in the hypnotic treatment of sexual dysfunction. *Australian Journal of Clinical Hypnotherapy and Hypnosis* 25:68–76.

ARAOZ, D. L., AND NEGLEY-PARKER, E. (1988). *The New Hypnosis in Family Therapy*. New York: Brunner/Mazel.

ARAOZ, D. L., AND SUTTON, W. S. (2003). *Reengineering Yourself*, 2nd ed. Gretna, LA: Wellness Institute.

BAK, R. C. (1968). The phallic woman. *Psychoanalytic Study of the Child*. 23:15–36. New York: International Universities Press.

BETTELHEIM, B. (1982). *Freud and Man's Soul*. New York: Random House.

BION, W. R. (1961). *Experiences in Groups*. London: Tavistock.

———— (1962). *Learning from Experience*. London: Heinemann.

BOHR, N. (1927). The complementary principle. In Bohr, N. *Essays on Atomic Physics and Human Knowledge*, pp. 77–91. New York: J. Wiley and Sons, 1958.

BOLLAS, C. (1987). *The Shadow of the Object: Psychoanalysis and the Unthought Known*. New York: Columbia University Press.

BOWEN, M. (1978). *Family Therapy in Clinical Practice*. New York: Jason Aronson.

BOWMAN, M. (2002). *The Last Resistance: The Concept of Science as a Defense Against Psychoanalysis*. Albany, NY: State University of New York Press.

BRANDCHAFT, B. (1992). The working alliance revisited: an intersubjective perspective. In A. Sugarman, R. A. Nemiroff, and D. P. Greenson, eds., *The Technique and Practice of Psychoanalysis*, vol. 2, pp. 323–339. Madison, CT: International Universities Press.

BRENNER, C. (1987). Working through: 1914–1984. *Psychoanalytical Quarterly* 58:88–108.

BREUER, J., AND FREUD, S. (1895). *Studies in Hysteria*. New York: Basic Books, 2000.

BROWN, D. P., AND FROMM, E. (1986). *Hypnotherapy and Hypnoanalysis*. Hillsdale, NJ: Lawrence Erlbaum Associates.

CAMPBELL, J. (1968). *The Hero with a Thousand Faces*. Princeton, NJ: Princeton University Press.

CAPRA, F. (1982). *The Turning Point*. New York: Bantam Books.

CAROTENUTO, A. (1982). *A Secret Symmetry: Sabina Spielrein Between Jung and Freud*. New York: Pantheon.

DEWALD, P. A. (1972). The clinical assessment of structural change. *Journal of the American Psychoanalytic Association* 20:302–324.

Diagnostic and Statistical Manual, IV–TR (DSM-IV-TR). (2000). Washington, D.C.: American Psychiatric Association.

DOR, J. (1999). *The Clinical Lacan*. New York: Other Press.

EDGCUMBE, R., AND BURGNER, M. (1975). The phallic narcissistic phase. *Psycho-Analytic Study of the Child* 30:161–180. New York: International Universities Press.

EDWARDES, A., AND MASTERS, R. E. L. (1963). *The Cradle of Erotica*. New York: Julian Press.

ERIKSON, E. H. (1950). *Childhood and Society*. New York: Norton.

ETCHEGOYEN, R. H. (1999). *The Fundamentals of Psychoanalytic Technique*, revised ed. London: Karnac.

FAIRBAIRN, W. R. D. (1952). *Psychoanalytic Studies of the Personality*. London: Tavistock.

——— (1954). *An Object-Relations Theory of the Personality*. New York: Basic Books.

FELDMAN, D. B. (2002). Whose "movie" is it anyway? Unscrambling projective processes in our work and in our lives. *NYSPA Notebook* XXIV(4):16–17.

FENICHEL, O. (1945). *The Psychoanalytic Theory of Neurosis*. New York: Norton.

FINLAYSON, R. (1998). *Nelson Mandela*. Minneapolis, MN: Lerner Publications.

FRANK, J. (2004). *Bush on the Couch*. New York: HarperCollins.

FRATTAROLI, E. (2001). *Healing the Soul in the Age of the Brain*. New York: Viking.

FRAWLEY-O'DEA, M. G., AND SARNAT, J. E. (2001). *The Supervisory Relationship: A Contemporary Psychodynamic Approach.* New York: Guilford.

FREUD, A. (1936). *The Ego and the Mechanisms of Defense.* New York: International Universities Press.

FREUD, S. (1900). The interpretation of dreams. *Standard Edition* 4:1–334.

———— (1905a). Three essays on the theory of sexuality. *Standard Edition* 7:125–245.

———— (1905b). Fragment of an analysis of a case of hysteria. *Standard Edition* 7:3–122.

———— (1912). The dynamics of transference. *Standard Edition* 12:97–108.

———— (1913). Totem and taboo. *Standard Edition* 13:1–126.

———— (1914a). On narcissism: an introduction. *Standard Edition* 14:67–104.

———— (1914b). Remembering, repeating, and working through. *Standard Edition* 12:145–157.

———— (1920). Beyond the pleasure principle. *Standard Edition* 18:3–64.

———— (1921). Group psychology and the analysis of the ego. *Standard Edition* 18:65–144.

———— (1923a). Two encyclopedia articles. (A) Psychoanalysis. *Standard Edition* 18:233–254.

———— (1923b). The infantile genital organization. *Standard Edition* 19:139–145.

———— (1925). An autobiographical study. *Standard Edition* 20: 3–75.

———— (1926). Inhibitions, symptoms, and anxiety. *Standard Edition* 20:77–176.

———— (1927). The future of an illusion. *Standard Edition* 21:1–56.

———— (1932). Why war? *Standard Edition* 22:197–232.

———— (1933). New introductory lectures on psycho-analysis. *Standard Edition* 22:3–182.

———— (1939). Moses and monotheism. *Standard Edition* 23:1–54.

FROMM, E. H. (1941). *Escape from Freedom.* New York: Henry Holt and Co.

———— (1951). *The Forgotten Language: An Introduction to the Understanding of Dreams, Fairytales, and Myths.* New York: Holt, Rinehart & Winston.

———— (1960). Psychoanalysis and Zen Buddhism. In E. Fromm, D. T. Suzuki, and R. De Martino, eds., *Zen Buddhism and Psychoanalysis*, pp. 77–141. New York: Harper & Row.

———— (1973). *The Anatomy of Human Destructiveness*. New York: Henry Holt and Co.

———— (1976). *To Have or To Be*. New York: Continuum.

FROMM-REICHMANN, F. (1950). *Principles of Intensive Psychotherapy*. Chicago: University of Chicago Press.

GITELSON, M. (1952). The emotional position of the analyst in the psychoanalytic situation. *International Journal of Psycho-Analysis* 33:1–10.

GLOVER, E. (1926). The neurotic character. *International Journal of Psycho-Analysis* 7:11–30.

GOLEMAN, D. (1998). *Working with Emotional Intelligence*. New York: Bantam.

GRAVITZ, M. A., AND GERTON, M. I. (1981). Freud and hypnosis: report on post-rejection. *Journal of the History of the Behavioral Sciences* 17:68–74.

GREENSON, R. R. (1967). *The Technique and Practice of Psychoanalysis*, vol. 1. New York: International Universities Press.

———— (1978). *Explorations in Psychoanalysis*. New York: International Universities Press.

HALL, C. S. (1954). *A Primer of Freudian Psychology*. New York: Penguin.

HEISENBERG, W. (1958). *The Representation of Nature in Contemporary Physics*. New York: Daedalus.

HORNEY, K. (1950). *Neurosis and Human Growth*. New York: Norton.

JOHNSON, S. M., AND WHIFFEN, V. E., eds. (2003). *Attachment Process in Couple and Family Therapy*. New York: Guilford.

JONES, E. (1933). The phallic phase. *International Journal of Psycho-Analysis* 14:1–33.

JUNG, C. G. (1956). Approaching the unconscious. In C. G. Jung and M.-L. von Franz, eds., *Man and His Symbols*, pp. 18–103. New York: Doubleday, 1964.

———— (1959). *The Basic Writings of C. G. Jung*. New York: Random House.

KAPLAN, H. S. (1974). *The New Sex Therapy*. New York: Brunner/Mazel.

KERNBERG, O. F. (1975). *Borderline Conditions and Pathological Narcissism*. New York: Jason Aronson.

———— (1976). *Object Relations Theory and Clinical Psychoanalysis*. New York: Jason Aronson.

———— (1980). *Internal World and External Reality*. New York: Jason Aronson.

KINSEY, A., POMEROY, W., AND MARTIN, C. (1948). *Sexual Behavior in the Human Male*. Philadelphia: Saunders.

KINSEY, A., POMEROY, W., MARTIN, C., AND GEBHARD, P. (1953). *Sexual Behavior in the Human Female*. Philadelphia: Saunders.

KLEIN, M. (1932). *The Psycho-Analysis of Children*. New York: Delta Books, 1975.

———— (1946). Notes on some schizoid mechanisms. In M. Klein, *Envy and Gratitude and Other Works*, pp. 1–24. New York: Delta Books.

———— (1955). *The Psycho-Analytic Play Technique: Its History and Significance*. New York: Simon & Schuster, 1975.

KLINE, M. V. (1958). *Freud and Hypnosis*. New York: The Institute for Research in Hypnosis Publication Society.

KOHUT, H. (1971). *The Analysis of the Self*. New York: International Universities Press.

———— (1977). *The Restoration of the Self*. New York: International Universities Press.

KRAMER, M. K. (1959). On the continuation of the analytic process after psychoanalysis (a self-observation). *International Journal of Psycho-Analysis* 40:17–25.

KRAMER, P. (1993). *Listening to Prozac*. New York: Viking.

KRIS, E. (1936). The psychology of caricature. *International Journal of Psycho-Analysis* 17:285–303.

———— (1938). Ego development and the comic. *International Journal of Psycho-Analysis* 19:77–90.

———— (1950). On preconscious mental processes. *Psychoanalytic Quarterly* 19:540–560.

LACAN, J. (1977). *Écrits, A Selection*, trans. A. Sheridan. New York: Norton.

LEVINSON, D. J. (1978). *The Seasons of a Man's Life*. New York: Ballantine.

——— (1996). *The Seasons of a Woman's Life*. New York: Knopf.

LEVY, S. T. (1984). *Principles of Interpretation*. Northvale, NJ: Jason Aronson.

LEWIN, B. D. (1933). The body as phallus. *Psychoanalytic Quarterly* 2:24–47.

LOTHANE, Z. (1994). The analyzing instrument and reciprocal free association. *Journal of Clinical Psychoanalysis* 3:61–82.

——— (1996). Psychoanalytic method and the mischief of Freud-Bashers. *Psychiatric Times*, December 1996, Vol. XIII, Issue 12.

MCGUIRE, W. (1974). *The Freud/Jung Letters*. Princeton, NJ: Princeton University Press.

MCWILLIAMS, N. (1994). *Psychoanalytic Diagnosis*. New York: Guilford.

——— (2004). *Psychoanalytic Psychotherapy*. New York: Guilford.

MEADOW, P. W. (2003). *The New Psychoanalysis*. Lanham, MD: Rowman & Littlefield.

MELTZER, D. (1973). *Sexual States of Mind*. Perthshire Strath Tay: Clunie Press.

MITCHELL, S. A. (2000). *Relationality: From Attachment to Intersubjectivity*. Hillsdale, NJ: Analytic Press.

MYERS, P. B., AND MYERS, K. D. (1993). *Myers-Briggs Type Indicator*. Palo Alto, CA: Consulting Psychologists Press.

NASIO, J.-D. (1998). *Hysteria from Freud to Lacan: The Splendid Child of Psychoanalysis*. New York: Other Press.

NEWIRTH, J. (2003). *Between Emotion and Cognition*. New York: Other Press.

OGDEN, T. H. (1982). *Projective Identification and Psychotherapeutic Technique*. Northvale, NJ: Jason Aronson.

PANEL. (1969). Problems of termination in the analysis of adults (reported by S. K. Firestein). *Journal of the American Psychoanalytical Association* 17:222–237.

PUNER, H. W. (1947). *Freud: His Life and Mind*. New York: Grosset & Dunlap.

RACKER, H. (1968). *Transference and Countertransference*. New York: International Universities Press.

REICH, W. (1933). *Character Analysis.* New York: Orgone Institute Press.

REIK, T. (1948). *Listening with the Third Ear.* New York: Farrar, Straus.

ROGERS, C. R. (1951). *Client-Centered Therapy: Its Current Practice, Implications and Theory.* Boston: Houghton Mifflin.

———— (1961). *On Becoming a Person.* Boston: Houghton Mifflin.

ROSSI, E. L. (1980). *The Collected Papers of Milton H. Erickson,* 4 vols. New York: Irvington.

RUSSIANOFF, P. (1982). *Why Do I Think I'm Nothing Without a Man?* New York: Bantam.

SAUL, L. (1972). *Psychodynamically Based Psychotherapy.* New York: Science House.

ST. CLAIR, M. (1996). *Object Relations and Self Psychology.* Pacific Grove, CA: Brooks/Cole.

SCHARFF, D. E. (1996). *Object Relations Theory and Practice: An Introduction.* Northvale, NJ: Jason Aronson.

SCHWABER, E. (1983). Psychoanalytic listening and psychic reality. *International Journal of Psycho-Analysis* 10:379–392.

SELIGMAN, M. E. P. (2000). Positive psychology: an introduction. *American Psychologist* 55:5–14.

SELYE, H. (1956). *Stress without Distress.* Philadelphia: Lippincott.

SIEGEL, A. M. (1996). *Heinz Kohut and the Psychology of the Self.* Philadelphia: Brunner Routledge.

SPOTNITZ, H. (1976). *Psychotherapy of Preoedipal Conditions.* New York: Jason Aronson.

———— (1985). *Modern Psychoanalysis and the Schizophrenic Patient,* 2nd ed. New York: Human Sciences Press.

STOLOROW, R. D., BRANDCHAFT, B. AND ATWOOD, G. E. (1995). *Psychoanalytic Treatment: An Intersubjective Approach.* Hillsdale, NJ: Analytic Press.

SULLIVAN, H. S. (1953). *The Interpersonal Theory of Psychiatry.* New York: Norton.

SUTTON, W. S. (1996). Self-hypnosis for stress management and self-exploration. *The Australian Journal of Clinical Hypnotherapy and Hypnosis* 17:91–97.

THALHEIMER, R. (1972). *Reflections: Bio-psychological, Psychoanalytic, Philosophical, Socio-political, and Personal.* New York: Philosophical Library.

TICHO, G. R. (1967). On self-analysis. *International Journal of Psycho-Analysis* 43:308–318.

TIMMERMAN, J. H. (2001). When religion is its own worst enemy: how therapists can help people shed hurtful notions that masquerade as good theology. *Journal of Sex Education and Therapy* 26:259–266.

VERHAEGHE, P. (2004). *On Being Normal and Other Disorders: A Manual for Clinical Psychodiagnostics.* New York: Other Press.

VILLOLDO, A. (2000). *Shaman, Healer, Sage.* New York: Harmony Books.

——— (1962). Psychoanalysis, scientific method, and philosophy. *Journal of the American Psychoanalytic Association* 10:617–637.

WAELDER, R. (1932). The principle of multiple function. In S. Guttman, ed., *Psychoanalysis: Observation, Theory and Application: Selected Papers of R. Waelder*, pp. 68–83. New York: International Universities Press, 1960.

WATKINS, J., AND WATKINS, H. (1997). *Ego States: Theory and Therapy.* New York: Norton.

WATSON, L. (1979). *Lifetide: The Biology of the Unconscious.* New York: Simon & Schuster.

WATZLAWICK, P., WEAKLAND, J., AND FISCH, R. (1974). *Change: Principles of Problem Formation and Problem Resolution.* New York: Norton.

WEINER, D. L., AND HEFTER, G. M. (1999). *Battling the Inner Dummy.* Amherst, NY: Prometheus Books.

WEISS, M., NORDIE, J. W., AND SIEGEL, E. P. (2005). Mindfulness-based stress reduction as an adjunct to outpatient psychotherapy. *Psychotherapy and Psychosomatics* 74:108–112.

WHITE, M. (1977). Sullivan on treatment. *Contemporary Psychoanalysis* 13:317–346.

WINNICOTT, D. W. (1965). *The Maturational Process and the Facilitating Environment.* New York: International Universities Press.

———— (1971). *Playing and Reality*. London: Tavistock, 1982.

WOLBERG, L. R. (1945). *Hypnoanalysis*. New York: Grune & Stratton.

YALOM, I. D. (1995). *The Theory and Practice of Group Psychotherapy*, 4th ed. New York: Basic Books.

ZUKAV, G. (2000). *Soul Stories*. New York: Simon & Schuster.

INDEX

Eros, 90. *See also* Death instinct;
Drive theory; Sexuality;
Thanatos
inner drives, 28–29
libido, 91
modern psychoanalysis, 39
spirituality, 93–95
superego, 91–93
Etchegoyen, R. H., 5, 191, 200
Existential anxiety, 53–58

Facilitator, group dynamics, 142
Fairbairn, W. R. D., 35, 38, 118, 141
Family and group therapy, 133–141,
163
case illustration (family therapy),
137–141
family dynamics, 135–137
group dynamics, 141–145
psychoanalysis, 133–135, 145–146
unconscious, 133
Fantasy, hypnosis, 108–109
Fear, anxiety, 50. *See also* Anxiety
Feldman, D. B., 141
Fenichel, Otto, 107, 190–191, 204
Fetishism, acting out, 206–207
Finlayson, R., 97
Firestein, S. K., 213
First-level psychoanalysis, xxiii
First-order change, second-order
change and, 57–58

Frattaroli, E., 28, 56, 78, 90–91, 178
Frawley-O'Dea, M. G., 231
Free association
hypnosis, 105, 107
unconscious, xxiii–xxiv
Free will, superego, 94–95
Freud, Anna, 33–34
Freud, Sigmund, xix, xxvi, 3, 4, 5, 7, 8,
18, 20–21, 26, 27, 28, 29, 30, 32,
33, 34, 36, 37, 39, 41, 44–46, 47,
49, 50, 53, 63, 69, 78, 80, 82, 90–
91, 101, 103, 104–105, 106–107,
116, 117, 119, 128, 144, 160, 165,
173, 174, 177, 180–181, 182, 189,
191, 193–194, 199–200, 201, 204,
205, 206, 210, 212–213, 214–216,
221, 222, 226–227, 230, 240
Fromm, E. H., 5, 12, 116, 174–175,
180, 212
Fromm-Reichman, F., 179

Gender identity, sexuality, 119. *See
also* Sexual orientation, Sexuality
Genital stage, personality types, 28.
See also Developmental theory
Gerton, M. I., 104, 105
Gestalt therapy, 41
Gitelson, M., 108
Glover, E., 194
Goldin, E., 25
Goleman, D., 101, 142